NEW TESTAMENT RHETORIC

New Testament ⮌
RHETORIC

An Introductory Guide

to the Art of Persuasion

in and of the New Testament

BEN WITHERINGTON III

CASCADE *Books* · Eugene, Oregon

NEW TESTAMENT RHETORIC
An Introductory Guide to the Art of Persuasion in and of the New Testament

Cascade Books
A Division of Wipf and Stock Publishers
199 W. 8th Ave., Suite 3
Eugene, OR 97401

ISBN 13: 978-1-55635-929-3

Cataloging-in-Publication data:

Witherington, Ben, 1951–
    New Testament rhetoric : an introductory guide to the art of persuasion in and of the
        New Testament / Ben Witherington III.

        x + 274 p.; 23 cm. Includes bibliographic references and index.

        ISBN 13: 978-1-55635-929-3

    1. Rhetoric in the Bible. 2. Rhetorical criticism. 3. Bible. N.T.—Language, style. I.
    Title. II. Series

BS2370 W7 2009

Manufactured in the U.S.A.

At this point Festus interrupted Paul's defense: "You are out of your mind, Paul!" he shouted. "Your great learning is driving you mad." . . .

Then King Agrippa said: "Do you think in such a short time you can *persuade* me to be a Christian?"

Paul replied: "Short time or long—I pray God that not only you but all who are listening to me today may become what I am, except for these chains."

       —Acts 26:24–29

All this is flashy rhetoric about loving you.
. . .
I want God, you, all friends, merely to serve my turn.

       —C S Lewis, from "As the Ruin Falls"

Contents

What Is Rhetoric?

Mention the word rhetoric and twenty-first century persons are apt to think of politics or mere verbal eloquence that is "full of sound and fury, signifying nothing" as the Bard said in Macbeth. Or perhaps they think of rhetoric in the sense it is used in C. S. Lewis's poem, "As the Ruin Falls" (see the frontispiece). This is unfortunate because rhetoric, specifically in its historical form of Greco-Roman rhetoric, provides us with an abundance of clues as to how the documents of the New Testament (NT) work, how they seek to persuade people about Jesus the Christ.

In this study, when I use the term "rhetoric" I am referring to the ancient art of persuasion used from the time of Aristotle onwards through and beyond the NT era in the Greek-speaking world to convince one audience or another about something. I am not merely talking about the use of rhetorical devices, though that is included, I am talking about all that went into convincing an audience about some subject. Rhetorical criticism, as I would define it, involves the study of the various sorts of uses of ancient Greco-Roman rhetoric in the NT by its various authors for various purposes. This sort of approach especially bears fruit in examining documents in the NT previously simply called letters, which on further examination are much more like rhetorical discourses or sermons than they are like letters. It also bears fruit in the examination of the Gospels and Acts especially in their speech material, and even in a document like Revelation where rhetorical techniques are used to structure the material and shape the polemic and apologetic going on there.

This brief guide book is intended to provide the reader with an entrance into understanding the rhetorical analysis of various parts of the NT, the value such studies bring for understanding what is being proclaimed and defended in the NT, and how Christ is presented in ways that would be considered persuasive in antiquity. In a sense, the art of rhetoric is the ancient art of preaching, and as St. Paul said, how shall any one hear the Gospel unless there is a preacher to convey it effectively? Consider this your invitation to investigate the ancient art of persuasion and how it is used in the NT and to see what insights and revelations it provides as we seek to understand the meaning of all the NT texts. The reader is encouraged to read the Annotated Bibliography to get a sense of how this companion to NT rhetoric differs from other guidebooks on the subject.

Pentecost, 2008

CHAPTER 1

The Oral Cultures of the Biblical World

THE RATIONALE FOR RHETORICAL CRITICISM

Ours is a text-based culture, a culture of written documents. You need look no further than your computer screens to verify this assertion. There could only be an Internet age if there was widespread literacy, which in turn leads to widespread production and reading of texts. It is thus difficult for us in a text-based culture to conceive of and understand the character of an oral culture, much less understand how sacred texts function in such an oral culture. Yet, however difficult, it is important that we try to understand such a thing, since all of the cultures of the Bible were essentially oral cultures, not text-based cultures, and their texts were in fact oral texts, which some might think is an oxymoron, but in fact it is not so.

The literacy rate in those biblical cultures seems to have ranged from about 5% to 20% depending on the culture and which sub-group within the culture we are discussing. Not surprisingly then, all ancient peoples, whether literate or not, preferred the living word, which is to say the spoken word. Texts were enormously expensive to produce—papyrus was expensive, ink was expensive, and scribes were ultra-expensive. Being a secretary in Jesus' and Paul's age could be a lucrative job indeed. No wonder Jesus said to his audiences, "let those who have ears, listen." You notice he did not ever say, "let those who have eyes, read." Most eyes could not read in the biblical period.

So far as we can tell, no documents in antiquity were intended for "silent" reading, and only a few were intended for private individuals to read. They were always meant to be read out loud and usually read out loud to a group of people. For the most part they were simply necessary surrogates for oral communication. This was particularly true of ancient letters.

In fact, most ancient documents including letters were not really texts in the modern sense at all. They were composed with their aural and oral potential in mind, and they were meant to be orally delivered when they arrive at their destination. Thus for example, when one reads the opening verses of Ephesians, loaded as it is with aural devices (assonance, alliteration, rhythm, rhyme, various rhetorical devices) it becomes perfectly clear that no one was ever meant to hear this in any language but Greek and furthermore, no one was ever meant to read this silently. It needed to be heard.

And indeed there was a further reason it needed to be orally delivered—because of the cost of making documents, a standard letter in Greek would have no separation of words, sentences, paragraphs or the like, little or no punctuation, and all capital letters. Thus for example imagine having to sort out a document that began as follows:

PAULASERVANTOFCHRISTJESUSCALLEDTOBEANAPOSTL
EANDSETAPARTFORTHEGOSPELOFGOD.

The only way to decipher such a collection of letters was to sound them out—out loud. There is of course the famous anecdote about St. Augustine and St. Ambrose. Augustine said that Ambrose was the most remarkable man he had ever met, because he could read without moving his lips or making a sound. Clearly, an oral culture is a different world than a largely literate text-based culture, and texts function differently in such a world. All sorts of texts were simply surrogates for oral speech. This statement applies to many of the biblical texts themselves.

It is hard for us to wrap our minds around it, but texts were scarce in the biblical world, and often were treated with great respect. Since literacy was largely a skill only the educated had, and the educated tended to be almost exclusively from the social elite, texts in such a world served the purpose of the elite—conveying their authority, passing down their judgments, establishing their property claims, indicating their heredity, and the like. But since all ancient people were profoundly religious, the most important documents even among the elite were religious texts.

What do texts in an oral culture tell us about their authors? It is too seldom taken into account that the twenty-seven books of the NT reflect a remarkable level of literacy and indeed of rhetorical skill amongst the inner circle of leaders of the early Christian movement. Early Christianity was not, by and large, a movement led by illiterate peasants or the socially deprived. The leaders of the movement mostly produced the texts of the movement, and the texts of the NT reflect a considerable knowledge of Greek, of rhetoric, and indeed of general Greco-Roman culture. This skill and erudition can only seldom be attributed to scribes, except in cases where scribes such as Tertius or Sosthenes (cf. Rom 16 and 1 Cor 1) had been converted and donated their skills to the movement. Even then, it appears they were largely just taking dictation from Paul.

The letters we find in the NT are mostly far longer than secular letters of their era. Actually they are *not in the main letters*, though they have epistolary openings and closings sometimes. They are in fact discourses, homilies, and rhetorical speeches of various sorts that the creators could not be present to deliver to a particular audience, and so instead they sent a surrogate to proclaim them. These documents would not be handed to just anyone. From what we can tell, Paul expected one of his co-workers such as Timothy, Titus, or Phoebe to go and orally deliver the contents of the document in a rhetorically effective manner. This would have been almost a necessity since the document would come without division of words or punctuation and so only someone skilled in reading such seamless prose; indeed, one who *already knew* the contents of the document could place the emphases in the right places so as to effectively communicate the message.

How then did a sacred text function in an oral culture? For one thing it was believed that words, especially religious words, were not mere ciphers or symbols. They were believed to have power and effect on people if they were properly communicated and pronounced. It was not just the sacred names of God, the so-called *nomena sacra*, which were considered to have inherent power, but sacred words in general. Consider for example what Isaiah 55:11 says: "so shall my word be that goes forth out of my mouth: it shall not return to me void, but it shall accomplish that which I please, and it shall prosper in the thing I sent it to do." The Word or words of a living and powerful God, were viewed as living and powerful in themselves.[1] One can then imagine how a precious and expensive document, which contained God's own words, would be viewed. It would be something that needed to be kept in a sacred place,

---

1. See Witherington, *The Living Word of God.*

like a temple or a synagogue, and only certain persons, with clean hands and a pure heart would be allowed to unroll the sacred scroll and read it, much less interpret it.

From what we can tell, the texts of the NT were treasured during the first century, and were lovingly and carefully copied for centuries thereafter. There is even evidence beginning in the second century of the use of female Christian scribes who had a "fairer" hand to copy and even begin to decorate these sacred texts. But make no mistake—even such texts were seen to serve the largely oral culture. Before the rise of modern education and widespread literacy, it had always been true that "In the beginning was the (spoken) Word."[2] All of this has implications for how we should approach the NT, especially the more ad hoc documents in the Pauline corpus and the other documents traditionally called letters in the NT, which often in fact are not letters. 1 John is a sermon with neither epistolary opening nor closing. Hebrews is an even longer sermon, with only an epistolary closing, but of course no listener would ever have considered it a letter on first hearing, because there were no signals at the outset of the document to suggest such a thing. Indeed, in an oral culture, opening signals are everything if the issue is what sort of discourse or document am I listening to. This is why Luke 1:1–4 is so crucial to judging the genre of that Gospel.

Given that the division between a speech and an orally performed text was more like a thin veil than a thick wall between literary categories it will not come as a surprise when I say that actually oral conventions more shape the so-called epistolary literature of the NT than epistolary ones, and with good reason. This was not only because of the dominant oral character of the culture, but also more importantly because the Greco-Roman world of the NT period was a rhetorically saturated environment, whereas the influence of literacy and letters was far less widespread so far as we can tell.

Here we need to come to grips with and understand an important fact: *the rise to prominence of the personal letter used as something of a vehicle for instruction or as a treatise of sorts was a phenomena which only really took root in the Greco-Roman milieu with the letters of Cicero shortly*

---

2. It is interesting that an important literate figure like Papias of Hierapolis, who lived at the end of the NT era, repeatedly said that he preferred the living voice of the apostle or one who had heard the eyewitnesses to a written document. In this he simply reflected the normal attitude of ancient peoples, literate or not.

before the NT era. Contrast this with the long history of the use of rhetoric going back to Aristotle, and use of it in numerous different venues. Rhetoric was a tool useable with the educated and uneducated, with the elite and the ordinary, and most public speakers of any ilk or skill in antiquity knew they had to use the art of persuasion to accomplish their aims. There were not only schools of rhetoric throughout the Mediterranean crescent, rhetoric itself was part of elementary, secondary, and tertiary basic education as well. *There were no comparable schools of letter writing* not least because it was a rather recent art just coming to prominence in the first century AD. Here we come to a crucial point.

Analyzing the majority of the NT on the basis of epistolary conventions—many of which did not become *de rigeur* nor put into a handbook until *after* NT times—while a helpful exercise to some degree, has no business being the dominant literary paradigm by which we examine the Pauline, Petrine, Johannine, and other discourses in the NT. The dominant paradigm when it came to words and the conveying of ideas, meaning, and persuasion in the NT era was rhetoric, not epistolary conventions. This is why I will say now that most of the NT owes far more to rhetoric and its very long-standing and widespread conventions than it ever owed to the nascent practice of writing letter essays, or letter treatises. Most of the letters of the NT, with the exception of the very shortest ones (2–3 John, perhaps Philemon) look very little like the very mundane pragmatic epistolary literature of that era. In terms of both structure and content, most NT documents look far more like rhetorical speeches. Some are in fact straightforward sermons, "words of exhortation" as the author of Hebrews calls his homily; some are more rhetorical speeches suitable for assemblies where discussion would then ensue (e.g., after dinner discussions at a symposium), but all are profitably analyzed in detail by means of rhetorical examination.

Not only so, but micro-rhetoric clearly enough shapes at least three things: 1) the *chreiai* (aphorisms) in the Gospels; 2) the speech summaries in Acts; 3) the way portions of a book like Revelation are linked together by catchword and A/B/A structure. In other words, rhetoric is not just something that illuminates Paul and other portions of the "so-called epistolary corpus" in the NT. It is a necessary tool for analyzing it all.

DEFINING RHETORICAL CRITICISM

At this juncture it will be well and wise to define more specifically what the phrase rhetorical criticism means in my view, and how it applies to the NT. Rhetorical criticism is by definition the study of rhetoric, whether ancient or modern, with a broad definition of rhetoric being the art of persuasion, though sometimes it has degenerated into the art of speaking well, or mere verbal eloquence. As applied to the field of NT studies, rhetorical criticism has been approached in two rather different ways by scholars. The first way, pioneered and championed by George Kennedy and Hans Dieter Betz and their students, is more of an historical enterprise, seeking to analyze the NT documents on the basis ancient Greco-Roman rhetoric, asking and answering the question of how the NT authors may or may not have used this art. Here we may speak of *how the NT authors adopted and adapted ancient rhetoric for their Christian purposes of communication.*

The second approach, growing out of modern language theory and modern epistemology, when it comes to the issue of texts and meaning, has been pioneered and championed by Vernon Robbins and his students, as well as William Wullener and others. This approach, rather than primarily looking for rhetorical structures embedded in the NT texts by NT authors, *seeks to apply certain modern rhetorical categories to the text* (e.g., categories such as "inner texture" or "intra texture"). Both the terminology and the method, as well as the theory of meaning of this latter approach has more in common with the "new" rhetoric of Heinrich Lausberg and others than with the rhetorical guidelines established by Aristotle, Quintilian, Menander, and other practitioners of ancient rhetoric. In other words, it is more an exercise in modern hermeneutics than in the analysis of the use of Greco-Roman rhetoric by the NT authors themselves. The methodological issue here is whether the NT should only be analyzed on the basis of categories the NT authors themselves could have known and used, or not.

In my view, both approaches can yield good insights into the biblical text, but the attempt to fuse the methods of old and new rhetoric confuses more people than it enlightens. In particular, I would insist that the primary and first task is to ask the appropriate historical questions about the NT text and what its ancient authors had in mind. When that is the prime mandate then only analysis on the basis of Greco-Roman or ancient Jewish rhetoric is appropriate, since ancient authors were completely innocent and ignorant of modern rhetorical theory and epistemology. Due to limitations of space, the remainder of this guide will explain more particularly rhetorical criticism in the Kennedy and Betz vein since the historical approach gives us a window into how and to what degree the NT writers actually used the ancient art of persuasion.

Most NT scholars at this juncture are quite convinced that micro-rhetoric can be found in NT documents, particularly in Paul's letters, but also elsewhere. By micro-rhetoric I mean the use of rhetorical devices within the NT documents—for instance the use of rhetorical questions, dramatic hyperbole, personification, amplification, irony, enthymemes (i.e., incomplete syllogisms), and the like.

More controversial is whether macro-rhetoric is also used in the NT. By macro-rhetoric I mean whether the overall structure of some NT documents reflects the use of rhetorical categories and divisions used in ancient speeches. Those divisions are as follows: 1) *exordium*; 2) *narratio*; 3) *propositio*; 4) *probatio*; 5) *refutatio*; and 6) *peroratio*. All six of these normal divisions of an ancient speech could be found in the three different species of ancient rhetoric: forensic, deliberative, and epideictic. But these different species of rhetoric served very different functions. Forensic rhetoric was the rhetoric of the law court, the rhetoric of attack and defense, and it focused on the past. Deliberative rhetoric was the rhetoric of the assembly, the rhetoric of advice and consent, and it focused on changing belief and/or behavior in the future. Epideictic rhetoric was the rhetoric of the forum and the funeral, the rhetoric of praise and blame, and it focused on the present. In any given ancient speech attention was paid as well to the issues of *ethos*, *logos*, and *pathos*, which is to say the establishing of rapport with the audience at the outset (in the *exordium*), the use of emotion charged arguments (*logos* in the *probatio* and *refutatio*), and finally the appeal to the deeper emotions (*pathos*) in the final summation or *peroratio*.

It is fair to say that those NT scholars who have done the detailed rhetorical analysis of all the NT documents have concluded that while micro-rhetoric can be found most anywhere in the NT, including in genres as varied as the Gospels or Revelation, that macro-rhetoric shows up only in the letters, homilies, and speech summaries (in Acts). In particular, Paul's letters, 1 Peter, and the homilies called Hebrews and 1 John reflect these larger macro-structures of rhetoric, often in great detail. The macro-structures however are used with some flexibility and they are enfolded within epistolary frameworks in some cases. Thus, for example, the beginning and end of Paul's letters do almost always reflect epistolary conventions and can certainly be categorized as a form of ancient letters. These epistolary categories, however, help us very little in analyzing the structure of the material if one is not dealing with the epistolary opening and closing elements (prescript, travel plans, opening or closing greetings). Furthermore, there was no ancient convention to have a "thanksgiving prayer" at the outset of an ancient letter, nor are we helped by lumping the vast majority of a discourse under the heading of "body middle," which tells us nothing really about the document and was not an ancient epistolary category any way. In other words, epistolary conventions and devices help us very little with the bulk of the material in the documents traditionally called NT letters. Here is where rhetoric has proved much more helpful in unlocking the structural and substantive intricacies of the majority of NT documents. Even Paul's letters were not meant to be privately studied. In the first instance they were surrogates for the speeches Paul would have made could he have been present with his audience. As such they partake of all the ad hoc characteristics of such purpose driven ancient speeches. They were intended as timely remarks, on target to affect belief and behavior of the various audiences. They were not intended merely as theological or ethical treatises. Rhetorical criticism helps us realize the dynamic and interactive nature of these documents.[3]

Having introduced the discussion of micro- and macro-rhetoric in the NT in this chapter we need to explain more fully what is meant by such terms, and other related ones. But first we must turn to giving a brief history of education and rhetorical training in the NT world. As we will discover, the teaching of rhetoric had a long and distinguished pedigree; indeed, there were whole schools in antiquity devoted to the subject in places like Alexandria, Ephesus, Athens, and Rome. Letter writing, however, was an art only beginning to be systematized, especially when it came to something like the letter essays of a Cicero or his later disciples. The oral and rhetorical culture dominated, and texts had to fit into its

---

3. Here we offer only a cursory discussion of the matters introduced in this chapter. We will go into much more detail on these matters in the chapter below, "Paul as a Rhetor and Writer."

paradigms, not the other way around. So let us consider ancient education at this juncture.[4]

QUESTIONS FOR REFLECTION

1. How do oral and text-based cultures differ?
2. Would rhetoric play a more crucial role in an oral or a text-based culture?
3. What does the use of normal means of persuasion in the NT say about the NT writers?

4. For a more detailed discussion of the matters raised in this chapter see the forthcoming Witherington, *Shifting the Paradigms.*

CHAPTER 2

Defining and Refining the Craft of Persuasion: The History and Practice of Ancient Rhetoric

RHETORIC REDUX—ITS HISTORY

Rhetoric, from the Greek word, *rhētorikē,* had a long and interesting history before any of the authors of the NT were ever born. Plato and Aristotle both discussed the matter, and took part in the debate about how to define what it was. Rhetoric was to play a crucial role in the birth of democracy in the Golden Age of Greece. This was so, of course, because in a democracy people had choices and had to be persuaded to pursue a particular course of action or adopt a particular policy in the Greek assembly (the *ekklēsia*). Aristotle for example insisted that rhetoric was so important that it was not fully separable from philosophy, and both Plato and Aristotle agreed that there were ethical issues involved in using rhetoric. The purpose of the various types of rhetoric should be furthering the good, the expedient, the noble, or the just (see for example Aristotle *Rhetorica* 2.19.26). Rhetoric was considered an art that required the honing of skills and the careful practice of the craft.

Aristotle, who wrote the first great treatise on rhetoric that is still extant, traces the beginnings of rhetoric to two Sicilians, Corax and Tisias, who are credited with developing the earliest rhetorical theory (see Cicero *Brutus* 46). Aristotle weighed in on the discussion of definitions by insisting that rhetoric was "the faculty of discovering the possible means of persuasion in reference to any subject whatsoever" (*Rhetorica* 1.2.1). By the time we get to Quintilian, the great summarizer and epitomizer of all things rhetorical both in the Greek and Roman traditions, rhetoric, while it has many definitions, is at bottom "the art of speaking well" (*ars bene dicendi* [*Institutio oratoria* 2.17.37]). But Quintilian was well aware that various definitions were in play (see *Institutio oratoria* 2.15 where he reviews them), and his own definition simply worked well in the Empire since democracies no longer existed. What is clear from studying the history of the terminological debate is that rhetoric was not just about informing people; it was about persuading and motivating them in various ways. The author of *Rhetorica ad Herrennium* stressed that the task of the rhetor was to address an audience in such a manner that as far as possible he secures the audiences agreement about something (1.2).

Though it is not completely clear at what point the division happened, there came to be two different approaches to rhetoric, one called Sophistic rhetoric and the other a more serious and substantive approach. Sophistic rhetoric was to rise in popularity during the period of the Roman Empire, not least because more and more orators were afraid of expressing contrary or controversial opinions and instead focused on being eloquent. The focus turned more to the form rather than the substance of the discourse. This is why Quintilian somewhat tamely defines rhetoric as the art of speaking well. This was closer to the Sophistic point of view than to the Aristotlean one that insisted that rhetoric had to do with philosophy and even the search for truth about something. Just how strongly many felt about Sophistic rhetoric can be shown by the strong, even vehement and sarcastic comments made about it. Philo, for example, called it mere "shadow-boxing" (*That the Worse Attacks the Better* 4), not a real contending for the truth of some substantive matter.

But this matter was not just of concern to the well-educated elite, like Philo. Rhetoric was a popular spectator sport in the first century AD. Most persons were either producers or consumers of some kind of rhetoric, and rhetoric had long been a staple of education, at all levels beginning with elementary education.

In elementary education, children would learn how to do rhetorical comparisons (called *synkrisis*) for the sake of the formation of their values—so they would know the difference between being a virtuous person and being a wicked one. They would also learn how to compose *chreia*, short pithy stories, which usually would have a memorable saying at or near the end of it—like for instance the story of Jesus' discussion with the wealthy young man which culminates with the famous: "it is easier for a camel to go through the eye of a needle than for a rich person to enter the Kingdom of God" (Mark 10:25). Rhetorical education would continue as the child got older and it was even made a staple item of higher education in Roman times. In fact, the rhetor came to be the person who dictated what was taught in higher education during the period of the Empire.[1] Rhetoricians were found in all the great cities of the Roman Empire, many of which also had schools of rhetoric or at least schools which made rhetoric one of the dominant subjects studied.

Education was of course by and large the privilege of the more elite members of society. It tells us something about the leaders of early Christianity that they could read and write, and various of them had rhetorical skills as well. Generally speaking rhetoric was part of the training of wealthy males seeking to enter the *cursus honorum*, climbing up the ladder of public office and pursuing a career in public life in one way or another, whether as a lawyer, a senator, an ambassador, a government employee, or the like. While there were a few examples of rhetorically trained and skilled women in antiquity, such as Hortensia, the daughter of the famous rhetorician Q. Hortensius Hortalus, who delivered a public oration to the triumvirs in 42 BC, arguing her own legal case, she was surely an exception to the rule and probably gained her training in the home. Women were not in general either encouraged or in some cases allowed to pursue "higher" education, which means that even wealthy women tended to lack rhetorical training beyond the intermediate or even *progymnasmata* level (see Quintilian *Institutio oratoria* 1.1.6).[2]

But the *progymnasmata* exercises were actually extensive. One learned how to deal with the following literary forms and verbally shape them in interesting and persuasive manners: Fable, Narrative, *Chreia*, Proverb, Refutation, Confirmation, Commonplace, Encomium, Vituperation, Comparison, Impersonation, Description, Thesis or Theme, Defend/Attack a Law. Some of these exercises were quite complicated and corresponded to specific elements in a speech of any of the three species of rhetoric. In addition, even early on there was training in declamation. One would be set a topic, sometimes trivial ("in praise of a flea" or "the shame of male baldness"), sometimes serious ("proposition—that the emperor deserves to be worshipped") and one would produce a speech to an imaginary audience about the matter.

Most ancient peoples used rhetoric and were avid consumers and critics of its more skilled practitioners. The more Sophistic styles were in

---

1. See my discussion in *Conflict and Community*, 39–43 and all the references there. See also especially Clark, *Rhetoric in Greco-Roman Education*.

2. Cantarella, *Pandora's Daughters*, 141, 214.

vogue, the more one was likely to hear epideictic rhetoric in the market place and elsewhere. It could be the most frivolous form of rhetoric, but also the most eloquent and aesthetically pleasing. Epideictic rhetoric was to be especially associated with the rise of the so-called second Sophistic in the second century AD, but those tendencies were already evident in the first century.

In an oral culture, orators might well make a considerable living, and some, like Herodes Atticus, who helped build the theater in the shadow of the Parthenon in Athens, became very wealthy indeed because of their gift of eloquence. Consider for example a papyrus fragment dating to about 110 AD, which reads in part, "Pay to Licinius . . . the rhetor the amount due to him for the speeches [in] which Aur[elius . . .] was honored . . . in the gymnasium in the Great Serapeion, four hundred drachmas of silver."[3] This was more than a Roman soldier's annual wages, according to the Roman historian Tacitus (*Annales* 1.17). The broad acceptance and indeed great popularity of rhetorical oratory is attested by important literary works that lionize orators, such as Athenaeus's *Deiphnosophistae* or Philostratus's *Lives of the Sophists*. Not only did the popular orators have many fans, they were widely imitated. It was the Sophists who were famous for their verbal pyrotechnics. They were the orators who made "news." This proved to be problematic for those who wanted to persuade audiences on some serious subject and who were unwilling to entertain or thrill the crowd with their verbal artistry. The alternative however was not to eschew rhetoric altogether, but rather to use it in a more substantive and sober manner, all the while castigating those "Sophists," who were not philosophically (or theologically) serious about what they were doing.

RHETORIC REDUX—ITS FORM AND PRAXIS

The art of persuasion had a multitude of rules and forms involved in its praxis; it will be well if we lay them out in some detail here. There were three different species of ancient rhetoric—forensic, deliberative, and epideictic. Each originally was used to address a particular social setting and had distinctive purposes. Forensic rhetoric, as the name suggests, was the rhetoric of the law court, the rhetoric of attack and defense, and

3. Sherk, *The Roman Empire*, 195.

it focused on things done in the past. This was the type of rhetoric most frequently practiced in the NT era. We hear samplings of it in the trials of Paul in Acts. Deliberative rhetoric was the rhetoric of the "assembly"— originally the democratic assemblies in Greece—and was the rhetoric of advice and consent, trying to get one course of action or another, one policy or another voted on in an affirmative manner. The temporal focus of deliberative rhetoric was the future since change was sought in some policy or action in the near future. Finally there was epideictic rhetoric, the rhetoric of display. Its social venues included the *agora* (for entertainment), the funeral (for encomiums or eulogies), or celebrations (e.g., the proconsul's birthday). This was the rhetoric of praise and blame—more praise than blame especially at funerals. Its temporal focus was the present. It did not seek to change beliefs, behaviors, opinions, or attitudes, but rather it sought to reinforce existing ones. It was possible to mix things up in a rhetorical discourse; for instance one could have an epideictic digression in the midst of an otherwise forensic discourse, but there was a certain way of doing this where one made clear one was digressing. We see this practice in 1 Corinthians where ch. 13 is an epideictic piece in praise of love in the midst of an otherwise deliberative discourse.[4]

During the period of the empire, epideictic rhetoric came to the fore, as flattery could get one advancement, or patrons, or at least noticed in a positive way. In a society that had a set, even rigid authority structure involving patrons and clients, with the Emperor being the biggest patron of all, the art of "sucking up" was the order of the day, not speaking truth to power. In such a setting it is no surprise that the rhetorical handbooks of the first century such as Quintilian's *Institutio oratoria*, which wanted rhetoric to be taken seriously, focused on forensic rhetoric, since it was the form of *substantive* rhetoric most frequently practiced in that era. What is especially interesting about the NT is that it more frequently exhibits deliberative rhetoric as it seeks to persuade people to change their beliefs and behaviors. It should be added that deliberative rhetoric was, however, still in play in the Roman Empire, not in democratic assemblies, but in ambassadorial missions when one group or country was negotiating with others to conclude some kind of pact or treaty.

---

4. On mixed rhetoric see the treatise *peri eschēmatismenon* in Dionysius of Halicarnassus, vol. 6 of *Opuscula II*. One can compare Demosthenes' famous *De corona* speech.

What is revealing about the predilection for deliberative rhetoric in the NT is that it suggests that the orator believes the audience is free to respond positively or not and, therefore, needs to be persuaded. In other words, good evangelism and good preaching involved persuasion, not manipulation and strong-arm tactics. It may well be very revealing that Paul repeatedly called the house meetings of Christians meetings of the *ekklēsia*—formerly the term for the democratic assembly; now the term for the assembling of Christians. Was this because Paul believed that the church was now the place where dialogue, discussion, and debate could still be carried on and lead to important conclusions about belief and behavior? I think so.

In the NT era, style often prevailed over substance when it came to rhetoric; much emphasis was placed on stylistic devices, figures of speech, colorful metaphors, exclamation, apostrophes, wordplay, and epigrams. These sorts of rhetorical devices are not lacking in the NT, but they are used to serve serious purposes about matters theological and ethical.

In regard to style, there were two major styles of rhetoric—the more reserved and formal Atticizing style, and the more florid and luxurious Asiatic style. We will have occasion to say a good deal about the latter since it turns up in abundance in the Pauline letters written to places in the province of Asia not surprisingly (i.e., Colossians, Ephesians, Philemon). In general Asiatic style tended to be more emotional, involving more colorful, longer sentences, lots of hyperbole, metaphors, and the like. Attic style was seen as more appropriate in some quarters but even Cicero preferred the Asiatic style for his Roman trials as it did a better job of stirring the emotions.

A normal rhetorical discourse had three basic emotional phases, dealing first with the issue of *ethos*, then *logos*, and finally attending to *pathos*. There was an appeal to the simpler and more surface emotions, such as a feeling of being hospitable or friendly, or the capacity for laughter in the opening of the discourse as the rhetorician sought to establish rapport and authority with his audience. *Ethos* was all about establishing the speaker's character and making clear he was trustworthy and believable. Lots of things could affect one's ethos. When the toupee of the rhetorician blew off in the agora in the middle of an otherwise compelling discourse he was having a bad ethos day, and his speech lost credibility. *Logos* refers to the real meat of the discourse, its emotion-charged arguments. In Greek arguments were called *pistoi*, interestingly enough. At the end of the discourse the rhetorician needed to appeal to the deep emotions—love or hate, grief or joy, anger or pity—and so create *pathos* in the audience in order for the hearers to embrace the arguments not merely intellectually but affectively as well. When that happened, the act of persuasion had achieved its aim of winning over the whole person or group—body and soul.

There was a normal structure to a rhetorical discourse, though certain elements could be rearranged or omitted in some cases. The taxonomy is as follows:

- The *exordium* is the beginning of the discourse, attempting to make the audience open and well-disposed to what follows.

- The *narratio* explains the nature of the disputed matter or the facts that are relevant to the discussion. This element could be omitted on occasion.

- The *propositio* or thesis statement is crucial and normally follows the *narratio* though sometimes it comes before "the narration." In a forensic discourse the essential proposition of both the prosecutor and the defendant might be laid out by way of contrast.

- The *probatio* enumerates the arguments for the proposition, supporting the speaker's case. This might be, but would not necessarily be followed by the *refutatio*, the refutation of the opponent's arguments. It is interesting that Paul tends to follow this taxonomy with some rigor. Thus, in Galatians the real bone of content is delayed until the allegory is presented in ch. 4 to create animus against the Judaizers, and in Romans Paul saves the refutation until chs. 9–11 where he refutes the suggestion that God has abandoned his first chosen people.

- Finally, the *peroratio* sums up or amplifies some major argument and/or makes a final appeal to the deeper emotions to make sure the argument persuaded.

BEYOND THE BASICS—CULTURAL SCRIPTS
AND ANCIENT PERSUASION

The psychological dynamics of any given culture are not only unique and particular, they are often difficult to assess. For example, what is considered humorous in one culture may well seem offensive in another, and

likewise what is considered persuasive in one culture may seem uncon-
vincing in another. It is not just a matter of trotting out ironclad rules
of universal logic. The issue is culture specific. I say this now because
a fair bit of the rhetoric of the NT will seem manipulative to us in our
post-modern situation. It will look like emotive arm-twisting as we shall
see when we examine in some detail Paul's tour de force argument in
Philemon. To some degree this reveals something important about ancient cultures: they were very different, and in various ways more emotive, than our cultures. A few words about the social world of the NT are
in order.

Ancient cultures were, to a far greater degree than most modern
cultures, collectivist cultures. By this I mean they did not promote in-
dividualism. Of course there were individuals, and indeed ones widely
recognized and of high status like an Alexander or a Julius Caesar, but
identity in the ancient world was largely established by what group one
was a part of and by factors like geography, gender, and generation. These
were all patriarchal cultures where the question "who is your father"
was crucial. This is precisely why the Gospel writers had to go to such
lengths to explain Jesus' origins. Have you noticed that people seem to
have no last names in the Bible? The very marker that most distinguishes
one person from another in our modern world hardly existed in biblical
antiquity. Rather, people were identified by their geographical point of
origin (Saul of Tarsus, Jesus of Nazareth, Mary of Migdal ["Magdalene"]),
or by who their father was (Simon bar Jonah, John son of Zebedee), or
occasionally by their religious affiliation or role (Simon the Pharisee,
Simon the Zealot).

Even in regard to the issue of salvation, which we tend to see as a
very individual matter, it is interesting to listen to how Paul talks about
it. He says, for example, in 1 Corinthians 12 that it is a matter of the
Holy Spirit baptizing a person "into the one body." One does not merely
become a new person. One is joined spiritually to a new group. Or in
Philippians 2:12–13 he literally says "work out *y'all's* salvation with fear
and trembling, for it is God who works in the midst of *y'all* (you plural) to
will and to do." I remember vividly the day it was brought home to me that
the "yous" here were plural in the Greek. Salvation suddenly went from
being an individual project to being a group exercise, and indeed salvation was something that God was working in and into the group and its
collective identity, especially as it met together as an assembly (*ekklēsia*).

How does this affect the rhetoric of the NT? It was much easier to appeal to the notion of group loyalty, group identity, the need for concord and unity within the group, because the cultural scripts of that culture had already undergirded such a value.

Another factor, which certainly affected the rhetoric, was the fact that ancient cultures had totally different economic systems than ours; in addition, they were not democracies. There was no free market economy in antiquity. People "got ahead" in life on the basis of patronage and client-age. It was a reciprocity culture—you scratch my back, and I will scratch yours. This presented enormous problems for Paul in Corinth, because deciding to work with his hands, having refused patronage, angered some of the more elite Christians in Corinth and led to trouble. Even more difficult was serving up the rhetoric of grace in a culture where it was believed that you did not get "something for nothing." It was all a matter of exchange. The idea that a human being, much less a deity would do an act of undeserved favor or give an unmerited benefit to someone, without either demanding or asking anything in return, made little sense in a reciprocity culture. Yet, this is how Paul depicted the nature of salvation and the God of grace. It surely must have been a hard sell in many quarters, requiring considerable rhetoric to persuade. All other deities were "payback" gods in antiquity. Why should the biblical God or Jesus be any different?

Thirdly, all ancient cultures were honor and shame cultures. At the top of the value hierarchy in an ancient culture was not the dyadic pair of "truth and falsity" or "life and death," but rather "honor and shame." The chief end in life was to obtain honor and avoid shame. If one needed to lie to achieve that end, so be it. If some needed to die to achieve that end, so be it. Establishing honor and avoiding shame was more important than truth, more important than life or death. How was one to change the cultural script so that truth was seen as the top value in the value hierarchy? This would take powerful rhetoric indeed. It did not mean that honor and shame, or life and death, did not continue to be very important to early Christians (see for example Paul's remarks in Philippians 1:20 about avoiding shame), but they were not as important as telling the truth about Jesus. The rhetoric of the NT calls for a trans-valuation of extant cultural values in various ways.[5] A good rhetorician knew that he

---

5. For a brief but helpful summary of the social world of the NT see Malina, *The New Testament World*; and de Silva, *Honor, Patronage, Kinship*.

had to start with a person or a group where they were culturally in order to lead them in a different direction. An appeal for group unity in Corinth was an easier sell in Paul's time than it is today precisely because of the collectivist nature of ancient cultures. It also accented just how badly the Corinthians had been behaving, following the rivalry conventions of the day and applying them to church life. In short, rhetoric in the ancient cultures of the NT era worked differently than rhetoric today, in various regards. The hermeneutical questions become difficult when one tries to transfer praxis from the early church to the church today, especially the church in the West, which unlike the Oriental church, does not have a collectivist and honor and shame foundation on which to build.

BEYOND THE BASICS—GOOD RHETORIC HUNTING

One of the more interesting facts that is unveiled when one does a detailed analysis of the rhetoric in the NT is that various of the authors of the NT, especially Paul and the authors of Hebrews, 1 Peter, and Luke, were capable of considerable sophistication (without becoming Sophists in the negative sense) in their use of rhetoric. We will have occasion to look at this in some detail in subsequent chapters. For now, it is enough to say that we find both elementary and more advanced rhetoric in the NT. But how should we approach this matter since on the surface what we have in the NT is Gospels, a history called Acts, letters, and an Apocalypse? On a superficial glance at the genre of NT documents, where do we find any rhetorical discourses?

The first and perhaps most obvious place would be to examine the various speeches we find in the Gospels and Acts. Do they reflect rhetorical conventions or not? Right off the bat, there must be a caveat. From what we can tell, the speeches in the Gospels and Acts, are mostly speech summaries, not full speeches. Indeed, various of the ones in Acts break off prior to conclusion as they are interrupted. Nevertheless, what is interesting is that a wide variety of such speeches, especially the ones in Acts, do indeed reflect rhetorical conventions and structures of various sorts. The NT writers obviously wanted their material to persuade people in a rhetoric saturated culture, and they shaped their materials accordingly.

Secondly, there was a dilemma for an orator who could not be present to deliver his oracle or discourse to the audience for whom it was intended. What was he to do? The answer was that he had to write down or have written his discourse, and send it off. Most often this was done using an epistolary framework, but sometimes even this was eschewed. First John, for instance, is very powerful epideictic rhetoric about Christian values; it has *no epistolary features at all.* Not at the beginning or end of the document or anywhere else in 1 John do we see epistolary conventions reflected. Similarly, consider Hebrews. Ancient documents were read aloud and from front to back. No one, hearing the opening of Hebrews in Hebrews 1, would ever guess this was a letter. They would assume it was a script for a speech of some sort. The fact that there are epistolary features at the end of the document simply confirms it was sent from a distance. It does not make it mainly a letter. Indeed, 95% of the document conforms to rhetorical and *not* epistolary conventions.

But what about Paul's "letters"? Here, clearly we have epistolary features at the beginning and the end of the documents. This is true enough, and some have argued that there are epistolary features in between. But the vast majority of the material in any of Paul's letters cannot be explained on the basis of epistolary analysis. What we have in the Pauline documents are letter discourses, meant to be proclaimed orally when the messenger arrives with the document in hand, rolls it out, and dramatically delivers it. Letter discourses have both epistolary features and rhetorical features, with some overlap at the beginning of the documents.

The epistolary prescripts and/or the "thanksgiving prayer" sections serve as the *exordium* for the discourse that follows, doing double duty. In fact, these sections, which establish the authority and ethos of the speaker and establish rapport with the audience function in more of a rhetorical manner than in an epistolary manner. For example, there was no epistolary convention to offer a long thanksgiving prayer at the opening of a letter—a brief health wish perhaps, but not a longer prayer. And more to the point, there was especially no convention to provide a preview of coming topics in the discourse via an opening prayer in a letter. A rhetorical *exordium*, however, regularly gave a preview of coming attractions. Once one gets beyond the opening few verses of Paul's letters, it is almost entirely rhetorical conventions that come into play and shape the various arguments that follow.

It needs to be stressed that all NT documents almost without exception, but perhaps especially the so-called letters, are ad hoc documents, written for specific audiences, at specific times, and addressing specific issues. One could argue that some are encyclicals such as Ephesians or 2 Peter, or that they had a broader audience in mind (say one of the Gospels), but in each case all these documents are addressing the tiny minority group in the Empire called Christians, whether that involves one or more than one house church group. The rhetoric of these documents is specifically Christian in character. The writers know they are "preaching to the choir." We have no NT documents written purely for outsiders, although we get a sense of what that would look like from some of the material in Acts and from the Fourth Gospel, which was written for Christians to use with outsiders "so that you might begin to believe Jesus is the Son of God."

Before we begin to examine in detail the rhetoric we find in the NT, one final point should be made. A key to understanding any rhetorical discourse, whether it is a full discourse like Romans or 1 John, or it is a speech summary like we find in Acts, is that one needs not only to determine the species of rhetoric in play (is it forensic, deliberative, or epideictic), but one needs to find the proposition and peroration of the discourse to find out what it is about and where the argument is going. One of the real benefits of rhetorical analysis of the so-called epistolary literature of the NT is that if we can find the proposition and peroration of a discourse, understanding the many and sometimes convoluted arguments that follow the proposition becomes much easier as we know the point and purpose of the discourse. Of course it is true that an epideictic discourse seldom has a proposition statement, since it is not trying to argue a particular case but rather praising an already approved and embraced matter or subject. Nevertheless, as we shall see, finding the opening thesis statement and closing summary is crucial when a document has such features; it is, in fact, a key to interpreting the document. Bearing these caveats, conditions, and suggestions in mind, we are ready to do more detailed rhetorical analysis of the NT itself.

QUESTIONS FOR REFLECTION

1. If you were asked to define ancient rhetoric, what would you say?
2. Reflect on the differing species of rhetoric and their time frames. How does knowing these things help you understand the content of a discourse?
3. What are some of the cultural differences between the NT world and ours that might affect how rhetoric works and what sort of rhetoric might persuade?
4. How does a commitment to truth change the way rhetoric might or could be used?

CHAPTER 3

Gospels of Persuasion—Mark and Luke

On first blush, it might not seem obvious that rhetoric has anything to do
with the four canonical Gospels. After all, at least three of these Gospels
seem to have been written by Jews, one perhaps by a God-fearer (Luke?),
and one might well ask the question that Church Father Tertullian was
later to ask—what has Jerusalem to do with Athens? In fact the answer is
"much in every way." The Judaism of the time of Jesus and Paul had long
since been Hellenized; this affected it not only linguistically, but culturally
as well. We even find strict Pharisees reclining at table with Jesus in the
Greco-Roman style in the Holy Land (Luke 7:36–50). Furthermore, Jews
were not only writing many documents in Greek, including their sacred
Scriptures (cf. the Septuagint), but even in their burial practices, we find
some first-century Jewish ossuaries with Hebrew or Aramaic inscriptions,
and some with Greek inscriptions. There was even a school of rhetoric in
Jerusalem where a Saul or a John Mark might well have learned rhetoric.

All four of our canonical Gospels seem to have been composed
in Greek. They were user-friendly for spreading the Good News from
Jerusalem right throughout the Empire, for clearly Greek was the lingua franca of the Empire in the first century, including its language of
commerce. If you were selling something or hawking a particular new
message for mass consumption, it had better be offered in Greek and
with rhetorical skill in order not to merely inform but persuade. In this
chapter, we will consider two of the earliest Gospels ever written—Mark's
and Luke's—and analyze them rhetorically. Though we will not be able
to analyze these Gospels in great detail due to space limitations, we hope
to demonstrate the rhetorical modus operandi of these writers by considering examples in each Gospel. What we will discover is that we find
varying levels of skill in Greek and rhetoric in these two Gospels—with
Mark being more primitive and Luke being more polished.

THE BEGINNING OF THE GOOD NEWS: MARK'S GOSPEL

Mark presents us with an ancient style biography of Jesus. The biographical genre in Greek and Latin literature of the era was quite popular to judge from the popularity of Plutarch's famous *Parallel Lives*, or Tacitus's *Agricola*, or Josephus's own biographical reflections. Of course the conventions of ancient biographies were in numerous ways different from modern ones.[1] Our concern then is with how rhetoric affected the shape and substance of ancient biographies. The answer is in several ways. In the first place, ancient biographies were mainly hortatory in character, by which I mean they were meant to teach lessons to audiences and inform not merely their views but their behavior. In other words, ancient biographies were exercises in persuasion, using storytelling and speeches to accomplish their aims. They were not disinterested investigations of the lives of ancient worthies. This being the case, it is no surprise that rhetorical conventions would readily come into play. This was all the more the case with what has been called the first true Christian book, which is to say, the first true narrative spawned by the Jesus movement that sought to further his following in various places and ways. The evangelistic aims of the earliest Christian movement made it all the more important that their "literature," however low brow or high brow, be gauged to persuade some audience about Jesus and the faith that was focusing on him. But how would rhetoric be used in service of this cause?

We can say from the outset, remembering that one of the elementary rhetorical exercises in the *progymnasmata* was forming *chreia*,[2] that even someone with only rudimentary training in rhetoric had been schooled to form small narratives in this way. It was precisely short pithy character-revealing and character-forming anecdotes from the life of the subject of the biography that we regularly find in Plutarch, Tacitus, and yes, in Mark's Gospel as well. One important point to be made about the forming of *chreia* is that it was an exercise in editing, an exercise in boiling down, not boiling up source material, streamlining larger more cumbersome accounts of things. The second-century church historian, Papias tells us that Mark in fact boiled down the memoirs of Peter and his

---

1. See Burridge, *What are the Gospels?*
2. On which see pp. 11–12 above. See also Mack and Robbins, *Patterns of Persuasion.*

preaching into manageable narratives.[3] In the age of papyrus and limited word space, there were several good reasons to boil down one's source material, and if one could do it in a rhetorically effective manner, the chances of the narrative persuading someone about something went up in a culture that was rhetoric-saturated and rhetoric-loving. Indeed, the use of *chreia* would signal to the audience that one *intended* to persuade in the account and not merely to serve as a chronicler of interesting events. It must be stressed that the author of Mark knew his limits. Not even the longest speech of Jesus in Mark's Gospel, Mark 13, the so-called Olivet discourse, appears to take the form of a rhetorical speech with its various functioning parts. Compared to Paul's "letters," Mark's rhetoric is more basic, more elementary; it is more a matter of micro-rhetoric than macro-rhetoric, with individual pericopes taking *chreia* form. This should not be seen as an attempt at mere verbal eloquence in spots, a sort of "verbal stucco-work" to use a phrase of Robert Taylor.[4]

The lists of elementary rhetorical exercises remained consistent throughout the Imperial Age, always containing the composing of *chreia*, along with the composing of other sorts of narratives such as fables or historical narratives. What is most interesting is that the exercises went from easiest to most difficult, from simplest to most sophisticated. On that scale, fable and general narrative came before and earlier than *chreia*. It should be noted that, in fact, what we find in Mark are exercises 2–4 on the scale of skill: narrative, *chreia*, and aphorism/parable, respectively. Jesus is portrayed as one who speaks in parables and aphorisms; the narratives about him sometimes appear of a more general historical sort and sometimes take the even shorter form of *chreia*.

Our author simply did not operate on the level of rhetorical sophistication we find in Hebrews or Paul's letters, but this does not make him a composer of non-rhetorical materials. This brings us to another point. Paul's letters clearly were meant to be declaimed and delivered orally in public. Mark 13:14 suggests that Mark's volume maybe the first Christian book meant to be read. The Evangelist says, "let the *reader* understand" not merely the hearer. The reference is to a singular or individual reader; although, the reader would likely have read it out loud to himself, so the

---

3. On what follows here, see the more detailed account in Witherington, *The Gospel of Mark*, 1–39.

4. See Taylor, *Groundwork of the Gospels*, 76 n. 1. Taylor was one of the first scholars in the modern era to recognize the *chreia* form in Mark's Gospel.

oral and aural dimensions were still in play. Mark's Gospel then is not intended as a collection of speeches but primarily as a narrative to be read. The further conclusion to be drawn from this fact is that Mark's Gospel is not to be seen as a sermon, though it contains fragments of preaching. Rather what is going on in Mark is the offering of persuasive teaching about Jesus that would supplement, not supplant the preaching, filling out the picture of who Jesus was and what his mission and ministry entailed. In other words, the old form critics like Bultmann and Dibelius were wrong. The Gospel of Mark is not *kerygma*; it is *bios* in rhetorical form. Mark's Gospel is in a sense the textbook that gathered up the memoirs and recollections of Peter and presented them in persuasive form. Indeed, the whole form critical approach to these Gospels is deeply flawed, for the Gospels do not amount to boiling up narratives from shards and bits of tradition and sayings of Jesus; on the contrary, Gospel writing was a matter of editing the material down in specific ways.

For example, Aphtonius the Sophist reminds his audience that a *chreia* is a *concise* statement of "memoirs, recollection, memoranda [the so-called *apomnemoneumata*]." While the recollection may go on at some length, the *chreia* is but an epitome, an edited-down version of the source which needs to be brief and pointed and so memorable in character. [5] As Taylor stresses, "*chreia* were about real, historical persons, and they intended to make a historical statement." This or that person said or did this or that memorable thing. For the composition of a true *chreia* "actual fact was demanded. If then the Gospels had not some guarantee of this kind, if they could not be shown to be ascertained history, they would have failed in their appeal."[6] In other words, the use of *chreia* implies a historical claim to an audience that knew how to read the rhetorical signals of the document. Equally importantly, *chreia* are not examples of maxims of a generic or general sort. *Chreia* arise from particular persons and situations, and relate some particular story or anecdote about their lives. We should not assume that Mark's modus operandi is any different from Luke's or Matthew's for that matter. When we look at the way Matthew and Luke handled their Markan source material, say for example with the miracles stories, we quickly discover that Mark almost always gives

5. Notice that Justin Martyr (*First Apology* 67) tells us the Gospels are based on memoirs. Luke 1:1–4 tells us the author is offering *diegesis*, which means longer less precise recollections or eyewitness accounts and early sermons that he has edited rhetorically.

6. Taylor, *Groundwork of the Gospels*, 78–79.

us the longer version of these stories, which Matthew and Luke edit down to make room for other material. Luke 1:1–4, for instance, indicates the author is using sources, and the examination of how he does so shows his historical and rhetorical methods.

If we grant then it is widely recognized that Mark used the *chreia* form (which we will consider examples of shortly), a further question arises as to whether we also find *ergasiae* or elaborations of the *chreia* form by added similar supplemental material. Let us consider the rules for expanding a *chreia*. Theon says one must first provide a brief introduction, use the *chreia* as the thesis of the segment, and then present a series of argument in order to support the thesis, using elaborations, digressions, and character delineations (*Progymnasmata* 215.10–15). Salyer argues that Mark 7:1–23, which does seem to be a combination of source materials, provides us with two *chreia* with expansions or elaborations of each.[7] For the most part however, Mark is comfortable and content to offer one simple *chreia* after another. Robert Fowler stresses: "Mark's rhetoric is not, like Paul's, the rhetoric of oratory, with its logical arguments and emotive appeals. Rather Mark's is the rhetoric of narrative,"[8] and mostly short narrative at that. This description follows the rules about *chreia* being short, precise, memorable, and ending with something of a bang at or near the end—a dramatic saying or deed that characterized or epitomized the person in question. Mark seems to have believed about his own narrative what John Milton once said about Jesus "Yet held it more humane, more heavenly, first/ By winning words to conquer willing hearts,/ And make persuasion do the work of fear."[9]

But, then of course, Mark also had to connect his various and disparate stories. How was he to do this? What were the rhetorical rules for connecting *chreia* together in something of a continuous narrative? Quintilian says that while long periodic sentences like one would find in a discourse were not necessary, in a narrative of some historical substance and subject matter what one wants is "a certain continuity of motion and connection of style. All its members are closely linked together . . . [like] people who link hands to steady their steps, and lend each other mutual support" (*Institutio oratoria* 9.4.129–30). Mark accomplishes the "motion"

7. Salyer, "Rhetoric, Purity and Play," 117–37 and 139–69.

8. Fowler, *Let the Reader Understand,* 63.

9. Milton, "Paradise Regained," 368.

dimension of this rhetorical advice by the prevalent use of his favorite adverb *euthus* ("immediately"). Used over 45 times and often conjoined with the word *kai* ("and"), the term, for the most part, means "and next." It is employed again and again, often at the beginning of sentences, to bind the narratives together. In other words, rhetorical considerations shape not only the editing of the memoirs down into *chreia* but also the connection of the various units into a narrative whole. It is of course also true that various other elements of micro-rhetoric show up in Mark (e.g., rhetorical questions, the use of irony and hyperbole, as well as various oral and aural devices) to make the narrative memorable. Now, however, we want to turn to some examples of *chreia* in Mark's account.

Mark's Chreia

Mark 6:1–6 can be called a characteristic example of a *chreia* meeting all the necessary rhetorical requirements. Not only is the narrative pithy and concise, it climaxes with a classic, memorable saying in v. 4. Furthermore, Mark uses this narrative to conclude the second major division in his Gospel with a story about the rejection of Jesus. The first major division ended with a similar story (Mark 3:6). Mark has a sense of rhetorical development, leading the reader from one climax in the narrative to another. I need to stress that Mark 6:1–6 is not an "ideal" scene, concocted on the basis of the climactic saying in v. 4. The saying, whilst apropos, does not suggest the sort of narrative about Jesus and his relatives that we find here. The story contains unflattering elements about the family of Jesus, which it is hard to imagine the church making up at some later time. It is also not really plausible that Mark would have invented the notion that Jesus was called "son of Mary" in this story, for on the one hand, this could be seen as a slur; on the other hand, Mark shows no interest in the notion of the virginal conception. Here then we are dealing with a story of historical substance, rhetorically shaped into a *chreia* form. Let us consider briefly the climactic saying or proverb in v. 4.

It is intriguing that the saying involved ever-narrowing circles of relationship: Jesus has no honor in his hereditary territory, in his wider kinsmen group, or even among the members of his own household. In an honor and shame culture there could hardly be a greater shame than to be dishonored within these three concentric circles. While it is not impossible that Jesus is quoting a traditional maxim (cf. "Physician heal thyself" and the parallels in Gospel of Thomas 31 and P.Oxy. 1.5 where that maxim is conflated with the physician maxim). The saying is based on the assumptions that those very people who should have most honored and given "face" to Jesus were failing to do so. Verse 5 goes on to suggest that the lack of "face" given reflected the lack of "faith" placed in Jesus, and so he was unable to do many mighty works in his hometown, except lay hands on a few sick people and heal them.

This *chreia* brings to light something crucial about the story of Jesus, and shows that Mark is not simply engaging in eulogistic rhetoric. There is a tragic dimension to the ministry of Jesus, when even one's hometown folks reject the prophet. Mark's account of Jesus' life is frequently stark and dark. This story is of a piece with that presentation.

Another very fine example of a *chreia* is the famous story about Jesus and the Syrophoenician woman in Mark 7:24–30. What is especially intriguing is that it climaxes with a *mot juste* not by Jesus but by the Syrophonecian woman ("even the dogs under the table eat the children's crumbs"). Jesus himself pronounces the benediction on her saying by concluding the discussion not only by giving the woman what she requests but by honoring her by making the direct connection between her words and his actions: "For such a reply you may go; the demon has left your daughter." This brings up a crucial point.

The old form-critical analysis completely fails to account for the form of this narrative. It is not built up from a saying of Jesus at all, but in fact, a saying of the Syrophoenician woman becomes the hinge that turns the tale. The story is, in fact, not generated out of saying; the story is about Jesus the exorcist, who even helps a foreign woman. Once more we should remember the words of Taylor that the use of the *chreia* form bespeaks the historical basis and seriousness of the story. This is all the more the case since on the surface of this story it presents us with an ethnocentric Jesus that seems to be at odds with other portraits of Jesus the exorcist in this Gospel (see for example the Gadarene demoniac story). In short, it is not likely to be a church creation.

One further example of a *chreia*—an elaborated one—must be examined: Mark 10:17–30, the familiar story of the so-called "rich young ruler" and his memorable encounter with Jesus. The heart of the story is the exchange between Jesus and the man, the querying of Jesus by the disciples, and of course, the famous "camel saying" of Jesus. As Ched Meyers has pointed out, this kernel of the story has been elaborated such that we have the following concentric structure:

A. Question about eternal life (v. 17)

B. Rich man cannot leave possessions and follow (v. 22)

C. Jesus' explanation, disciples' reaction (twice!) (vv. 23–26)

B'. Disciples have left possessions and followed (v. 28)

A'. Answer to eternal life question (v. 30).[10]

There appears to have been a story about Jesus and this man that Mark has taken and used as an opportunity to add in some additional teaching of Jesus about the sacrifices of discipleship and its relationship to everlasting life. In addition, we actually have yet another surprising and potentially offensive saying of Jesus that the church would not likely fabricate. Jesus' abrupt response to the man, however much he may love him, is: "Why do you call me good? No one is good but God alone." The rhetorical question is followed by a succinct and surprising answer. This could suggest that Jesus saw himself as neither good, nor God, but it should not be viewed that way. The saying is deliberately provocative meant to help the man rethink his assumptions about things.

As in so many *chreia*, attention is meant to be focused on the climactic saying of the sage or prophet in question. Verses 23–24 are carefully phrased: "With what difficulty will those who have wealth enter the Kingdom of heaven." This is followed by the key aphorism where Jesus is deliberately contrasting the largest animal with the smallest hole in that part of the world. The point is that salvation is not obtainable even by the most strenuous of human efforts. While Jesus is not saying it is impossible for a rich person to be saved, he is saying it is very difficult, and only God could accomplish it. This is of a piece with Jesus' other teachings on how wealth can be an obstacle to final salvation and cannot simply be seen as an uncomplicated blessing from God. Wherein lies the rhetorical elaboration? Perhaps in the introduction of the question about eternal life, or perhaps in the enumeration of the commandments, or perhaps in the further discussions with the disciples at the end of the tale. In any case the heart of the matter is the dialogue with the man and Jesus' famous camel saying. While we could multiply examples of *chreia*, especially from the controversy stories in this Gospel, it will be well if we turn to the parables in Mark briefly, because "parables" were not just the provenance of Jewish sages. They were a normal part of the rhetorical

10. Meyers, *Binding the Strong Man*, 272.

arsenal of those who had been trained in the *progymnasmata*, and Jesus' parables could quite readily be presented in a helpful rhetorical form.

Mark's Parables

Ancient writers and readers in the Greco-Roman world treated a parable as a form of rhetorical *synkrisis*, comparison, or comparative illustration of sorts. Parables were used to clinch a rhetorical argument and persuade someone to do or think something. This raises the very good question as to whether Mark, writing largely to rhetorically aware Gentiles perhaps in Rome, has edited Jesus' parables in a rhetorically adept manner.

It was Aristotle who seems to have first taken *paraboloi* as a subclass of proof called *paradeigma*, or paradigm, which makes its point indirectly through comparison or contrast (*Rhetorica* 2.20.1ff.). Aristotle contrasts these sorts of illustrations taken from everyday life to historical examples, which are called *pragmata* or *exempla*. Quintilian basically echoes what Aristotle says on the matter, agreeing that parables draw on common experience. Further, he distinguishes "parables" from comparisons that in essence draw on "fables." Quintilian's view is that they are most effective when their external referents are apparent and immediate, and so lack the opacity of a true metaphor (*Institutio oratoria* 5.11.22–30). A metaphor is just a stylistic device, rhetorically speaking, but a parable can be an actual inductive proof. Quintilian says that inanimate objects can certainly be used in parables, and in fact he uses the example of sowing a seed as a good example of a proper comparison or illustration by parable (*Institutio oratoria* 8.3.74–75). I doubt that Mark, operating in Rome, was unaware of these sorts of suggestions, for he begins his examples of Jesus' parables by presenting us with the parable of the sower in Mark 4, rapidly followed by two other seed parables: the seed growing secretly and the mustard seed.

Let us consider then Mark 4 from a rhetorical point of view. "Parables" as a form of "paradigm" were used to further deliberative arguments where the aim was to get the audience to embrace something that was beneficial or useful to their praxis, and thus, they were used to enhance the persuasiveness of the argument (see *Institutio oratoria* 3.8.34; cf. Aristotle *Rhetorica* 3.17.5). What then is Mark's audience being shown by Mark 4 that is useful or beneficial to know in deciding on their future course of action? Surely the point of these parables is that it is the disciples job to "sow far, and sow good" the good seed of the Gospel of the Kingdom, but leave the outcome of the sowing in God's hands, realizing that the outcome of an act of persuasion involves factors beyond just the speaker's skills in rhetoric. It also involves the receptivity of the audience, the competing factors in their lives, and also the silent work of God giving growth and harvest.

In deliberative oratory, the ethos or authority of the speaker is crucial (*Institutio oratoria* 3.8.13). Thus, in Mark 4 we have not only the stress on Jesus as the great teacher both to those outside and the insiders as well, but we have the saying "whoever has ears let them hear ... " that is clearly the pronouncement of an authority figure who believes his words carry inherent weight and wisdom.

If we ask about the rhetorical exigency or obstacle being overcome here, it must surely be the discouragement of the proclaimers and persuaders in the audience who have experienced failure of various sorts after sowing the Gospel. The parable is realistic in that it suggests a wide variety of failures or falling short, but then stresses that the good outcomes far outweigh the variety of failures. Unreceptiveness, shallow reception, temporary reception squeezed out by competition, and finally a bumper crop of real fruit are each mentioned in turn.

Mark's audience faces a world largely unreceptive to the Gospel. Mark must persuade them to continue to sow the seed, in spite of this fact. He does so by stressing that Jesus faced the same challenges and rejection. Why should the audience expect it to be otherwise with them? In fact he stresses that there has not been a failure of the sower or the seed when someone does not accept the Good News, rather what determines the outcome is the various states of the soil. This is "useful" and practical information for proclaimers, and should affect their decision to go on spreading the message abroad. They can take heart knowing there will, in due course, be at least some positive and permanent fruit of their labors. The very way this chapter is framed suggests that the audience, despite opposition, must not hide their light under a bushel, but carry on with the sowing. Much more could be said along these lines but this must suffice in our discussion of Mark. Mark's rhetoric may be elementary, but it is no less effective for that. It involves not just the use of small rhetorical devices, like rhetorical questions or irony, but larger skills in forming *chreia* and their elaboration and editing parables into skillful collections that meet certain deliberative purposes of the Evangelist. It involves, as well, structuring narratives so that they are effectively and rhetorically linked to provide flow to the sequence of stories. While the so-called "first Christian book" may not have been the most sophisticated rhetorical effort of early Christians, it was, nonetheless, an effective one to judge from the fact that it was placed in the canon despite Matthew's Gospel re-presenting 95% of Mark's account. We must turn now to Luke's rhetoric.

LUKE'S RHETORICAL SKILLS

It is really quite unfair to compare what is going on in Luke-Acts to what is being attempted in Mark's Gospel, when it comes to rhetoric. It would be like comparing a high school graduate with someone who had a postgraduate degree in the same major subject. Mark's Greek is not the eloquent and able Greek of Luke, and Mark's rhetorical abilities are more elementary than Luke's. Each should be evaluated on their own, not least because Luke is trying to accomplish something quite different than Mark. He is not merely trying to persuade some person or persons about some aspects of the life, person, and works of Jesus. Luke is trying to present a whole salvation history from just before John the Baptist's birth, somewhere between 4–6 BC, to about 60 or so AD, when Paul arrived in Rome, staying there two years under house arrest. Luke is operating as a rhetorically informed and skilled Hellenistic historian, who also knows and writes informed by the historical material in the OT (and in the Macabbean literature as well). He is our only historian among the NT writers, and our only Gospel writer who chose to write a sequel, so far as we know. His two-volume work should be seen as an historical monograph, and this in turn means his Gospel should not be seen as an ancient biography. There are a few good reasons for this position.

First, Luke's Gospel begins with an historical, even a scientific prologue (Luke 1:1–4). No one would ever guess from the first chapter of this book that it was about Jesus. Ancient writers—because of the orality of their documents and because of writing using *scriptum continuum*, an unending stream of letters and words without many, if any, divisions—knew that they had to send signals in the first few lines of a document as to what sort of document it was and what it would be about. Luke 1:1–4 says nothing about Jesus; it speaks of the "things that have happened amongst us." Indeed, that will be Luke's focus throughout his historical project—

events, significant historical events, events of salvific significance as the Good News of Jesus spreads from Galilee to Jerusalem, and then from Jerusalem to the world, even to the heart of the Empire in Rome. Luke's first volume has centripetal motion, "going up to Jerusalem," staying there at the end of the first volume. The second volume moves centrifugally from Jerusalem through the provinces to Rome, the heart of the Empire. The issue is about the progress of the events and message of the Good News, not just telling the story of Jesus, though that is crucial. Indeed, it is the catalyst of all that follows it in the second volume—that and the falling of the Spirit on the church once Jesus ascends. When we are dealing with Luke-Acts we are dealing with the rhetoric of history—nothing less and nothing else. But, it is a particular kind of history: Good News history or salvation history.

Luke, alone of the Evangelists, bothers to provide us with a back story before telling us about Jesus. Luke alone is really interested in historical causality, at least on occasion. Luke alone gives us historical synchronisms, synching up the micro-history of his main story with the macro-history of the Empire (see Luke 2:1–3; 3:1–3; and Acts 18:1–3). It is as a rhetorical historian that we must evaluate Luke and his literary accomplishments. Here we must say something about what sets apart ancient Greek history writing during and after the time of Alexander from modern history writing—namely the influence of rhetoric and rhetorical conventions.[11] Even as early as the time of Aristotle, rhetorical concerns, the desire to persuade and make one's narrative appealing, were affecting how Greek history was being written. So much did the tidal wave of rhetoric influence things that by the first century AD there were actually "historical" works that owed more to declamation and rhetorical concerns than actual study of sources and consulting of eyewitnesses. A very good example of this would be 4 Maccabees, which is nothing other than a use of some historical stories in order to score various emotive and rhetorical points, pulling out all the rhetorical stops to create pathos in the audience. In the Roman tradition another good example of this tendency would be Livy, who saw the transition from Republic to Empire. Livy spent more time following the rhetorical example of Cicero and adapting the literary qualities and composition of his work than on study

---

11. For a general introduction to rhetoric in Luke-Acts see Kurz, "Hellenistic Rhetoric," 171–95.

and comparison of source material. This is noteworthy not least because his work includes various long rhetorically interesting speeches, most of which he could not have been present to hear.[12]

But Luke is telling us something very important about both his historical and rhetorical intentions in Luke 1:1–4. Unlike a Roman historian like Livy, who tended to write what he wrote from the luxury of his armchair, without bothering to do any detailed research or consulting of eyewitnesses, Luke is telling us that on the one hand he intends to write history in the tradition of a Thucydides or a Polybius, a tradition that involved detailed consulting of sources and eyewitnesses, but on the other he intends to write in as rhetorically effective a manner as is possible, as demonstrated by the eloquence of this very sentence, which some have said is the finest Greek rhetorical prose in the entire NT.

More importantly, Luke is reminding us that there was no ancient historical convention that suggested it was fine simply to create speeches for one's heroes, making them up out of whole cloth. A historian could be lazy, or a historian could be diligent as the good Greek and Hellenistic one's were, but nowhere was it a literary convention for such historians to avoid the hard work of doing research and finding out both what had been said and what had been done. The reference to consulting the servants of the Word, the preachers and traditioners who passed the teaching of Jesus and his disciples along, is not accidental. Luke did this. But what would this entail?

In an age before tape recorders or video cameras, while some important speeches of rhetoricians, Emperors, and lawyers were taken down nearly verbatim when possible, most speeches were not. What we have in the speeches in Luke-Acts, which most reflect Luke's rhetorical skill, is at most summaries of speeches, with rare possible exceptions. The most Luke could hope to recover was the main or salient points of some of these speeches in many if not most cases. Thereafter, it would be his task to fill out the speech in a way that was consistent with and fairly represented the epitome that he knew. He needed to be sure to make the speech appropriate to both the speaker and the occasion. Luke probably did not engage in the free composition of speeches, but he surely did edit and amplify his source materials in ways that would have been deemed rhetorically appropriate for historians in that age and of his ilk.

12. On all this see Witherington, *The Acts of the Apostles*, 40–41.

Luke had to balance two essential elements of good, rhetorically sensitive, ancient history writing: fidelity to the truth and at the same time attention to perfection of the style of the narrative—*narratio* but also *exornatio*.[13] We must stress that ancient works, including ancient historical works, were meant to be heard and, therefore, rhetorical attention had to be paid to things like rhythm, assonance, and alliteration, all of which made the narrative listenable at length. One must also assume that Theophilus, who is called noble, was a socially elite, well-educated person interested in Luke's accounts. He may well have been Luke's patron, but whether he was or not, he was definitely a person who knew rhetoric and would appreciate efforts to make the narrative rhetorically effective and persuasive.

One of the most interesting rhetorical features of Luke-Acts is that Luke shows at length that he has the skill to vary the style of his Greek according to the person speaking and the subject matter. For example, the Greek of Luke 1–2 is highly Semitic, intending from the outset of giving the impression of the Jewishness of the subject matter. Similarly, in Acts, as H. J. Cadbury demonstrated long ago, the style of the narrative, which begins in Jerusalem, begins in Semitic fashion, but the further one gets into Acts, the closer one gets to Athens (Acts 17) and Rome, the less and less Semitic and the more and more Hellenistic the Greek becomes.[14] This did not happen by accident. It is probable that Luke is courting a listener who knows the cadences of the LXX and so in his freedom to use Semitisms in Luke 1–2 and Acts 1–12 he is deliberately archaizing and suggesting that the history he is writing is a continuation of salvation history and just as important as that found in the LXX. Christianity is not to be seen as a totally new religion, but rather one grounded in and linked to a religion of hoary antiquity. Luke is highly skilled in Greek, and knows various styles and how to use them well. Form and content were expected to co-inhere, and style was supposed to be a function of genre and rhetorical purpose or intent.

Polybius reminds us that serious historians had the tasks of both informing *and* persuading, following the conventions of deliberative rhetoric most of all, and if one was doing an apologia, forensic rhetoric as well. We certainly find both in Acts, particularly in the speeches. Aristides

13. See North, "Rhetoric and Historiography," 234–42, here especially 242.
14. See Cadbury, *Style and Literary Method of Luke*.

informs us that in writing a history the rhetorical art should especially be evident in the preface or proem (see Luke 1:1–4) and in the speeches. Here is how he puts the matter: "While the flowing and loose structure is appropriate for narrative and emotional passages, the periodic structure is appropriate for declamations [i.e., speeches] and *proemia* and arguments" (*Ars rhetorica* 1.13.4). Let us consider then Luke's proem or *exordium*.

Luke's Exordium: Luke 1:1–4

As we have already noted, Luke 1:1–4 has been called the best Greek sentence in the whole NT. Since an elevated subject was thought to deserve an elevated style, this sentence incorporates a whole series of impressive multi-syllable Greek words not found in the rest of Luke-Acts (e.g., *epeidēper, diēgēsis, anatazasthai, plērophorēmenos, autoptas*). Yet still, as Quintilian instructs and as is appropriate in an *exordium*, Luke writes in a clear and direct manner in this sentence (*Inst.* 4.1.34). What should be said about some of the impressive words in this proem is that they were in various cases almost technical terms in Greek historiography.

The task of the historian, according to Polybius, was to teach and persuade the lover of knowledge by means of recounting true deeds and words worthy of learning and even emulating (2.56.11). Luke does not suggest he is going to be like the more Sophistic historians, more interested in entertaining and giving pleasure rather than instructing and persuading. No, Luke wants his audience to be clear about the "things which have happened amongst us." He wants Theophilus to know an orderly account, not least because there were apparently various previous such accounts, and some confusion might be possible. Luke seeks to set the record straight about "these important things which have happened."

Notice that nowhere in this introduction is any mention of Jesus or his life. Both Luke 1:1–2 and Acts 1:1–2 mention a narration of deeds and words—not just any kind of deeds and words but rather "things that have been *fulfilled* among us." That is, Luke will discourse about events that came to pass according to some sort of divine plan, and so were fulfillments of divine promises, prophecies, or even predictions.

The term *historia*, for which the obvious English transliteration is "history," refers to an investigation, or as Aristotle puts it "the investigations (*historiai*) of those who write about deeds" (*Rhetorica* 1.4.13). Luke must meet the requirement of Greek history writing to produce a sequential narrative of crucial events, and in the course of the presentation, bring order to the account, helping the audience see the significance of these particular events deemed worthy of chronicling. Mere reporting was not enough—explaining in an orderly and rhetorical manner was required. At the end of the first volume, Luke 24:44 speaks of all things written about Jesus being fulfilled or at least needing to be fulfilled. One must conclude that this term "fulfilled" is a shorthand for saying that salvation events, promised in Scripture, were being accomplished, beginning with the life of John the Baptizer and continuing right on to the open-ended conclusion of Acts, where we find the Word spreading unhindered in Rome through the efforts and auspices of one Saul of Tarsus. Fulfillment was to be an important refrain in Luke-Acts (Lk 1:45; 4.21; Acts 2:15, 21). The coming of the Kingdom brings the age of fulfillment.

One highly rhetorical example of how to use this announced theme of fulfillment and suggest a pattern of historical recurrence, which demonstrates that we are not dealing with mere coincidence but rather a divine plan in history, can be briefly mentioned at this juncture. Consider what is happening in the first paradigmatic speech of Jesus after the Prologue in Luke 4, a speech that sets up the subsequent events and shows them to be a fulfillment of a particular Isaianic Scripture interpreted by Jesus in his home synagogue.[15] Luke has carefully structured this material so that the narrative that follows this sermon will demonstrate how the Scripture he cites here (Isa 61:1–2) is fulfilled.[16] We can see this from the following:

Luke 4:18–19/Isa 61:1–2	Luke 4:38–44	Luke 8:1–15
Preach Good News (18)		Preach and proclaim Good News (1)
Recovery of sight to the blind (18)	Jesus heal's Simon's mother-in-law (38) and sick (40)	Healing evil spirits and illnesses in women (2–3)
Set at liberty the oppressed (18)	Demons cast out (41)	Example of exorcism: Mary (2)
Proclaim the acceptable year of the Lord (19)	Preach Good News to other cities (43)	Parable of the sower (4–15)

15. And as is often noted the parallel speech of Peter in Acts 2 and the events surrounding it set in motion the narrative in Acts as well.

16. See the discussion in Witherington, *Women in the Earliest Churches*, 128–29.

A good *exordium* would be a compact introduction hinting at much that was to come but not showing the writer's hand before due time. It foreshadowed but did not give yet a foretaste. Luke's prologue is masterful in this very way, leaving the hearers longing for more, and so leading them directly into the narrative that follows. Quintilian would have been proud of this opening, but then so would Polybius for its rhetorically adept sort of history writing. We are fortunate at this juncture that many have now recognized the rhetorical skill and prowess of Luke, as well as his historical acumen, and so increasingly this prologue is being appreciated for what it is. Consider, for example, the essential thesis of a recent doctoral dissertation by Clare Rothschild, who argues that the Lukan "patterns of recurrence, prediction, use of the expression *dei* ('it is necessary') and hyperbole . . . are elements of Hellenistic rhetorical historiography with counterparts in other Hellenistic and early Roman period histories. As the rhetorical techniques of these historians, they are in direct support of the prologue claims to accuracy and truth, not undermining the genre of the work as historiography in favor of theological readings, but supporting such a designation."[17] In other words, the preface sets up the expectation that rhetorical history writing with rhetorical patterns will follow, and indeed they do. It is in order to turn now to one other feature of Luke's Gospel that especially reveals his rhetorical hand, namely, his way of presenting Jesus' parables.

Luke's Rhetorically Shaped Parables

It needs to be recognized that *parabolē* is a term for a comparison or comparative illustration from at least the time of Aristotle if not before.[18] If Luke was indeed dealing with a rhetorically informed Gentile audience, one would expect it to read his parables with a recognition of the way the term was used in Greco-Roman rhetoric.

As we mentioned when dealing with Mark's treatment of parables, Aristotle in his discussion of the matter (*Rhetorica* 2.20.1ff.) treats parables as a sub-class of comparative proofs which he calls paradigms (*paradeigma*). These are artificial inductive proofs which make their points by means of the comparison or through illustration. Parables can

17. Rothschild, "Luke-Acts and the Rhetoric of History," xiv.
18. See McCall, *Ancient Rhetorical Theories*, 1–23.

be distinguished from fables (called *logoi*) in that they are shorter comparisons that draw on actual historical examples. They are then comparisons drawn from everyday life or common experience. Rhetorically their function is to prove or support the veracity of the general proposition being advanced. It would be in order to ask in the case of Luke what is/are the general propositions Luke is seeking to advance about Jesus and salvation history that could be supported or "proved" by the use of some of his distinctive parables, such as the parable of the Good Samaritan or the parable of the Prodigal Son? Also, are their signs when Luke has taken over parables from Mark or elsewhere that he has edited them so they will be more rhetorically useful to support the case he is advancing? We will return to address these questions shortly.

Let us consider briefly what Quintilian has to say about the matter of parables. Quintilian agrees with Aristotle that a *parabolē* is rightly seen as a sub-category of paradigms drawn from common experience and used as an auxiliary to inductive proofs. His view is that they are most effective when they have as little metaphorical qualities as possible, but rather speak in plain language where their referents are immediately apparent (*Inst.* 5.1.30ff). He obviously would not have been enamored with modern theories about parables as giant metaphors.

If, for example, we were to read the parable of the Good Samaritan as a rhetorical unit with Quintilian's strictures as a guide, we would assume: 1) Jesus is actually talking about Samaritans, priests, Levites, and Jews in general, these are not figures for something else; 2) he is actually trying to answer the time-honored Jewish question about the nature and scope of neighborliness in the context of a tense multi-ethnic situation; and 3) he is probably seeking to deconstruct certain parts of the holiness code which would prevent one from fulfilling the higher obligation to love one's neighbor.

But of course there is also the possibility in rhetoric that a parable would be used as a figure of thought. However, if one reads, for example, *Rhetorica ad Herenium* closely it becomes clear that even as a "figure" a parable is not some sort of enigmatic metaphor but an analogy, linked very closely to the historical illustration or the example (4.48.61). As a figure, however, a parable has as its function not the clinching of a proof but clarifying or making a point more vividly. Quintilian likewise disassociates parables from metaphors and links them closely with historical analogies (*Inst.* 4.1.70 and 6.3.61–62).

In general it needs to be said that it is not the length of a parable or its specific form (is it more like a straight analogy, or more like a brief narrative) that makes a parable a parable from a rhetorical point of view but rather *the content is determinative*-- it must involve a comparison from everyday life, whether elaborated at length or not, whether involving a story element and so a plot, or not. It is also germane to add that rhetoricians like Quintilian also specified that in general a parable should be, more often than not, about things or concepts rather than about persons (which would be an historical example). In a passage of obvious relevance to the Lukan version of the parable of the sower in Luke 8:4–15, Quintilian says:

> If you wish to argue that the mind requires cultivation, you would use a comparison drawn from the soil, which if neglected produces thorns and thickets, but if cultivated will bear fruit; or if you are exhorting someone to enter the service of the state, you will point out that bees and ants, though not mere dumb animals, but tiny insects, still toil for the common good. (*Inst.* 5.11.24)

What we learn from this discussion is that though we do have some uniquely Lukan parables that have a plot and so can be called "narratives," the fact that we also have some that seem to be simpler analogies shows that Luke, in agreement with the rhetoricians of his day did not define parable as a plot-driven narrative, unlike some modern parable scholars. Equally striking is the fact that the ancient rhetors urged that good parables were not characterized by multiple layers of dark meaning and so were not oblique but rather were the contrary—clear illustrations of the principle or proof being argued for on other grounds as well.[19] Quintilian is emphatic at this point—the metaphorical quality of the parable must be kept to a minimum (*Inst.* 5.11.22).

One wonders if Luke, in taking over Mark's discussion about the secrets of the Kingdom (see Luke 8:9–10), intends his own audience to see a clear contrast between inside information and outsiders being given parables. The point here to be stressed is that the emphasis on parables for the public would not be a surprising point for a Gentile audience that was rhetorically informed; the assumption would be that these were rather straightforward analogies intended for public consumption. It must also

---

19. See the excellent discussion by Young, to whom this entire section is indebted, in his fine dissertation, "Whoever Has Ears to Hear," 120–26.

be stressed that the first parable that Luke presents in Luke 8 is in fact the parable of the sower, a form of which Quintilian himself uses to show how a rhetorically adept use of parables might transpire.

There is a good deal more that could be said along these lines, but perhaps we may end this discussion by suggesting a list of desiderata for the future study of Luke's parables in a rhetorically informed way: 1) a careful examination of what Aristotle, Cicero, Quintilian, Demetrius, and others say about parables needs to be undertaken; 2) this should be followed by a systematic study of all of Luke's parables to see how and to what degree the rhetorical discussions may affect Luke's presentation; 3) one needs then to assess whether in fact Luke seems to be using parables as auxiliary proofs or comparisons that help make his points, in good rhetorical fashion; 4) a reassessment of the use of the parable as metaphor theory needs to be undertaken *vis-à-vis* the rhetorical discussion—it is doubtful Luke himself will have viewed parables in this light; and 5) one ought to undertake an especially close re-examination of the uniquely Lukan parables in light of the rhetorical discussions, as well as the re-dactional differences between Luke's and Mark's (or Q's) presentations of a common parable, to see if the differences seem to reflect rhetorical conventions and aims.

AND SO?

We have sought in this chapter only to present the flavor of the rhetoric of Mark and Luke, and we have deliberately not dealt with how Luke handles speeches in a rhetorical manner. We wanted to reserve that discussion for the next chapter when we look at Acts. Enough, however, has been said to show that both Mark's and Luke's Gospels reflect rhetorical concerns and features in various ways: Mark in a more elementary manner; Luke in a more sophisticated manner. Luke shows the ability to shape not merely brief narratives or parables in rhetorical ways, but indeed, his whole ac-count, beginning with his Prologue and carrying on through the whole of the two volumes, is shaped rhetorically. He is a rhetorical historian. Mark by contrast is writing a biography of Jesus, and is able to use the skills learned from the *progymnasmata* to shape *chreia*, elaborate several of them, rhetorically edit parables, and even make some rhetorical com-parisons (*synkrisis*) along the way. The comparison between the camel and the rich man, while comic, is also tragic. But, there is very little that could be called comic about the multitude of speech summaries we find in Luke's second volume. Luke is a serious historian, and his editing of the speeches he uses reflects it. To these we now turn.

QUESTIONS FOR REFLECTION

1. How do Gospels reflect rhetorical concerns even when they are not dealing with speech material?
2. What does the use of the *chreia* form tell us about the seriousness of purpose of the Evangelist?
3. Are *chreia* examples of "invention" and so boiling up narratives from scratch, or are they examples of boiling down and editing more extensive source material?
4. How does Luke's Prologue reflect the rhetorical conventions about a "proem"?

CHAPTER 4

Early Christian Homilies:
The Rhetorical Speech Summaries in Acts

While it is certainly possible to analyze the speeches in Luke 1–2 on the basis of ancient rhetorical conventions,[1] what comes of such analysis is lots of evidence of micro-rhetoric, but not evidence of macro-rhetoric, particularly the skeletal form that one usually finds in ancient Greek speeches. This is not entirely a surprise because Luke the historian does indeed go out of his way to avoid anachronism. It would be inappropriate to have Mary sing the Magnificat in a manner that would suggest it was composed according to what Aristotle and his successors said about the structure of such epideictic oratory. The mother of Jesus may have known a few words of Greek, but a rhetorical education at that level was surely not a part of her history, nor is it even likely she spoke to Elizabeth in Greek. Surely, it would have been in Aramaic.

But when we turn to the speeches, or better said, speech summaries in Acts we are in a different ethos and context altogether. Here the Christian movement is on the rise and setting out to do persuasive evangelism, or at least that was the hope. It will serve us well to analyze reasonably closely what Luke does with his speeches in Acts as we assess his rhetorical skills, aims, purposes, and interests.

Before we do so, it is important to stress that Luke does not just conceptualize these speeches in rhetorical ways. As we said in the last chapter *he conceptualizes his whole historical project in rhetorical ways.* For example, Bruce Longenecker has recently demonstrated at length how Luke uses the chain-link rhetorical technique of repetition and overlapping material to bind Acts 1 to Luke 24. Likewise, in Acts 11–13, we find the transition from the focus on Petrine narratives to the focus on Pauline

---

1. I have had a doctoral student of mine do just this sort of an analysis.

narratives, and at both the mid-point of the first half of Acts (Acts 8) and the mid-point of the second half (Acts 19:21–41), this technique is used. The following unit and its subject is introduced before completing the first unit, and so there is an anticipatory-retrospective feature to the narrative at major junctures in the story-telling.[2] We should expect then, that the rhetorically shaped speeches have been contoured in similar ways to the rhetorically shaped narratives.

THE SPEECHES IN ACTS: AN OVERVIEW

Scholars have known for some time that the excerpts or summaries of speeches in Acts reflect rhetorical skill and conventions. Satterthwaite has shown that Luke's choice and arrangement of material in Acts, most especially the speeches, shows a good familiarity with rhetorical conventions in regard to invention, arrangement, and style—three of the main things one needed to attend to in order to be persuasive in the Greco-Roman world.[3] Lest we think that the rhetoric in and of the speeches in Acts simply reflects the rhetoric in the source material, though no doubt there is some truth to that, Soards has shown at length that whatever source Luke may have used for these speeches, he has made them his own in terms of style, vocabulary, syntax, and the like.[4] The other side of this balance is what the classics scholars and ancient historians tell us—there was no literary convention or permission simply to invent speeches for one's characters in a historical narrative, rather "the principle was established that speeches were to be recorded accurately, though in the words of the historian, and always with the reservation that the historian could clarify."[5]

Once more we must remind ourselves that what we have is Luke's edited down or précis versions of these speeches, and so the fact that they still reflect the rhetorical macro-structure or speech outline is surely in significant measure attributable to Luke. And here at the outset, we should note a feature of the speeches in Acts that set them apart from those in Thucydides' earlier Hellenistic history. "In Thucydides, speeches func-

2. Longenecker, *Rhetoric at the Boundaries*, 165–205.

3. Satterthwaite, "Acts against the Background of Classical Rhetoric," 337–79.

4. Soards, *The Speeches in Acts*.

5. See the helpful discussion in Fornara, *The Nature of History in Ancient Greece and Rome*, 145–55, especially here 145.

tion as a commentary on events. In Luke-Acts, speeches are an essential feature of the action itself, which is the spread of the Word of God."[6] It is God's living, powerful, and persuasive Word, which changes things, sets the story in motion, and transforms people. The early Christian movement was a movement focused on and impelled by the proclaimed Word. It is thus no wonder that Luke the historian devotes over one third of his whole narrative in Acts to speeches—some 365 verses out of about 1000; 295 of these verses occur in the some twenty-four speeches usually discussed by scholars. If one wants to be absolutely complete there are actually some 27–28 speech summaries in Acts, plus some eight partial speech summaries and three dialogues. To get a sense of how much emphasis is placed on speeches in Acts, there are twice the density of speeches in Acts compared to what we find in Tacitus's *Annales* or Herodotus's *Histories*, eight times as much as we find in Thucydides' *History of Peloponnesian War*, and sixteen times as much as we find in Polybius's *Histories*.[7]

We must of course bear in mind that it was seldom possible for someone to remember or take down speeches verbatim in antiquity, and in any case, various of the speeches in Acts are not the sort that scribes would have been busily recording, not being the speeches of major political, religious, or socially elite figures. There was thus room for Luke to make his speech source material his own, and to seek to make each summary rhetorically appropriate to the speaker, the occasion, and the subject matter.

Let us consider then the distribution of speeches in Acts and their ascribed sources:

A. Eight speeches by Peter—chs. 1, 2, 3, 4, 5, 10, 11, and 13

B. Two speeches by James—chs. 15 and 21

C. One speech by Stephen (the longest single speech)—ch. 7

D. Nine speeches by Paul—chs. 13, 14, 17, 20, 22, 24, 26, and 28

E. Four longish speeches by non-Christians—5:35–39 (Gamaliel); 19:35–40 (town clerk in Ephesus); 24:2–8 (Tertullus); and 25:14–21, 24–27 (Festus).

---

6. Aune, *The New Testament in its Literary Environment*, 125.

7. Soards, *Speeches in Acts*, 183 n. 3. This is reckoning things only on the basis of the major speeches in Acts—the big 24. If we count everything the disparity is even greater.

It should be apparent that the speeches in category E are not in any case the kind Christians would memorize or takes notes on, though the latter two may have been summarized in court proceedings. Furthermore, apart from the Miletus speech in Acts 20 and the defense speeches beginning in Acts 23, Luke was not likely present to hear these speeches. Then too, the missionary speeches of Peter and Paul do sound alike at points (cf. Peter's in ch. 2, 3, and 10 with Paul's in ch. 13), even to the degree of using the same proof texts in similar settings, which may in part be put down to knowing the same basic kerygma and testimonia or catenae of OT texts that would be useful for persuasion, especially about Christ. One of the mistakes that must not be made is fretting too much over the fact that the speeches of Peter and Paul in Acts seldom sound like the Peter and Paul of their letters. The lone exception to this is of course the speech to the Ephesian elders in Acts 20. There is a reason for this exception—this is the only speech addressed to Christians by either Paul or Peter, and of course the letters are *all* addressed to Christians. The rhetoric is different because the audience is quite different in Acts and in the letters.

Upon analyzing the speeches closely, it becomes apparent that Peter is portrayed as carrying the burden of persuasion in the first half of Acts, while Paul picks up where Peter left off in the second half. Note as well that James's speeches come just at or after the crucial hinge or turning point in the narrative and help set the church off in a new and better direction, having resolved the first major crisis that threatened to divide the church. In general, speeches do indeed come at crucial junctures in the narrative and either precipitate or are part of the action, and in terms of literary effect the speeches help bind the whole narrative of Acts together. That we have speeches in Jerusalem, Athens, and the like shows that Luke is concerned to make clear the Gospel was proclaimed in major places in the Empire, and so Luke selects representative material, to show how the Gospel was rhetorically effective in different sorts of settings.

Of all the speeches in Acts, the one that sounds least Lukan is Stephen's speech, and this may reflect that in this case Luke relied on more source material here than elsewhere, perhaps source material from Paul himself. Whatever their ultimate sources, the speeches are masterpieces in miniature. F. J. Foakes-Jackson puts it this way: "Whatever these speeches may be, it cannot be disputed that they are wonderfully varied as to their character, and as a rule admirably suited to the occasion on which they were delivered. Luke seems to have been able to give us an extraordinarily accurate picture of the undeveloped theology of the earliest Christians, and enables us to determine the character of the most primitive presentation of the Gospel. However produced, the speeches in Acts are masterpieces and deserve the most careful attention."[8] They reveal that Luke is a skillful rhetorical historian concerned that in both form and substance this material be an accurate reflection of the early Christian art of persuasion. At this juncture we must turn to look at some samples in a bit of detail.

THE PERSUASIVE POWER OF PENTECOST—ACTS 2:14–42

One of the more common rhetorical practices of Hellenistic historians when it came to speeches was archaizing—giving the feeling that the discourse was given in a style and diction of an earlier time or period. In fact historians like Dionysius of Halicarnassus would imitate the much earlier style of the speeches in Thucydides. Luke is well aware of this rhetorical device meant to give an air of authority and antiquity to a passage, and he uses it here and elsewhere. Luke, however, is not working with a figure like Aeneas or brave Achilles. He is working with a Jewish speaker speaking on Jewish subjects to an almost entirely Jewish audience, while quoting the Hebrew prophets, Joel in particular. Thus here, in Acts 2, and later in Acts 13 we have the form of archaizing called Septuaginalizing, the making of a speech to sound like the biblical diction of the LXX. The rhetoricians had a term for why this needed to be done. It was a matter of "suitability" and they called it *prosōpopoia* or "impersonation" of an earlier and famous speech style. Lucian had this to say about the matter: "let his language suit his person and subject [and so] you can play the orator and show your eloquence" (*How to Write History* 58).

Bearing in mind that Luke is presenting a Greek epitome of a speech that may have been spoken in Aramaic or possibly Koine Greek, and in either case spoken with a Galilean accent, he is thus not able to directly mimic the effect of such a situation. Nevertheless, he wants to suit the speech to the speaker and the importance of the occasion, and he does so by Septuaginalizing the diction here, conveying the sense that Peter too spoke like the prophets and Scriptures of old. What this suggests about Theophilus is that perhaps he knew the LXX, perhaps like Luke

---

8. Foakes-Jackson, *The Acts of the Apostles*, xvi.

he had been a God-fearing, high-status Gentile before Luke wrote these accounts for him.

The type of rhetoric we find in Peter's speech here is forensic, the rhetoric of defense and attack, beginning more with the former (doing an *apologia*) than the latter. Thus, vv. 14–21 refute the charge of drunkenness, and vv. 22–36 go on the attack, indicting some Jews for killing Jesus. By this rhetorical move the innocence of the former group is shown, putting the latter group now on the defensive, with the result that many are heart-stricken and ask what they must do now. This in turn prompts what can be called a second brief speech that is deliberative in form telling the audience the proper course of action to take in the immediate future that will be to their benefit. This second speech as well prompts an appropriate response (vv. 41–42 showing that the rhetoric was effective). In the course of all this, Peter is presented as being like a trained orator, standing tall and lifting up his voice (v. 14), which is to say taking the typical stance of the orator, particularly the rhetorician.

One of the interesting features of the rhetoric of the first speech is that we do not find a full *exordium* or introduction to the speech, but that was not absolutely necessary when the audience did not need to be lulled into a favorable listening posture so that they would willingly listen to the speech that followed (see Quintilian *Inst.* 3.8.7; 4.1.5–6). Luke Timothy Johnson notices the skill in the two little speeches we find here: "By no means is the speech a casual collection of assertions. It is a rhetorically sophisticated argument, involving refutation of common opinion (that the disciples could be drunk . . . or that David was speaking of himself in the psalms) (2.29–30); an appeal to eyewitness testimony (of the apostles); and an appeal to scriptural prophecy concerning this event (2.17–21), and its cause (2.25–35)."[9]

Peter is presented as being a good and careful orator gradually establishing increasing rapport with his audience whom he first addresses as "men Jews" or "Judeans" (v. 14), then "men Israelites" (v. 22), and then finally "men, brothers" (v. 29), to which the audience responds in kind (v. 37).[10] In such a speech much rests on the ethos and authority of the

9. Johnson, *The Acts of the Apostles*, 54. Black, "The Rhetorical Form of the Hellenistic Jewish and Early Christian Sermon," 1–18, rightly recognizes the use of the two different rhetorical species in these two little speeches.

10. Notice that this very same progressive direct address device is used by Paul in Acts 13:16, 26, 38.

speaker, and so what we find here is the speaker bases what he says on "inartificial proofs," that is proofs from ancient authorities (such as the Scripture) that both the speaker and the audience respect, and from eye-witness testimony. Luke reminds Theophilus in this first lengthy example of speech material that it is a summary, and so he tells him "and he testi-fied with many other arguments" (v. 40a) which Luke does not present here. The audience knows then that this is but a sampling of the persua-sion and so it is not a shock when Luke portrays Peter as going directly from an argument to the peroration—with the stirring up of pathos, the deeper emotions—"save yourselves from this wicked generation." The audience's situation is suddenly seen as grave and requiring immediate response and action.

While editing and paraphrasing a speaker was a well-known rhe-torical art that was part of basic rhetorical training and exercises,[11] Luke's rhetorical skill is shown not merely in editing but also in how Luke pres-ents the two parts of this speech (or these two little speeches) so they have a certain unity and coherence, using the rhetorical technique called amplification, where one repeats an idea, but with variation, using dif-ferent language to say the same or a similar thing. Thus, in v. 21 we have "to call upon the name of the Lord," which is another way of speaking about what we find in v. 38, where we are told about being baptized in the name of Jesus Christ. Or again, the promise in vv. 17–18 prepares us for the reference to the promise of receiving the Spirit in v. 38, and the final exhortation in the *peroratio* in v. 40b reiterates the conclusion of the Joel prophecy in v. 21. It is not for nothing that this first real speech in Acts has been called a rhetorical masterpiece.[12] Peter in a short space of time has accomplished two major rhetorical aims: (1) defending the moral vir-tue of his fellow Christians who are responding to the Spirit falling upon them, and (2) going on the offensive and calling the Jewish audience to repentance, baptism, and conversion to Christ. Peter is depicted here and throughout the first half of Acts as the spokesman for the Jerusalem Jewish Christians, that is until James takes over after Acts 11–12. The authority he has is charismatic, or Spirit empowered and impelled, but Peter is depicted as harnessing the Spirit's inspiration, guidance, and power in a rhetorically effective discourse. This will be the first of many such discourses in Acts, beginning with a bang, and with more than a

11. See e.g., Cadbury, "Four Features of Lukan Style," 87–102, especially here 92.

12. R. E. Zehnle, *Peter's Pentecost Discourse*, 37.

hint that it is the Spirit (and not primarily the education) that inspires good and effective rhetoric.

ORATORIA INTERRUPTUS: LUKE'S TECHNIQUE

One of the readily discernable features of the way Luke handles his speech material is that speeches tend to be concluded by way of interruption, or at least the speech appears to be unfinished (cf. 7:54; 10:44; 17:32; 22:22; 26:24). Doubtless some of these speeches *were* interrupted since they dealt with emotive and volatile issues, at least when it came to Jewish Christians trying to persuade non-Christian Jews about Jesus. But, it is fair to say that some of this is simply good rhetorical technique, artfully making up for the limited source material. Luke, it must be remembered, believed these speeches were both part of the actions and prompted the action, and when the latter was the case, there was often an interruption of the speech, sometimes even by the Holy Spirit for instance when Peter was addressing Cornelius and his family (10:44).

If we ask why Luke the historian, with surely limited speech source material, would nonetheless spend over a third of his narrative on such material, Colin Hemer provides us with a clear answer and rationale for this phenomenon: "the author of Acts displays an interest in direct speech that is not readily paralleled in other ancient literature. The reason for this preoccupation is not difficult to understand, however; the progress of the good news is the very subject of the book of Acts and preaching of that word (and the words spoken in opposition to it) is therefore the heart of the matter, not merely illustrative material as it might be to authors who write about history of nations or the cause and effects of war."[13] Early Christianity is about the spread and progress of the Word by means of the Spirit and the Spirit's spokespersons. In order to see exactly how skillfully Luke uses his source material and the device of "interruption" let us briefly consider Acts 4:8–12.

We are told at the outset in v. 8 that Peter began to speak once he was "filled with the Holy Spirit." Luke surely is using this phrase here not to refer to the spiritual level or degree of sanctification of Peter. He is using the same sort of language we find in the LXX, to indicate that Peter like the prophets of old was inspired to speak God's word, prompted and guided by that same Spirit. Notice the way the phrase is used throughout

13. Hemer, *The Book of Acts in the Setting of Hellenistic History*, 418.

Luke-Acts to indicate the prophetic character of the speaker and speech (Luke 1:15, 41, 67; 4:1 Acts 2:4; 4:31; 6:3, 5; 7:55; 9:17; 11:24; 13:9).

When we examine Acts 4:8b–12 closely what we discover is basically a reiteration of the major elements of the sermon summaries already presented in Acts 2–3. This brings up an important point. The "Christian" speeches in Acts must be examined in the context of the ongoing and developing narrative, as they are meant to have a cumulative effect. By this I mean that after Acts 2 sometimes Luke will repeat themes in speeches, but only allusively, because he has already established the theme in an earlier speech. These speeches, as we find them now in Acts, are meant to have a cumulative effect on the audience and should not be seen as isolated phenomena, however they functioned in the original historical setting. Nowhere is this more apparent than in the threefold account of Saul's conversion in Acts 9, 22, and 26, which includes one third person account and two first person ones. The effect of what we learn about Paul both from the speeches and the narrative is meant to be cumulative, with some new facts showing up for the first time in Acts 26. The rhetorical technique of "amplification" or "accumulation" is in play, and we will need to attend to it shortly, to see the full rhetorical force of what Luke is doing there.

This speech of Peter's in Acts 4:8–12 can be said to be forensic in character and to be an example of speaking truth to power. The setting here is more apropos for a forensic speech since Peter is addressing ruling and judicial authorities; indeed, the speech serves as something of a defense of the faith and Peter's actions. The rhetorical exigence that prompts the speech is the authority that Peter has to do what he is doing.

The speech begins in a respectful fashion with Peter addressing the audience as "rulers of the people and elders," which serves to establish some rapport with the audience, attempting to make them more receptive to what will follow. Overall the speech is not highly polemical in character, though it is adamant about defending a point of view—v. 12 could hardly be more emphatic. This particular speech summary does not rely on detailed proofs but rather chiefly on the ethos of Peter himself: he is a man of godly character full of the Spirit, which despite his lack of being a learned man, gives him both power and *auctoritas*—the term *exousia* of course referring to both of these things. The speech does, however, also rely on *parrēsia* or free speech. This was an important earmark of rhetorical authenticity—the stating clearly, plainly, directly, without subterfuge or fear of the relevant facts. At issue here is the character of Peter's deed—what is a *good* deed? Verse 9 indicates that the main thing at issue is the performance of the miracle.

Notice as well the establishment not only of the eschatological message about Jesus, "whom you crucified but whom God raised from the dead," but also the fact that now the time of ignorance is over, and so the regular refrain "let it be known." Once it is "known" there can be no more excuse for ignorance, bad behavior, or lack of response. Verse 11 further makes clear Jesus' own character, since the issue of ethos is crucial here. Jesus was selected by the ultimate Divine Authority for great things though he was rejected by human authorities. Luke is using Ps 117:22 here, which was previously used in Luke 20:17 at the end of the parable of the vineyard. Luke's modifications are noteworthy. A stone cannot be "scorned," but a person can be, and so, Luke has changed the verb in v. 11 to "scorned" to unmask the attitude of the authorities before whom Peter stands. The words "by you" are also added before "builders" to make clear that the allusion is directly perceived to be fingering the immediate audience and their behavior. Calling them "builders" was appropriate since these very men were still in the process of having the Herodian temple completed.

One rhetorical technique we find a good deal in the speeches in Acts amounts to a sort of emphatic throwing down the gauntlet. The opposite of this would be the rhetorical technique called *insinuatio,* where one merely hints at the real bone of contention at the outset and reserves until much later dealing with it. Here we have the opposite of that in v. 12, where we find the dramatic statement, "There is no salvation in any other, for no other name under heaven is given among human beings by which we must be saved."

The reaction of the audience to this exercise in "free speaking" is amazement, according to v. 13, and, like in the Gospel when the crowd is amazed, this does not mean that they are convinced or are responding in faith. It cannot be over-emphasized the importance of the term *parrēsia* and its cognates in Acts (cf. 2:29; 4:13, 29, 31; 28:31; and in the noun form 9:27–28; 13:46; 14:3; 18:26; 19:28; 26:26). This was not merely a way of saying that the speaker was brave or bold, it indicates that his rhetoric is plainspoken and not sophistic. The term is almost always used to show how the Gospel was preached to Jews in Acts. What might be interesting to a person like Theophilus, however, is the fact that this term was regularly used about and by Greek philosophers over and over again, if they were exemplars of "free speaking" as the Cynics were often credited with being. Peter thus appears like a mighty rhetor in a potentially hostile setting. Luke is careful however not to suggested that Peter was an illiterate person incapable of such powerful rhetoric. Peter and John are called *aggramatoi* and *idiōtai*, with the former having the basic sense of "without letters" (i.e., not learned, no "higher" education; cf. John 7:15). What is meant here particularly is no formal training in the Law or rhetoric, the skill in presenting it persuasively in public. In other words, Peter is viewed as the opposite of a trained scribe and rhetor. The second term means a private person, one who is not initiated, but we might use the term "layperson" in a religious context such as this. Here is where we point out that v. 19 suggests that Peter spoke with Spirit-inspired rhetoric and eloquence, something he did not obtained through long hours of study in Jerusalem. The amazement of the audience then is caused by their failure to recognize the source of this eloquence and authority.

But not only is Peter presented as a powerful rhetor, he is presented here, and would have been viewed by Theophilus, as a formidable philosopher who echoes even Socrates as a brief look at v. 19 will show. If we compare both 4:19 and 5:29 to the recorded words of Socrates, the echo becomes clear. Socrates, when on trial in Athens before the Athenian judges was ordered to stop teaching his philosophy. His response was "I shall obey God rather than you, and while I have life and strength I shall never cease from the practice and teaching of philosophy" (Plato *Apology of Socrates* 29d). The trial of Socrates was of course famous throughout the ancient world. Luke is suggesting that the trial of Peter should be seen as a trial of no less great a moment and a no less great man. Luke is suggesting that Christianity is an equally noble philosophy with equally powerful rhetoric and its heralds will not be silenced, but rather they will engage in "free speech," telling one and all about the Christ. The apostles will not be kept from being witnesses, even if they must give their lives for it. Perhaps the echo of Socrates is meant to foreshadow that end for Peter. But if death is barely on the penumbra of the discussion here, it comes center stage in the speech of Stephen and the reaction to him, as we turn to the tale of the first true Christian martyr.

THE RHETORIC OF THE MARTYR:
STEPHEN'S SPEECH (ACTS 6:8—8:3)

Stephen is introduced into the discussion in Acts at 6:5 and Luke spends no little time on his story, giving more space to his speech before the Jewish authorities than to any other speech or figure in Acts. This must surely indicate something of the importance Luke assigned to this particular speech and event in early Christian history. In fact, the story in Acts 7 brings to a climax the tale of three trials before the Sanhedrin in Acts 4–7, with escalating results: warning, flogging, and the last ending in stoning. There can be little doubt that Luke sees the martyrdom of Stephen precipitating a crisis, the first major one, for early Christianity.

For one thing, this is the first time that "the people" and not just the authorities turn against the followers of Jesus. For another, this event causes various Christians to flee from Jerusalem and persecution, which in turn leads to the evangelism of other places. Already the words of the later church father Tertullian, that "the blood of the martyrs is seed for the church" were coming true. Luke thus shows that in various cases it was crisis events and not human planning that led to the spread of the church from east to the west. Luke must make very sure to demonstrate that Stephen's death was both travesty and tragedy, and so at the outset he stresses that Stephen is full of "grace" (*charis*) and power, and he had, like Jesus, performed various signs and wonders among the people. Stephen had been involved both in the internal life of the Christian community and its external witness as well, perhaps especially in the synagogue of the Hellenists in Jerusalem.

Scholars have often noted, rightly, that Luke goes out of his way in Acts 6:8—8:3 to indicate how Stephen's demise closely parallels that of his master Jesus. This is an important point, not least because Luke will not take his narrative far enough to draw detailed parallels between the demise of Jesus and that of Peter, and the demise of Paul is only foreshadowed through dreams and hints in the narrative. Here then is the parade example that Luke will give full·rhetorical attention to demonstrate that "if any one would come after me, let him take up his cross *daily* (only in the Lukan text) and follow me." Furthermore, like Jesus, Stephen through his speech places himself in the long line of holy persons, chiefly Joseph, Moses, and the later prophets, who were of great character and stature and were full of grace, power, and inspired words. We should enumerate here the notable parallels between the passion of Jesus and of Stephen. It is the mark of an adept rhetorical historian that Luke can craft his narrative so the parallels are evident without becoming obtrusive or seeming forced.[14]

1. Trial before the high priest/Sanhedrin	Mark 14:53 and par.	Acts 6:12 and 7:1
2. False witnesses	Mark 14:56–57 / Matthew 26:60–61 / *not in Luke*	Acts 6:13
3. Testimony about the destruction of the Temple	Mark 14:58 / Matthew 26:61 / *not in Luke*	Acts 6:14
4. Temple "made with hands"	Mark 14:58 / *not in Luke*	Acts 7:58
5. Son of Man saying	Mark 14:62 and par.	Acts 7:56
6. Charge of blasphemy	Mark 14:64 / Matthew 26:63 / *not in Luke*	Acts 6:11
7. High priest's question	Mark 14:61 / Matthew 26:63 / *not in Luke* (but see "they" in Luke 22:67)	Acts 7:1
8. Committing one's spirit to God	*only in Luke 23:46*	Acts 7:59
9. Crying out with a loud voice	Mark 15:34, 37 and par.	Acts 7:60
10. Interceding for the forgiveness of executioners	*only in Luke 23:34*	Acts 7:60

There are many striking features of this list. Two of the items (8 and 10) are found only in Luke-Acts, but five of the items are found in Acts and the other Synoptic accounts of Jesus' death but not in Luke's. It seems we have compelling evidence that Luke had in mind Acts while he was writing his Gospel: the themes and subjects he did not have full room for at the end of a dwindling piece of papyrus he resolved to take up in the account of Stephen's execution in the second volume. He writes up the passion of Stephen drawing on the Markan account of Jesus' passion. The end result is that Stephen's demise looks like the end of the Jesus narrative in Mark and Luke combined. This may mean that Theophilus knew both the Markan and now the Lukan accounts.

14. The following analysis is found in Hill, *Hellenists and Hebrews*, 59.

Modern scholarly rhetoric too often counts more than reality when it comes to interpreting a controversial text like the Stephen speech. While Luke clearly tells us that the witnesses against Stephen are *false witnesses* (6:11–14), we are asked by scholars to believe that their charges against Stephen are true—namely that he really was a radical critic of the Law and the Temple as well—even though the speech of Stephen does not really support the former idea at least in any real way. One NT scholar opines that the charges in 6:11–14 were indeed false "but not in the sense of being contrary to fact."[15] Were this not enough, we are in addition asked to believe that Stephen is a representative theological critic of the Law speaking for the Hellenists in general, even though nothing at all in Acts 6–7 suggests this conclusion. On the basis of this tenuous and flimsy hypothesis, F. C. Baur and his successors built a whole theory of early Christianity pitting the "Hebrews" over against the "Hellenists" in the early church, that is the more conservative Aramaic-speaking Jewish Christians over against the more liberal Greek-speaking Diaspora Jewish Christians, also based in Jerusalem. Stephen and Paul (after his conversion) are then portrayed as the good guys in this tension, whereas James and the Judaizers are on the distaff side of things. This can only be called a severe misreading of the evidence.[16]

If one sees execution by legitimate authorities in an honor and shame culture as a grave injustice, then considerable rhetoric needs to be brought into play to redeem the man's honor, especially since many ancients believed that how one died most revealed one's true character. Stephen died as a supposed blasphemer of God's Word and God's character. It is thus no surprise that in the conclusion of the narrative portion of the story leading up to Stephen's speech, Luke emphasizes the godly ethos of the man Stephen. According to 6:15 Stephen reflects the character of the divine, for we are told that the Council stared at him intently and saw a face that looked like the face of an angel. The point of this expression (cf. Esther 15:13 [LXX]) is to convey that the person reflects God's glory and character as a result of being close to or in the very presence of God (see the effect of Moses' close encounter with God at Sinai in Exod 34:29–35; see also 2 Cor 3:7–18). The point in the Stephen narrative is divine endorsement, inspiration, and vindication, as we see at the end of

15. Scharlemann, *Stephen,* 102.

16. See the discussion in Witherington, *Acts of the Apostles,* 257–65 and the lengthy discussion in Hill, *Hebrews and Hellenists.*

the story when Stephen has a vision of being received into the presence of Christ the Son of Man in heaven.

What then are we to make of the lengthy Stephen speech itself and its powerful rhetoric? In the first place it needs to be seen that Stephen is not offering an apologetic speech, defending himself against false charges, nor in essence is this speech critical of either Law or Temple per se. Rather it is *people critical*, which is to say critical of those Jews who have down through the ages rejected God's prophets and messengers and their messages; it is also critical about some of the naïve assumptions about God dwelling in temple buildings made by human hands. The speech comes to the boiling and breaking point when Stephen accuses his present audience of being like those earlier stiff-necked and hard-hearted Jews who would not listen to God's Word. In other words, Stephen is not on the defensive in this speech, he is on the offensive.

It is my conviction that the main reason this speech has been so often misunderstood is that scholars have failed to recognize its forensic character and rhetorical shape, and failed to understand the force and direction of this sort of rhetoric used in the way it is seen to be used here. There is in addition a failure to recognize how the different rhetorical parts of the speech function.

The first point to be stressed is the audience of this speech is not neutral, but rather it is hostile. The rhetoric must rise to meet the situation. This in turn makes the rhetorical technique of *insinuatio* necessary. A certain amount of indirection is needed if the audience is going to listen to this discourse at all. This speech is long precisely because of the adoption and adaptation of this technique. It takes a good deal of building up before Stephen can really broach the real bone of contention. If it is to persuade at all it cannot be just pure polemics; it must solicit and garner some approval of the audience along the way.

Thus it is that Stephen sets out to establish common ground with the audience, demonstrating that he shared a common heritage with his auditors, and that they are also a part of a tragic history of partial acceptance and partial rejection of God's message and the messengers he has sent to Israel. There is irony in the story of course, because the very action taken against Stephen precisely makes his point—his death reveals that indeed some Jews are uncircumcised of heart.

Dupont provides us with the most convincing rhetorical analysis of this speech:[17]

1. *exordium*—v. 2a (vey brief in nature)

2. *narratio*—vv. 2b–34 (long narration of the pertinent facts)

3. *propositio*—v. 35 (the theme is announced)

4. *probatio*—vv. 36–50

5. *peroratio*—vv. 51–53.

As is true of most rhetorical pieces, the first part of the speech needs to be more positive in order to establish the speaker's authority and establish rapport with the audience. Then the "narration of relevant facts" prepares for the argument proper, *but is not the argument*. This is where various scholars have gone wrong in analyzing this speech. The argument proper does not begin until v. 36. Finally, the peroration offers the appeal to the deeper emotions. If one does not understand the rhetorical function of each part of the speech, then one will misinterpret what Stephen is saying at one juncture or another.

Stephen's rhetorical strategy in this speech relies heavily on a source of inartificial proofs that he and the audience respect, namely the LXX. There are some ten quotes or allusions to the LXX in this speech. It is entirely possible that Saul of Tarsus was present to hear this speech, which would then explain where Luke, the sometime companion of Paul, would have gotten the extensive material. It is probable that the speech was indeed originally spoken in Greek, but it is also probable that it was longer than this; the rhetorical shaping and outline of the speech may owe as much to Luke as to Stephen. Two preliminary questions are in order at this point: Is the speech Law critical and is it Temple critical? On the former score we actually have very little direct evidence on which to base a decision, but at Acts 7:38, Stephen calls the Law "living oracles," which is surely a positive endorsement of its divine character. Furthermore, Stephen sees Moses as a positive paradigm of a righteous prophetic figure. More importantly, the history of Israel's disobedience to the Law is brought up at the end of the speech as *a cause of guilt*, which in turn strongly indicates that Stephen does not see the breaking of the Law as a good thing. Finally, Stephen builds his case using the Pentateuch positively, indeed he mainly cites texts from the Pentateuch to make his

17. Dupont, "La structure oratoire du discourse d'Etienne (Actes 7)," 153–67.

points, especially Genesis and Exodus. Stephen's single most telling indictment of his audience is that they do not keep the Law (v. 53). The only reasonable conclusion from all this is that Stephen and his speech are not Law critical. What about the Temple?

Let it be said first that if Stephen is Temple critical, such a view seems to go against the grain of the way the Temple is presented in the rest of Luke-Acts. Luke 1–2 presents the Temple in a positive light, and we are told that Jesus taught there day after day (Luke 22:53). It is true that Jesus predicts the dismantling of the Herodian Temple in Luke 21:6, but this does not constitute criticism of the temple cultus per se, as even a cursory reading of the Qumran literature demonstrates. The issue is not the Temple as such but the Herodian character of it. In Acts 2:46 worship in the Temple precincts is seen in a positive light, even as a positive trait of the earliest Christians, not just Jews in general. The early teaching and healing by the apostles in the Temple in Acts 3–4 further presents the Temple as a holy and positive venue. The point is this—there is nothing in all of Luke's Gospel and in Acts 1–6 that prepares us for Stephen's speech being a criticism of the Temple concept and cultus per se.[18]

No doubt, the main reason it is assumed that Stephen's speech is Temple critical is because of the contrast between things made with human hands and things made by God; perhaps, secondarily, there is an assumed contrast between the tent of witness and the house that Solomon built for God. We need to note that this amounts to suggesting that the criticism of the Temple does not begin until v. 40, even though the more polemical part of the speech begins in v. 35 and is clearly aimed at and directed against God's people rejecting their leaders. It is also overlooked that the contrast between tent and house does not parallel the contrast between made by human hands and made by God, since the tent as well was made by human hands. Indeed we even hear of the tent of Moloch in v. 43. "Tent" itself is not presented as a positive category contrasted to temple.

A careful rhetorical analysis of the grammar shows that the real contrast in the speech does not come at v. 47, but rather with the "but" at v. 48, which in turn means that the contrast is about true and false thinking

18. Even in the book of Hebrews, a powerful rhetorical sermon, the author does not replace the temple concept with something else, but rather says the Tabernacle is obsolete because Christ the priest and sacrifice has made it so. There is now a heavenly tabernacle on which to focus. See pp. 195–210 below.

about God's own presence. As David deSilva has shown at length, what Stephen is arguing for and about is that God transcends human structures, *not that God's presence cannot be found in human temples.* God does not "dwell in," by which is meant "is not confined to" temples.[19] Robert Tannehill, in a wise analysis of this speech, stresses that Acts 7:48–50 simply involves a warning that God cannot be confined or restricted to a temple. Using Isaiah 66:1–2, the transcendence of God is stressed instead, with a reminder that God is not dependent on anything humans can make or do for God. God's location cannot be defined by building God a temple, and indeed humans cannot really make anything vital for God, for God is not in need of anything. This same view will be later argued by Paul for an Athenian audience in 17:24–25, which makes evident it is an important Lukan theme.[20]

If we are wondering whether this speech of Stephen is something of an anomaly, the answer must be no. In fact, it is very similar to the speeches given in crisis we find in other ancient historical works (e.g., Thucydides *History of the Peloponnesian War* 1.3.68–70 and 2.6.35–47, and even more tellingly Josephus *Jewish War* 5.376–419). In Josephus various precedents from the Bible are related to explain to the residents of Jerusalem why they are in the current dilemma of being surrounded by the Roman army. In other words, our speech, like others, is typical of those given at a crucial historical juncture, and like them as well, the speech is depicted as changing the course of events. Stephen's speech is the proverbial straw that breaks the camel's back, leading to persecution of the church and the scattering of many of its members, which causes the narrative of salvation history to finally turn its focus to a variety of other places than just Jerusalem.

If we ask how a rhetorical analysis of this speech helps us avoid the pitfalls that have often plagued the interpretation of the speech, we can respond, "much in every way." By the proposition in v. 35 we learn that God's people tended to reject God's spokesman: "who made you ruler and judge?" This clearly signals that this speech intends to be people critical, not Law and Temple critical. Secondly, the peroration in vv. 51–53 reinforces that this is the theme of the speech, for there Stephen accuses the audience directly of being like their ancestors: stiff-necked, always re-

19. Sylva, "Meaning and Function of Acts 7.46–50," 261–75.
20. Tannehill, *The Narrative Unity of Luke-Acts,* 2:93.

sisting the Holy Spirit, always persecuting or killing the righteous prophets, including the Righteous One, Jesus. The *coup de grâce* in v. 53 in fact
reinforces Stephen's positive view of the Law—"you who have received
the Law which was put into effect through angels but have not obeyed
it!" Again, this is clearly people not Law critical. The Law by contrast has
heavenly agents putting it into effect; it ought to be obeyed by God's people. Once one has identified and closely studied the proposition and the
peroration, then the rest of the speech makes much better sense. Because
it was required in a forensic speech in a way that a *narratio* was not necessary in a deliberative speech, one realizes that there will be a rehearsal of
facts relevant to the accusations Stephen will make. One also realizes that
the actual argument will not begin until after the proposition in v. 35. The
trajectory or drift of the actual argument can only be assessed by starting
with v. 36. The "facts" are crucial to the "acts" of persuasion, but they are
not the "acts of persuasion," the so called *pistoi* or proofs.

Much more could be said along these lines about this wonderful
and fascinating speech, but this must suffice. It is rhetorical in character
through and through, and its proper rhetorical analysis helps us understand its cut and thrust and character. Luke presents us more nearly here
with a full speech, and a full rhetorical outline is more in evidence here
than elsewhere in Acts. The other speeches are much more summaries
than this one is. We must examine several more at this juncture.

RHETORIC FOR THE SYNAGOGUE—ACTS 13:13–52

Luke is of course ever conscious of his space limitations, and accordingly he must be selective in the speeches he chooses to present and the
amount of each speech he uses. Accordingly he chooses representative
speeches—a Christian speaking to a synagogue audience in the Diaspora,
a Christian speaking to his fellow Christians in Jerusalem at the first great
Christian Council meeting, a Christian speaking to a pagan audience
in Athens, a Christian speaking to his own fellow Christian leaders in
Miletus, and the defense speeches in Jerusalem and Caesarea that lead
to the climax and conclusion of the book of Acts. We must give some
attention to each of these speeches in turn, though more briefly than the
examination of Stephen's speech.

Acts 13:14 tells us that while Paul and his company are in Pisidian
Antioch on the Sabbath in the synagogue, the synagogue rulers ask them

if they would offer a *logos paraklēseōs*, a word of exhortation to the people
(cf. Heb 13:22). This not only reveals how Luke rhetorically characterizes
the speech which follows, it reveals what was expected, namely a piece
of deliberative or epideictic rhetoric (in this case, the former) meant to
urge a change in belief and/or behavior (in this case, both, as the focus on
behavior in vv. 40–42 shows). This is Paul's first great oration in the book
of Acts. Luke intends to go out of his way to make clear how able Paul was
as a rhetor. Paul not only knows how to shape a speech rhetorically, he is
even depicted as using the typical hand gestures of a rhetorician (13:16).

This speech can be divided up rhetorically as follows: 1) *exordium*,
v. 16; 2) *narratio*, vv. 17–25; 3) the *propositio*, v. 26; 4) the *probatio*, which
includes the use of inartificial proofs from Scripture, vv. 27–37; and 5)
the *peroratio*, vv. 38–41, introduced by the turn to direct address in v.
38 ("to you"). In fact, direct address is used three times in this speech to
signal new divisions (v. 16—"men Israelites"; v. 26—"men brothers"; and
at v. 38). These markers simply reinforce the rhetorical divisions already
in place.

This speech could hardly be more different in character than the
one Paul gives in Acts 17, before the Areopagus. In ch. 13, he is addressing a Diaspora Jewish audience. The speech reflects early Jewish patterns
of argumentation, in particular he uses the *gezerah shewa* technique,
where texts are chosen and welded together on the basis of the use of a
key common term, assuming that the usage in each text can illuminate
the exegesis of the other. For example, at 13:34 the text referring to holy
things and the further text referring to holy ones are allowed to interact
and cross-fertilize.

A lengthy *exordium* was unnecessary in a speech like this since Paul
could assume he is addressing an audience of fellow Jews *at their invitation*. He did not have to labor to establish rapport with them. We have
here, as in the Stephen speech, a review of salvation history as part of the
"facts" shared in common; however, Paul starts at a different juncture in
the story. Here the focus is on the Jews' election and the formative events
of the Exodus. Most striking is the omission of any real attention to Moses
himself, unlike in Stephen's speech. It is interesting that we have in this
speech a definite attempt at the periodization of history: the 450 years
referring to 400 in Egypt, 40 wandering back to the land, and 10 years to
conquer the land. Verse 20, then, refers to the period of the judges up to
the time of Samuel.

Verse 21 continues the historical review with reference to the monarchy and in particular a focus on King David. Verse 22 shows the blending technique of using Scripture where three different texts are brought together to characterize David—"I have found David" (Ps 89:20), "a man after my own heart" (1 Sam 13:14), "who will do all I want him to do" (Isa 44:28). It is surely not an accident that Paul says David was "raised up" by God for Israel, since he will go on to characterize that latter day Davidic figure Jesus in like manner. Verse 23 brings us rapidly to the point—the seed of David, namely Jesus was brought to Israel as a savior, just as God promised.

In vv. 24–25 the story backtracks to include John the Baptizer, presumably because he called all Israel to a baptism of repentance. In short, he made clear Israel was estranged from God and needed to turn back to God. This reference also makes clear that John is not the messianic figure, but the one who prepares for Jesus' coming. Verse 26 stresses that the message of salvation was for both Abraham's descendants and the God-fearers in their midst. Here we see the ignorance theme. The point is not polemical, but rather to emphasize that with knowledge comes responsibility to respond to Jesus properly. Verse 29 stresses all that happened to Jesus was foretold in Scripture, and so was part of God's plan. Paul rehearses the basic kerygma about the death, burial, and resurrection of Jesus, and equally importantly the appearances of Jesus to various witnesses who had traveled with Jesus from Galilee to Jerusalem, and who now were his heralds. Paul does not refer to himself receiving an *appearance* of Jesus. One suspects this is because the focus of Paul's task was not on being a witness to Jews in Israel, although he is addressing Jews here.

Verse 33 is quite interesting because of its similarity to the creedal material we find in Romans 1:3–4 about Jesus being a descendant of David according to the flesh, but raised by God's Spirit from the dead and thereby appointed and anointed to be Son of God in power, having been Son of God in weakness prior to that point. Here in Acts 13, as in Romans 1 and unlike the Synoptics, the king's coronation ode (Psalm 2) is connected with the resurrection *not* with Jesus' baptism.

Verse 35 is even more intriguing because it shares a common Scripture citation with what Peter offers in Acts 2:31–32, and v. 36 is also quite close to Peter's speech. We note that Luke, by repeating citations and themes in these speeches, seeks to show how the original unity of the church described in Acts 2:42–47 and 4:32–35 continued to play out in the rhetorically effective proclamation of its leaders. The point being that the reference in the psalms could not be to David himself because he not only died, his body experienced corruption. By contrast, Jesus did not lie with his ancestors for generations, but was raised shortly after death. The purpose of this whole analysis and argument was to get to the exhortation in vv. 38–41. Since Jesus is the messiah and savior, the audience must not make the same mistakes about Jesus that the Jewish authorities in Jerusalem did.

The peroration (vv. 38–39) should probably be seen as two different ways to say the same thing. Through this man Jesus release from sins is proclaimed to Paul's audience for all who will believe in him. It would appear that Luke is trying to portray the early message of Paul, who appears to be saying that Christ's death can even justify a person from deliberate high-handed sins, for which the Law of Moses made no provision of atonement. Paul finishes with a flourishing final warning, citing Habakkuk 1:5 where Israel was warned about the rise of the Babylonian king and the threat of destruction.

This first message was actually received quite positively. The congregation in v. 42 urges Paul to speak to them again. Luke clearly knows some of the major themes of Paul's preaching for we hear of Paul exhorting those who followed him out of the synagogue to continue in the grace of God. Much more could be said, but this must suffice. Let us turn to another speech given by a Jewish Christian, who adeptly uses the Scriptures to address other Jews and includes comments about Gentiles.

CONCILIAR RHETORIC—ACTS 15:13–21

James is an enigmatic figure in the book of Acts who gradually rises to the top of the leadership pole in Jerusalem. In Acts 15 he is presented as taking charge and making the final judgment that was meant to settle the issue of the basis for Gentiles to participate in Christian community with Jews. James's speech is in fact a very brief speech summary followed by stipulations. The speech is directed to all Christians present, from Judaizing Pharisaic ones all the way to Paul and his adherents. It is an attempt to bring concord in a somewhat rancorous debate. Speeches attempting to persuade an audience to unity and embrace concord are deliberative in character, which is what we find in this text (see also 1 Corinthians).

Once more, there is little or no need to establish ethos or rapport with the audience since James is already respected by the whole group present at this meeting, and so we have the briefest of *exordiums* ("men, brothers") as there was no need to work up to a fraternal address as in Acts 2 and 13. Verse 14 provides the very briefest of *narratios*; it becomes clear that Luke has edited James's speech so that he picks up where the exhortation of Peter left off. In the main, James provides an inartificial proof, citing a previous written sacred text in vv. 16–17 as a further argument in favor of the case that Peter has already begun to make about how the Gentiles could and should be a part of God's people, without first becoming full-fledged Jews. The issue then becomes what will be required of Gentiles so that they can fully participate in Christian fellowship, not be second class citizens, and be fully accepted by Jewish Christians. The proof from Scripture is seen as so definitive that from it James is able to both draw a conclusion and reach a decision that resolves the dilemma. In short, James is not portrayed as just another rhetor, as Paul, Barnabas, and even Peter are. He is portrayed as the final arbiter and judge of the situation. A rhetorician can only propose policy, but an arbiter can dispose and determine a policy.

Sometimes the authenticity of this speech has been objected to on the grounds that it cites the LXX version of Amos 9:11–12. This is overlooking that the Diaspora portion of the audience would have required that the discussion be in Greek, and it further overlooks the Jewish practice of the period where one would choose between the Hebrew and Greek version of a text, depending on which one better made one's case. This was considered legitimate and normal rhetorical practice even in a judicial setting. As Richard Bauckham so rightly puts it: "Thus, there is not the slightest difficulty in supposing that a Jewish Christian exegete, familiar with the Hebrew text of the Bible, but writing in Greek, should have welcomed the exegetical potential of the LXX text of Amos 9.12 as a legitimate way of reading the Hebrew text of the verse."[21] To this one can add that there are actually various verbal similarities between this speech and what we find in the homily of James, so there are good reasons to ascribe this speech to him.

One can notice the Semitic character of the discourse here. Firstly, Peter is called Simeon not Simon, for the only time in Luke-Acts. Luke

---

21. Bauckham, "James and the Gentiles," 160–61.

is interested in ethnographic and linguistic differences as a historian and so he uses a Semitic form to characterize James as he speaks of a fellow Palestinian Jew. James backs up both the activity of Peter in going to Cornelius, and also the clear divine imprimatur displayed in those events. The essence of the Scripture citation is to make the point that God returns to rebuild the tent of David *in order that* all other peoples may in fact seek the Lord. In short, the eschatological restoration of God's people always, in God's plan, was intended to attract Gentiles to seek the one true God.

The textual variants of importance in the citing of Amos 9 are that in the Hebrew text it speaks of "possessing the remnants of Edom," whereas the LXX speaks of "the remnants of Adam" and so all humankind "seeking" God. These two variants arise from two different vocalizations of two key words. The verb "will possess" in the Hebrew becomes "will seek" in the LXX, and Edom becomes Adam in the LXX. In the case of the latter, the Hebrew radical would be the same for either word, the difference being in the vocalization of the word. It is even possible that the LXX is offering the more correct and original reading of the Hebrew, as opposed to the later Masoretes' rendering of Amos 9, but probably not since Amos elsewhere shows interest in the fate of Israel's neighbors including Edom (see Amos 1:1; 2:1).

There is no need to dwell on the Decree, which comes at the end, as it is not part of the speech per se, but rather is based on the speech. Nevertheless, the Decree attempts to say that Gentiles must stay away from pagan temples where the abominations of idols exist; the list refers especially to idolatry and immorality that transpired there in the context of idol feasts. If the Gentiles want to partake in Christian fellowship and meals, they must give up these other polluting sorts of religious meals and the behavior that accompanied them. The issue here is social and religious venue, more than it is menu.[22] Once more we have a speech that precipitates and supports an action. In this case, the speech and the action are both by the same man. Luke admits that the church had struggles in handling the diversity issue, and at the same time, he seeks to make evident that the matter was resolvable through the judicious interpretation of God's Word coupled with persuasion based thereon.

---

22. On which see Witherington, *Acts of the Apostles*, 460–63.

RHETORIC FOR PAGANS—ACTS 17:22-31

It is certainly not surprising that Luke would insist on presenting us with a rhetorical speech summary of what Paul said in Athens, since of course it was seen as the home of rhetoric and Greek philosophy as well. The content of the speech is of course indebted to Greek philosophy and poetry, but the form is shaped by Greek rhetoric. One of the unfortunate things that has happened is that this speech has been so over-analyzed in regard to its content that insufficient attention has been paid to its rhetorical form and setting.

As Luke tells the tale, Paul has for some time been speaking in the agora, and even interacting with Greek philosophers, and Luke is patiently building a portrait of a Paul who can stand toe to toe with the great intellectuals of the age, even in Athens. In fact, Luke in this passage will portray Paul as something of a new Socrates for his age. Both the Epicureans and the Stoics he discourses with are not all that impressed with Paul's attempt to enter the Athenian marketplace of ideas and make a difference. In v. 18, for example they call what he is offering *spermalogoi* (literally "seeds of words"), someone who is a conveyor of snippets or sound bites of knowledge or of religious ideas, but they also suggest he is proclaiming new deities or gods (called *daimoniōn*), a dangerous thing to do in Athens without official approval. Verse 19 then must be allowed to have its full force in how we evaluate what follows, because it involves a Socratic allusion—Socrates was accused of proclaiming new, foreign, and thus false deities.

Paul being hauled before the Areopagus should not be seen as Paul appearing before the Athenian Socratic club on some hill called Mars Hill to have a friendly debate. No, Paul is appearing before the city council (note the reference to council member Dionysius the Areopagite). Paul has been hauled before an official meeting in order to be examined on this new religious teaching. This council had the responsibility to monitor and regulate religious customs and discourse, as a part of preserving city order and peace. It acted as a court, dispensing verdicts and judgments. That Paul was dragged before this august body forcibly, according to the narrative, indicates we must see this as an adversarial and indeed forensic situation. Note the further allusion to Socrates in v. 20—Paul was accused of proclaiming strange or new deities. Verse 21 could hardly be clearer, as we have one of Luke's rare intrusions into the narrative to make an editorial comment. The Athenians are portrayed as busybodies and intellectual dilettantes, spending all their time speaking or hearing new things and playing intellectual games. The council then is not to be seen as a group of truth seekers. While Paul may well not be appearing in a formal trial setting, he is appearing before an initial investigatory hearing, which could lead to a trial, and so the setting should still be seen as forensic. Paul is portrayed as angry in presenting forensic arguments of attack and defense for the sake of the Gospel.

The speech can be divided up as follows: 1) the *exordium* including a notable and ironic *captatio benovolentiae* ("I see that you are very religious")—vv. 22–23a; 2) *propositio*—v. 23b; 3) *probatio*—vv. 24–29; and 4) *peroratio*—vv. 30–31. The *narratio* is omitted from this speech summary presumably because its content has already been covered in the narrative in vv. 18–19 (namely the charges that Paul is guilty of new and false religious teaching).

The major rhetorical exigence or obstacle Paul must overcome of course is that he is a preacher of theological ideas the Greeks did not accept—in particular the notion of resurrection from the dead, coupled with the idea of a final judgment by the one true God. These ideas were so difficult for Greeks that Paul quite wisely follows the procedure known as *insinuatio*—saving the real bones of contention until near the end of the speech—to make sure he has established rapport with the audience before introducing difficult ideas. Even then the ideas prove to be so volatile that the outcome is largely predictably negative.[23] Paul tries to overcome the problem by resorting to much pathos in the peroration—all people everywhere need to repent for the world will be judged in righteousness on a day fixed by the true God, and judged by a man suited to the task as was shown by God's raising him from the dead. These last remarks were of course a bridge too far, not least because they implied (not unlike the words said to Caiaphas by Jesus in Mark 14:62) that the Areopagite judges would one day be judged by a higher court and authority.

Sometimes this speech has been seen as rather un-Pauline in character, but in fact if we pay attention to the hints in 1 Thessalonians 1:9–10, this appeal to turn from idolatry to the one true God seems to have characterized Paul's missionary preaching. We must remember that

23. On this whole technique and how it could be used by Paul in both speech and letter discourse see Witherington, *Conflict and Community*, 429ff.

Paul's letters are not addressed to outsiders. It may well be the case that Paul is attempting a *tour de force* argument, denying he is introducing new deities into Athens. No, says Paul, he is simply proclaiming a deity that Athens has been honoring unaware at its altars to unknown gods. If this argument was accepted, it would imply that Paul had no need to buy a piece of land, erect a new altar, and set up new sacrifices for this God, which would be the normal procedure when establishing a new cult in Athens. Paul says no, the deity he is referring to is self-sufficient, does not need sacrifices anyway, and does not dwell in temples.[24]

It should be noted that this speech summary is carefully crafted, reflecting micro-rhetoric as well as macro-rhetoric. For example, it exhibits alliteration, assonance, and paronomasia. Furthermore, the speech reflects knowledge of local customs. While we might think it strange that Paul begins with the words "men, Athenians" when he is in fact addressing Areopagites only, it was a rhetorical convention to begin speeches in Athens in this way (see e.g., Aelius Aristides *Orationes* 1), and the context suggests that more than just the council heard the speech anyway (see v. 33).

There are many subtleties to this speech. It seems to toggle between flattery and rebuke, with some of the language being deliberately ambiguous. For example, the term *deisidaimonesterous* could be understood as either a positive comment ("you are very religious") or a negative one ("you are very superstitious," the clear use in Acts 25:19). In fact Paul goes on the attack and suggests that while the Athenians should know better, they are in fact too superstitious and ignorant in religious matters, building altars for gods they do not even know the names of in order to cover their bases. It is interesting that Lucian warns against trying to be too complimentary when offering a discourse before the Areopagus as it would have the opposite of the intended effect, producing ill-will rather than goodwill (*De gymnasium* 19).

Paul seems to be suggesting in this speech that, while the Athenians have an inkling that there is a one true God, they do not truly know or have a relations with this God, and equally importantly they do not appropriately acknowledge the true God. This is not much different from what we find in Romans 1:20–23. God has revealed the divine nature in

---

24. See the fascinating discussion in Winter, "On Introducing Gods to Athens," 71–90, here especially 84–87.

all of creation, but humanity, though it has a notion of this, has chosen not to acknowledge the true God. Both here and in Romans 1 Paul suggests an image of pagans groping around in the dark trying to find the true God. While natural theology is affirmed, it is seen as inadequate to transform human beings and produce an adequate response in them to the true God—hence the need for proclamation based on special revelation. Rhetorically, Paul is insisting that offering such discourses as this one is essential to true religion. It cannot just be derived from observing and reflecting upon nature.

There has been considerable debate among scholars as to just how Christian this apologetic speech is. Is Paul really affirming natural theology or is he in the main condemning idolatry and insisting at the end of the speech that special revelation is necessary for true religion? Here is where recognizing the forensic character of the speech makes a difference, helping one realize that v. 23b is the thesis statement—"what you (blindly) worship as unknown, I am going to proclaim to you." Clearly this speech is meant to be critical of idolatry, not merely affirmative of natural theology. Indeed, as the thesis statement shows, proclamation of special revelation is needed for them to be able to make sense of the behavior they already exhibit. Greek ideas are taken up and given a new Judeo-Christian context and sense. We should not see this as an exercise in diplomacy but ultimately rather a call for conversion. The audience has been worshipping a what and not a who, and they needed to be enlightened about the who question. Socrates had once discussed whether human beings could serve or offer the gods anything they needed (Plato *Euthyphro* 12e–15e); Paul here does the same.

There is ever so much more we could say about this remarkable speech summary,[25] but it must suffice to comment briefly on the peroration, which should not be seen as a tacking on of a Christian ending to an otherwise non-Christian speech. The speech is monotheistic throughout—there is one God who seeks to unite the world as one people through his emissary, Christ. The speech calls for the audience to renounce their pagan past and their superstitions. Athens is called to repent of its bad theology, which suggests that God is somehow dependent on human priests, altars, sacrifices, rituals, images, and the like. The speech suggests that the times of ignorance, whether blissful or not, were over, and now

25. For which see Witherington, *The Acts of the Apostles*, 516–35.

was the time of repentance, of religious decision, for a day of judgment was coming.

It must be stressed that the outcome of this speech should not be seen as total failure. Though Paul in v. 33 leaves the council without endorsement, he did not leave without a witness to the true God in Athens. There were others besides the council listening, and we are told that at least one Areopagite, Dionysius was persuaded, and one woman, Damaris, perhaps a foreigner or a "companion" to a high status Athenian, was as well. All had not been for naught in Athens; Paul had survived to preach another day. If one fails to note the rhetorical signals that a forensic speech is being given here and that its thrust is corrective, not laudatory, one will misjudge the substance of the speech. This has all too often led to exaggerating the difference between the Paul of the letters (i.e., 1 Cor 1 and Rom 1) and the Paul who appears in this text in Acts. If we want to see a Pauline speech that is sometimes thought to be laudatory and epideictic in character we must turn to Acts 20.

RHETORIC FOR CHRISTIAN LEADERS—ACTS 20:17–38

Our next to last port of call in this journey through speech summaries in Acts will be to examine what Paul said when he docked at Miletus, summoned the Ephesian elders, and gave them something of a valedictory or farewell address. It is not an accident that this is the one speech in Acts where we find Paul addressing Christians at length, niether is it a surprise that in this one speech Paul sounds rather like the Paul of the letters.

Some scholars have claimed that Paul in Acts 20 sounds like the Paul of the later letters (e.g., Philippians or Ephesians) or even the Pastorals, but this assertion is basically untrue. The speech actually has many echoes of the earlier undisputed Pauline letters, as we shall see. But there may be another reason why this speech sounds to some scholars like "the later Paul." Luke may have been the person who wrote down the Pastoral Epistles for Paul, using his own style and diction; indeed, there are a few Lukanisms and Lukan themes in this speech (e.g., the language about repentance, the emphasis on the kingdom of God, the quoting of a Jesus' saying, and the image of God's people as a flock who need shepherding and protection from predators).[26] Bearing these things in mind, let us turn to the speech itself.

26. See Witherington, *Acts of the Apostles*, 611. For further discussion see also

Term/Concept	Acts 20	Paul's Letters
• Reminder of how he lived when with the audience	vv. 17–18	1 Thess 2:1–2; Phil 4:15
• Paul's work called "serving the Lord"	v. 19	Rom 1:1; 12:11; Phil 2:22
• On refusing to claim anything for self	v. 19	2 Cor 10:1; 11:7; 1 Thess 2:6
• On his fears / showing personal concern	v. 19	2 Cor 11:24–26; 1 Thess 2:14–16
• Taught from house to house	v. 20	Rom 16:5; Col 4:15; Phlm 21
• Profitable teaching	v. 20	Gal 4:16; 2 Cor 4:2
• Preaching to both Jew and Greek	v. 21	Rom 1:16; 1 Cor 9:20
• Faith in our Lord Jesus	v. 21	Rom 10:9–13
• Paul's uncertainty about his future	v. 22	Rom 15:30–32
• Lack of attempt to preserve his own life	v. 24	2 Cor 4:7—5:10; 6:4–10; Phil 1:19–26; 2:17; 3:8
• Paul's task—preach the gospel of grace	v. 24	Gal 1:15–16; 2 Cor 6:1
• Being innocent of converts' blood	v. 26	1 Thess 2:10

One of the tell-tale signs that this speech is certainly more Pauline than Lukan is the reference to salvation by the blood of Jesus (v. 28), the only such reference in Acts and a nice parallel with Romans 8:31. Furthermore the discussion about invaders from without and predators within in vv. 29–30 can be paralleled in 2 Corinthians 10–13, Philippians 3:2–6, or Romans 16:17–20. There is nothing un-Pauline about the speech, though some of the vocabulary is not specifically Pauline. The important point to be noted is that *most* of the parallels mentioned above come from letters written prior to the date when this event is likely to have happened, namely sometime in AD 56–58, which is to say the parallels come almost entirely from the undisputed Paulines. The case for labeling this a Paulinist but not a Pauline speech is weak, and even the reference to elders can be considered Pauline since it is a term he will have known and used in his life as a Pharisee, and in any case we already

---

Witherington, *Letters and Homilies for Hellenized Christians.*

see such Jewish terms being applied in the church in Philippians (1:1–2). We have the term *episkopoi* here in v. 28 as in Philippians 1.

Much has been made of comparing this speech to earlier farewell speeches (Gen 49, Josh 23–24, and especially 1 Sam 12) but more proximately it should be compared to what Jesus says in Luke 22:14–38. There is, however, a significant difference between the speech in Acts 20 and previous last will and testament sorts of speeches. This speech focuses on final advice and farewells; it is not given on the eve of the death of the apostle. The issue is Paul's final departure from Asia, not his near impending death. Acts 19:21 provides the context in which Paul has now accomplished what he came to do in the region and needs to move on to Rome, stopping first in Jerusalem with the collection. This is a farewell address, not a really premature self-delivered funeral oration.

At this point the rhetorical analysis of the speech helps us to understand it. Is the content of this speech intended to praise and eulogize Paul? It is possible to see this speech as something of a piece of epideictic rhetoric, but there are some real problems with such an analysis.[27] The issue that has to be determined is *how* the example of Paul functions in this speech. Does it function to set an example that the speaker wants the audience to follow, changing or modifying their present behavior, or does it simply function to laud Paul in the present? Surely it is intended as a guide for the future conduct of the Christian leaders in Ephesus known as elders. In addition, epideictic rhetoric is mainly about praise or blame and emotions, and not about mounting arguments, whereas this speech not only has arguments it even has a shortened syllogism, known as an *enthymeme*, in vv. 26–27.

Because the audience is very well known, a lengthy *exordium* was quite unnecessary, as Paul already had rapport with them. So after a very brief opening, the speech in essence starts with a *narratio* (vv. 18–21), reminding the audience of Paul's life while he was in Ephesus, a topic appropriately revisited in the final appeal. The function of this *narratio* is to establish what sort of conduct would be beneficial and useful for the audience to follow. After a transitional remark about the present in v. 22a, we have a discussion about Paul's future in vv. 22b–25. The key transition, however, comes in v. 25 with the reference to the audience not

---

27. For this sort of conclusion see Watson, "Paul's Speech to the Ephesian Elders," 184–208.

seeing Paul again, creating pathos and setting up the arguments found in vv. 26–30 (note the transitional word *dioti* in v.26).

In essence Paul argues that he has discharged his duty to the audience and set them a good example; it is now up to them to begin to follow that example. This leads into the dramatic *peroratio* in vv.31–35, revisiting Paul's behavior while in Ephesus (vv.33–34) to seal the emphasis on imitation. That appeal to imitation is sealed with a final sanction by quoting a word of Jesus—"it's more blessed to give than to receive" clearly ending on a deliberative note urging a particular course of behavior for the audience. The speech achieves it desired result and the story concludes with a scene full of pathos in vv. 36–38. One of the giveaways that this is a deliberative speech summary is the emphasis on Paul's having done what was *sumpherontōn* (useful, beneficial) while with the audience. Paul recognizes his impending absence will cause a problem for the audience, so he prepares them in advance for when they must lead without his help, and follow his example when he is no longer around. Imitation was at the heart of ancient education, the rhetoric of imitation was deliberative in character.

How does this rhetorical analysis help us understand this speech summary? In the first place it makes clear that this speech is not an example of "inoffensive self-praise," nor an attempt to lionize Paul after his death. Luke, to be sure, sees Paul as one of his heroes in the faith, but the point of this speech is not to prepare the immediate audience for his demise, but rather to prepare them for the transition to full leadership of the church in Asia. Secondly, the material in the *narratio* which crops up again in the peroration shows how the example of Paul functions in this speech—as an implicit call to go and do likewise. Paul is not distinguished as the great apostle, whom none could imitate, much less equal. To the contrary, here is advice for elders that they can and should follow, even in Luke's own day. The advice is specific, showing the Ephesian elders how to shepherd their own flock. In a world full of takers and reciprocity conventions, Paul advances the unconventional wisdom of Jesus: giving and serving even with no thought of return. And here we have reached the heartbeat of the Christian message about grace—undeserved benefit, unmerited favor. There are other speeches in Acts where Paul is not preparing others to lead and follow his example, but rather to serve as his personal apologia and defense. We turn to those speeches as we bring this chapter to a close.

WHERE SPEECH AND NARRATIVE RHETORICALLY
COINHERE: ACTS 9, 22, AND 26

We have been saying all along that Luke is a rhetorical historian, by which
is meant that rhetorical devices and techniques affect the way he does
narrative as well as speeches. Nowhere is this more evident than when
one examines the threefold account in Acts of Paul's conversion: once
told in a third person narrative in ch. 9, and then twice over-epitomized
in speeches in the first person in chs. 22 and 26. What we will see is
that the later speeches are meant to amplify and add to the earlier narrative, or put the other way around, the later speeches presuppose what has
been said in the earlier narrative and in various ways reinforce its major
thrusts. It will be well to lay out the parallels between these three texts
before we examine them briefly.

Triple Anatomy of a Conversion

9:1–19 (third person)	22:1–16 (first person)	26:1–19 (first person)
Luke's summary from talking with Paul	In Hebrew/Aramaic (v. 2) [Paul's Greek summary given to Luke?]	Spoken by Paul to Festus (vv. 1–3), with Luke present
Saul, with letters from high priest to synagogues, authorized to bring Christians back to Jerusalem (vv. 1–2)	Letters from high priest and council to bring back Christians to Jerusalem for punishment (v. 5)	Authorization from the chief priests (v. 10)
Light from heaven flashed about him (v. 3)	At noon, great light from heaven shone about me (v. 6)	Midday, light from heaven, shining around me and those with me (v. 13)
Fell to ground and heard a voice (v. 4)	Fell to ground and heard a voice (v. 7)	We all fell to the ground, I heard a voice saying *in Hebrew* (v. 14)
"Saul, Saul, why do you persecute me?" / "Who are you, sir?" / "I am Jesus, whom you are persecuting." (vv. 4–5)	"Saul, Saul, why do you persecute me?" / "Who are you, sir?" / "I am Jesus of Nazareth, whom you are persecuting." (vv. 7–8)	"Saul, Saul, why do you persecute me? It hurts you to kick against the goads." / "Who are you, sir?" / The Lord said, "I am Jesus, whom you are persecuting." (vv. 14–15)

9:1–19 (third person)	22:1–16 (first person)	26:1–19 (first person)
"Rise, enter the city. You will be told what to do." (v. 6)	"What shall I do, sir?" / "Rise, go into Damascus. You'll be told all that is appointed for you to do." (v. 10)	"Rise, stand on your feet. I have appeared to you for this purpose, to appoint you to serve and bear witness to the things in which you have seen me and to those in which I will appear to you. Delivering you from the people and from Gentiles, to whom I send you, to open their eyes that they might turn from darkness to light . . ." (vv. 16–18)
Men stood speechless, hearing a voice, seeing no one (v. 7)	Men saw light, but did not hear voice of one speaking to me (v. 9)	——
Saul arises. Can see nothing. Three days without sight and food. Led by hand into Damascus. (v. 8)	Paul cannot see due to brightness of light. He is led by hand of companions into Damascus (v. 11)	——
Vision of Ananias (vv. 10–16)	Ananias (no vision mentioned; v. 12)	(no mention of Ananias)
Ananias lays hand on Saul. "Jesus sent me that you may regain sight and be filled with the Holy Spirit." (v. 17)	"Brother Saul, receive your sight" (v. 13) / "God of our fathers appointed you to know his will and see the just one and hear a voice from his mouth. You will be a witness to all people of what you have seen and heard." (vv. 14–15)	——
Something like scales fall from Saul's eyes. He regains sight and is baptized. (v. 18)	"Rise and be baptized, and wash away your sins, calling on his name." (v. 16)	——
Saul takes food and is strengthened (v. 19)	——	The above was a heavenly vision (v. 19)

One of the questions that should be asked when analyzing a rhetorical historian like Luke is *to what degree are the rules about forming a rhetorical narratio shaping the way Luke thinks about editing and shaping his larger narratives themselves.* This question is something of a pressing one once we notice the similarities between the narrative account in Acts 9, and the speech material in Acts 22 and 26. In fact it needs to be stressed that the rhetorical approach to narrative, especially when one has limited space, involves asking questions such as what are the necessary and pertinent facts that absolutely ought to be conveyed in a narrative. Secondly, since one is attempting to persuade the audience about something, what facts help one accomplish one's aims with this particular audience (in this case Theophilus)? Is it an accident, for example, that Luke goes out of his way to talk about some of the more high status persons who have converted to Christianity in different settings, and stresses that Christianity is not at odds with a person being a Roman citizen and showing respect for Roman law? Probably not. One of the things Luke as a rhetorical historian is unlikely to do is offer interesting but rhetorically irrelevant or insignificant details in his narrative. Everything is included with the view to persuading the audience about various matters. In short, the material is purpose-driven and tendentious in shape.

One of the interesting obvious conclusions from a close analysis of the three accounts above is that the heart of the dialogue between Jesus and Saul is basically the same in each account, whereas everything else is allowed to be a bit different from account to account, with the apparent intent that the three accounts have a cumulative effect. Details are added in later accounts to the earlier one(s) not merely for the sake of stylistic variety but in order to keep the audience interested in the account, even though it involves considerable repetition. Repetition in ancient education, including rhetorical training, was a way of stressing what was crucial or important and what ought to be learned. Having three accounts of Saul's conversion stresses just how crucial that event was to the spread of the Gospel and the development of earliest Christianity.

Another crucial insight into what is going on in these three accounts is that it is clear the speeches in Acts 22 and 26 are not simply additive or examples of amplification. For example, the speech in Acts 26 is a compressed speech that leaves Ananias entirely out of the account. The speech in Acts 26 also cannot be the basis of the account in Acts 9 and Acts 22. If Luke was present for any of these speeches, it would perhaps have been the one in Acts 26, but the accounts in Acts 9 and 22 cannot be said to be a reduced or edited form of Acts 26. There is the further complication that while all three accounts are now in Greek, we are told that the speech in Acts 22 was spoken not in Greek, but in the "Hebrew tongue," which likely means Aramaic. Luke will have had to rely on Paul relating to him what was said on that occasion.

Differences of purpose in the three accounts do help explain some of the differences we find in Acts 9, 22, and 26. For example, in Acts 26 Paul presents himself as a prophetic figure called of God, whereas in Acts 22 the point is to present himself as a good Jew and a former Pharisee, and thus as one who is a faithful follower of Abraham. One of the things that counts in favor of these three versions speaking about actual occurrences is the obvious differences in the accounts. If Luke was just making up the speeches in Acts 22 and 26, we would have expected them to conform a bit more closely to the introductory account in Acts 9.

The following is the essential list of things on which all three accounts agree and on which they report: 1) Saul was authorized by a priestly authority or some priestly authorities in Jerusalem to do something against Christians, and as the story goes on, the implication is that it was against Christians in Damascus; 2) while Saul was traveling to Damascus, Saul saw a light and heard a voice; 3) the voice said "Saul, Saul why do you persecute me?"; 4) Saul answered: "Who are you sir/lord?"; 5) the voice replied "I am Jesus whom you are persecuting." Thus, all three accounts confirm that Saul had an encounter including a real communication from Jesus in the context of a bright light which turned Saul from an anti- to a pro-Christian person. This summary comports with what we find in Galatians 1–2 and 2 Corinthians 3:8 and 4:6 when Paul alludes to his own conversion. In both sources, conversion and call come at the same juncture for Saul, though it is important to add that the name change does not come at the point of conversion and is not part of that process. Rather it comes when he begins to be a missionary to Gentiles, including one of high status named Sergius *Paulus* (see Acts 13:9). Luke is not simply trying to present an apologia for Paul in Acts, but rather he aims to reveal Paul's crucial role in the spread of the Gospel and the development of the Christian movement. What is crucial about Paul from Luke's vantage point is not his distinctive theology (for what Paul says sounds much like what Peter says in Acts), but rather his crucial historical role in the Gospel spreading from Jerusalem to Rome. This in turn may help explain why there is no reference to Saul being commissioned to be a missionary to the Gentiles in ch. 9, whereas this commissioning is emphasized in chs. 22 and 26. The historical role of Saul is emphasized in the latter two accounts, whereas his conversion is more the focus of the earliest account.

Is there evidence of literary and rhetorical freedom within limits in these three accounts? Yes. The reference to "kicking against the goad [a wooden stick with metal spikes]"—meaning it is fruitless to struggle against one's destiny—in ch. 26, involves a Greek idiom, not a Hebrew one. While the idiom might be familiar to an Agrippa or a Festus, it is hardly something that one would expect on the lips of Jesus in Aramaic. Either Luke or Paul inserts it into the speech to help explain things and indicate Saul was struggling against God. If we need further evidence of limited literary license, the commission that comes to Saul from Ananias in Acts 22 comes directly from Jesus in Acts 26. Both of these examples were within the bounds of best practices of responsible rhetorical historians.

The matter of rhetorical focus or perspective comes into play when in 26:14 we read that "we fell to the ground" (emphasizing Paul was not alone when this happened to him and that to some extent it affected his compatriots), whereas in Acts 9 and 22 only Saul falls to the ground—indeed, 9:7 says the others stand. The third account is simply a shorter generalization of the earlier ones on this score. The point is the others saw and heard something, though they did not have the full experience Saul did. Only he saw a person and heard a voice. They saw a light and heard a sound of some sort. Luke is likely telling Theophilus that what happened to Saul was not a purely subjective experience, not the product of an overactive imagination.

We need to bear in mind as well that all the speeches prior to Acts 20 tend to have a deliberative cast and function, but after the farewell speech in Acts 20, the speeches all have a forensic character. Since the narrative and the speeches are meant to be mutually reinforcing this is not a surprise. Prior to Acts 20 we have narratives about evangelism, missionary work, discipleship. After Acts 20 we have narratives about apologetics, defense of the faith, and the like. The speeches and the narrative work together and co-inhere to achieve the rhetorical aims of Luke.

Keeping the above things in view, we are better able to consider the rhetorical character of the speeches in Acts 22 and 26 now. Let us begin with the defense speech before the Jewish crowd in Acts 22:1–22, and note that the other long defense speech is before a Jewish authority, Herod Agrippa II, in 26:2–29. In between there is a brief but telling hearing before the Sanhedrin that aborts due to the division Paul causes by raising the issue of his belief in resurrection. It is extraordinary that while the defense speeches are given to Jews, Paul is on trial before Gentile authorities and under Roman law. That is to say, Paul does not direct major defense speeches either towards Felix in 24:1–23 or Festus in 25:6–12, though Festus is present at the speech given to Herod Agrippa II.

The first defense comes impromptu when Paul is accused of being an Egyptian, or a zealot of some sort. He must establish that he is not a rabble-rouser and is indeed a Jew, in fact a well-educated Jew of high status "from no mean city." Thus Paul states from the outset in Acts 22 that he is indeed a Jew and a citizen of a city that has a high honor rating—Tarsus in Cilicia. Tarsus was an important center of Hellenistic culture and education, including rhetorical education (cf., Strabo *Geographica* 14.5.13–15). Since ancient peoples believed that where one came from partly dictated who one was on the social scale, the higher the honor rating of one's birth place, the higher honor derived by its native sons and citizens. It is interesting that Paul mentions his legal citizenship to the Roman tribune (22:2) but not to the crowd. One of the reasons Paul is allowed to address the mob is that he has equal or higher social status than the tribune himself, as Paul has made clear. Paul shows respect to the tribune, speaks an educated man's Greek, has revealed some of his pedigree, and honor claims to the tribune, so his being allowed to speak is plausible. Paul commands immediate respect from the audience because he addresses them in their native tongue—Aramaic (which left Claudius out of the conversation most probably).

Paul then trots out his best attributes in his *narratio* in order to better defend himself. It was paramount that Paul establish his ethos at some length with a hostile crowd in order to command some respect and at least a partial hearing. The rhetorical handbooks are all clear that it was crucial for a defendant to be portrayed as a person of good moral character from the outset. For if the defendant "is believed to be a good man, this consideration will exercise the strongest influence at every point in the case" (Quintilian *Institutio oratoria* 4.1.7). What follows from this is that Luke's interest in Paul's life and character, especially in the last third of Acts, reflects Luke's own rhetorical and apologetical purposes to defend the Gospel and its major exponents. In other words, Acts 22–26 is not biography for its own sake, but rather biography as defense. The speeches are an essential part of the story, not merely commentary on the story, because the story is about the spreading and defending of the Word.

The key to understanding the rhetoric in Acts 22 is that we are dealing with an interrupted speech. Paul never gets past his personal *narratio* before he is interrupted. There is an *exordium* in vv. 1–2 and a *narratio* in vv. 3–21 but that is all—he had not yet reached the stage of proofs, much less a peroration. Had proofs been added we would have expected a defense of the conduct of Paul and Trophimus in the Temple, as well as a defense of Paul's teaching. We have neither. *Rather the speech is interrupted, as in Acts 17, at its most contentious point.* What the speech accomplishes by *narratio* is to make clear who Paul is and is not, and especially to make clear he is not a Jewish apostate, but rather a fellow zealot for God and even the Law.

Paul's rhetorical strategy is to appear "patriotic." This he accomplishes in part by choosing to address the crowd in Aramaic, and in part by what he says to establish he is a good Jew. Secondly, he establishes rapport both with the audience and the Jewish tradition by calling them "fathers and brothers" (cf., 7:24, also before a hostile audience). Paul states as well from the outset that he will offer a reasoned *apologia* (v. 1b), thus signalling that only forensic rhetoric should be expected thereafter, including a lengthy statement of the facts—the *narratio*. What is remarkable is that Paul establishes rapport not merely by making clear he is a fellow good Jew, but even that he was a fellow persecutor of heresy.

Furthermore, Paul is seeking to show he is not merely a Diaspora Jew, but one raised and educated in Jerusalem (vv. 3–5). His Tarsian citizenship was merely hereditary; there was no implication that he might have been involved in pagan religion while young. No, says Paul, I was raised and received my religious education in Jerusalem, sitting at the feet of the great Gamaliel himself (see Acts 5:34). Paul was no average Pharisee either once he became one as a teen. He seems to have been extremely zealous for the Law, perhaps modeling himself on the example of Phineas (Num 25:13) and his successors the Maccabees. Paul then, in vv. 6–11, recounts his visionary encounter on Damascus road. This depicts Paul as a highly religious Jew. Ananias is not spoken of as a Christian convert but as a devout Jew, like members of the hostile audience Paul is addressing. Ananias is seen as a gifted and pious man who helps Paul recover his sight. "Brother" here means fellow Jew, whereas in the account in Acts 9 Ananias is depicted as a Christian. The rhetorical shaping of the story in Acts 22, being cognizant of the audience and their likely response, is evident. Notice as well that the name Jesus does not occur on Ananias' lips (he speaks only of the God of our ancestors), but rather Paul is just exhorted to get up and be baptized, washing away his sins, something John the Baptizer could have easily said to Saul. As well, Paul leaves out the bit of the story about his having to leave Damascus because of opposition from Jews.

Paul speaks of a vision he has had in which Jesus has told him to go far away and preach to Gentile nations, fulfilling as it were the calling of Jews to be a light to the nations (Isa 49:6). But this reference to a mission to Gentiles is not well received at all, and despite Paul's rhetorical care and eloquence, the speech does not accomplish its intended end. As a defense speech it is a failure, as it produces the opposite of the intended effect. The crowd wants to lynch Paul, not exonerate him. This leads to the further intervention of the tribune.

Scholars have long recognized the forensic cast and language of Acts 22–26, even though properly speaking there is no formal trial mentioned before Acts 24. Paul's hearing before the Sanhedrin that follows the incident in the Temple precincts is just that—a hearing. What needs to be stressed is that since Paul is in the custody of Claudius Lysias from the outset, Roman procedures, not Jewish ones, are to the fore and controlling the process. That means the hearing before the Sanhedrin is part of the "discovery" or *cognitio* phase. No one from the Sanhedrin assumes the role of plaintiff before Acts 24, and even then the Roman authority is trying to discern whether Paul is guilty of a chargeable offense under Roman law. What is most crucial about the pre-trial hearing before the Sanhedrin is the adroit rhetorical move of Paul in which he sets the terms for all future discussion of the matter by defining what the *real issue or main bone of contention* is. Quintilian rightly stressed that in a forensic process the statement of facts, or the *narratio*, is crucial to the case for "a statement of facts is not made merely so that the judge may comprehend the case, but rather *so that he may look upon it in the same light as ourselves*" (*Institutio oratoria* 4.2.21). Paul, throughout Acts 22–26, is presented as a very effective rhetor, who at the outset successfully defines the terms of the following discussion.[28]

---

28. On the forensic character of all of Acts 22–26 see Neyrey, "The Forensic Defense Speech," 210–24.

The audience Paul must impress in this first hearing is Claudius Lysias, not the Sanhedrin, and the letter Claudius writes (cf. 23:29 to 24:21) demonstrates that Paul has succeeded in this rhetorical aim. Rhetors need to know who their real audiences are. The Roman official sees the real issue in the very way Paul wants him to see it. This in turn means that we must not see Paul's speech before the Sanhedrin as an example of Paul being clever by using a divide and conquer tactic. It is not just that Paul does not want to be judged by the Sanhedrin (though that is true), it is that he does wish to be judged by the Roman authorities, and to that end he is not afraid to say things that will cast the Jewish authorities in a divided and mixed light. This is of course because if Paul can successfully convince the Romans that this is squabble over Jewish beliefs and laws, and not any sort of serious or treasonable offense so far as Roman law is concerned, then Paul as a Roman citizen will be in a good legal position, as Roman law was heavily weighed on the side of its citizens against all others.

Even more interesting is the skillful way that Paul moves the issue from his person being on trial to the Gospel itself being on trial. The crucial thing is not so much for Paul to defend himself as to give a positive presentation of the Gospel before the authorities; thereby, fulfilling the mandate or promise given him by Jesus himself at his conversion.

Luke has carefully edited Acts 22–26 so that gradually we move from more general or generic to more specific in the "witness" of Paul on behalf of the Gospel. For example, Paul begins by speaking generally about hope and the resurrection of the dead (lit. plural "dead ones," 23:6). This discussion is continued at 24:15, 21, and again at 26:8, *but only at the end of the judicial process do we hear about the resurrection of Jesus in particular.* Paul's full Christian witness then does not come until Acts 26, after which we have the missionary appeal to Agrippa and Festus 26:27–29. This makes clear what we could have already surmised, namely that Luke intends the effect of these scenes to be cumulative with the Word to some extent, driving the action. Wisely, Paul leaves the more objectionable and specific subjects and material until last, following the advice of the rhetors about *insinuatio* as a way of dealing with difficult subjects only after having long since established the good will of the audience. In other words, we see the same rhetorical move here as in Acts 17 before the Areopagus. Paul then is depicted as providing an exemplum of how Christians should bear witness before neutral or hostile audiences.

The speech fragment or summary that we find in Acts 23 is indeed forensic or judicial in character. Paul does not address the audience as his superiors, but rather as his fellow Jewish brothers. Paul says he has always lived as a good citizen unto God (see Phil 1:27). Paul is more concerned about his Christian than his civic duty. Though things get off to a rocky start (Paul insults the high priest after he is unnecessarily struck in the face; then, when he is told it is the high priest, Paul self-effacingly quotes Scripture against himself). Then suddenly, having observed that there were both Pharisees and Sadducees present, Paul blurts out that he is a Pharisee, son of a Pharisee on trial because of his hope of the resurrection of the dead. Paul speaks in such general terms about the matter that the Pharisees in the audience (probably a minority) could assent to the proposition. Why does Paul suddenly make this brilliant move? Because Sadducees were in the majority, and had the high priest as their leader. Paul knew he could not get a fair trial from such a high priest as Ananias, who was known to be violent and ruthless with his foes according to Josephus (*Jewish Antiquities* 20.31, and on Ananias's unethical conduct even in regard to tithes see 20.205–13). Paul means to rally a few Jews to his side and stir up a "dissension." Verse 9 indicates various Pharisees stood and said they found nothing wrong with Paul and his words.

After the initial rhetorical sparring comes the trial proper recorded in Acts 24. Luke presents it to us as a rhetorical duel between two master rhetoricians—Tertullus and Paul. The chapter can be divided into three parts: 1) the prosecution (vv. 1–9); 2) the defense (vv. 10–22—which is much longer); and 3) the aftermath (vv. 22–27). Tertullus seems to be a hired Roman advocate, and the procedure followed is the looser *extra ordinem* one where the advocate for the prosecution is able simply to allege "facts" without formal proofs. It is then left to the judgment of the proconsul or another Roman official to decide the matter. Tertullus, representing the Sanhedrin, gives a formal rhetorical speech in which the charges are laid out. Paul has to answer for himself. He has no defense attorney.

Luke gives a summary of Tertullus's speech as follows: 1) *exordium* vv.2–4 which is long and suggests that buttering up the judge is seen as most essential; 2) a brief *narratio* alleging criminal facts; 3) the *peroratio* urging the governor to act by investigating Paul himself. What is entirely missing is formal proofs. It appears Tertullus thought he could prompt the governor to act on the basis of the sheer force and eloquence of his rhetoric and his "gravitas" and ethos. The *exordium* should not be seen as mere flattery since it is closely linked to the narrative of alleged facts which follow. Tertullus is also relying on the fact that he is making serious political accusations of the sort that, if true, would force Felix to act. Unfortunately for Tertullus, he had not read Claudius Lysias's report.

Felix is praised as one who had brought much peace to the region in contrast to Paul who is characterized as stirring up sedition and trouble. Felix, in addition, is praised for his foresight or "providence," by which is meant flexible use of the law to preserve order. Paul is being painted as a troublemaker like the Egyptian. This *exordium* played just the right notes which should have sounded like music to the ears of this governor. He is praised for his "usual graciousness" in listening to the Jewish leaders when they alleged charges about the likes of Paul. There are basically two charges—fomenting a riot in Jerusalem as a ringleader of a dangerous sect, and attempting to profane the Temple. According to Cicero, alleging seditious actions was exactly the right thing to allege in criminal proceedings, and in fact either of these charges, if proved, could warrant the death penalty (see Cicero *De inventione rhetorica* 2.516—8.28). It appears that at the end of the speech there is a rather bold and bald-faced lie. If Tertullus is suggesting Paul was taken by the Temple police in order for the Jewish authorities to claim jurisdiction in the matter, this is false and Felix knows it from the report of Claudius Lysias. While the peroration in v. 8 may seem strange to us, in fact the exhortation to Felix to examine or better said "interrogate" Paul for himself and find out what he has done wrong is precisely what one would expect in this looser Roman form of dealing with problems. Felix, at least for the moment declines to do this, and instead bids Paul to make his defense.

Paul says he will gladly do so before someone who has been ruling over Israel for many years (five to be exact). Paul's *exordium* in v. 10 is both briefer and more factual than that of Tertullus, and indeed Paul seems to think he has the upper hand, and is, thus, exuding confidence. The appeal he makes to the governor's knowledge and experience is appropriate since in this sort of procedure the matter becomes a judgment call of the governor, not a matter of elaborate consulting of rules. Paul seems to be relying on what he already knows about the disruptions in the region and how the Nazarenes had never been a party to that in the past. Verse 11 provides a brief *narratio* with vv. 12–20 being the actual response to the charges, and there is a brief peroration in v. 21. Paul in fact takes the trouble to rebut the charges point by point:

1) he had not been in Jerusalem but 12 days, hardly time to start a revolution;

2) the Jewish authorities had certainly not found him disputing with anyone in the Temple nor stirring up the crowds either in the synagogues or in the city in general;

3) they had no proof he profaned the Temple, nor that he was a "plague throughout the world." The issue is what they could prove, not what they alleged, and since they had not bothered to bring any Asian Jewish witnesses, who made the initial observation of Paul in the Temple, with them their case was weak. In a striking rhetorical move in v. 14, Paul makes a confession, but what he is confessing is not a crime at all—professing faith in Jesus. Hereby he testifies before officials about Jesus.

4) Paul indicates that far from being simply a sectarian person, he in fact shares the same hopes in God of resurrection as many other Jews. Indeed, the one charge the accusers could substantiate is that there had been a disagreement over this very theological matter, which was of no concern to Felix at all. In a master stroke then, Paul makes his accusers witnesses for him as they could attest he had debated with them about a theological matter.

Felix simply adjourns the session without rendering judgment, but Luke tells us he has "a more accurate knowledge of the Way," which in turn suggests he knows these charges are basically bogus, as he had been in Israel for five years and had no evidence that Nazarenes were rabble rousers. The cumulative portrait of Paul in all these proceedings build up a portrait of a rhetorically adept Paul who is able to defend himself, even against an experienced rhetor. But Felix does not decide the issue, rather leaving Paul languishing in house arrest, that is until Herod and Bernice come on the scene, taking us to the final defense speech of Paul in this sequence.

The speech of Paul in Acts 26 should not merely be seen as the climax of the sequence of hearings in Acts 22–26, but also the climax of all Paul's speeches in Acts. It could be seen as something of a summary of the Christological message of Acts as well. This speech is more substantial than various of the previous speech summaries and takes up most of the chapter (vv. 1–32), being the longest apologetic speech of Paul in Acts. Several factors help us view this crucial and climactic speech correctly. First, Paul is not operating in the same forensic mode he was in Acts 24. He is not rebutting charges point by point. Secondly, this is, however, an apologia, being more a defense of his life than of his recent actions in the Temple. The primary audience for this speech is not Festus but rather Agrippa, as the references to him in vv. 2, 19, and 27 show, and in fact, v. 1 states it is Agrippa who gives Paul permission to speak. This means it is primarily a Jewish speech, at a hearing, not a formal defense at a trial. Here then Paul presents his personal testimony to Agrippa, and to "both great and small" who are present (v. 22). Paul is being portrayed as a model evangelist, even an evangelists of Jews, including high status and royal Jews like Agrippa. The interest in the salvation of the Jews continues right to the end of the book of Acts.

Granting that we have forensic rhetoric at some length in Acts 26, what role is Paul playing? It would appear he plays the role of witness on his own behalf, seeking to establish his ethos and good character; he is not a defendant rebutting charges. The whole speech leads to the dramatic peroration in which Paul with much emotion urges even Agrippa to become like he is, except of course for the chains. In the end, Festus gets frustrated and Agrippa goes on the defensive.

In some ways the speech in Acts 26 is the most rhetorically elegant in all of Acts, reflecting careful attention to both elements of rhetorical style and content.[29] We are probably meant to think that Paul had time to prepare for this speech, whereas the one in Acts 22 was impromptu. Paul is shown to be an orator of some distinction.

The rhetorical structure can be outlined as follows: 1) *exordium*, vv. 2–3; 2) *narratio*, vv. 4–21; 3) *propositio*, vv. 22–23; 4) the formal proofs are once more omitted, in part because Luke has let us know what they are already in Acts 22–25, and also they are briefly alluded to in the *narratio* and *propositio*; 5) brief *refutatio*, vv. 25–26; followed by 6) the *peroratio* in vv. 27 and 29. The speech is interrupted twice (vv. 24, 28) and in both cases continues. The interruptions then are not to be seen as a literary device indicating Luke ran out of evidence. The bulk of the speech is a simple *narratio* of facts/events leading up to the point when Paul became

---

29. On the finer points of rhetoric here see Witherington, *Acts of the Apostles*, 737.

a captive (see v. 21). Paul then is establishing he has been a sincere Jew all along who became and remains a witness for Jesus, the Jewish Messiah and Savior of Gentiles. It is interesting that Paul does not seek to deny the salient facts of his life—he has always been a zealot of sorts for his religious convictions—and indeed, he rehearses them again here, explaining this by the fact that he continues to be a witness for Christ.

It is important to notice Luke stresses that Paul was not just an able orator, he was a rhetorically trained one. Thus in 26:1, as elsewhere, Paul is depicted as stretching out his hand to his audience, the gesture of a trained rhetor, as he begins his speech, something already hinted at in the beginning of Paul's other speeches in Acts. Verse 1 also tells us that Paul began to give an *apologia* for himself. The speech opens with the suggestion that he will discuss all the things non-Christian Jewish officials have accused him of, although as the speech proceeds it becomes clear that this is an example of rhetorical hyperbole for he does not discuss the issue of his defiling the Temple by bringing a Gentile into it, nor his upsetting Jews in the Diaspora. Here again we have an excellent example of the rhetorical tactic of redefining what the real issue is, which Paul insists has to do with the essence of the Gospel, identified as the hope of Israel and involving resurrection (see v. 23). Part of Paul's rhetorical strategy is to convey the idea that Agrippa is a pious and knowledgeable Jew. He is called an expert in the *ethos* (i.e., customs) and disputes of the Jewish people. He knows the religious parties, their beliefs and practices, and so Paul urges Agrippa to settle in and listen patiently to the discourse (which suggests it will not be short).

Using a bit more rhetorical hyperbole, Paul begins the speech proper by suggesting that "all the Jews" know his character or way of life since the time of his youth—"Jews" could mean Jewish officials in Jerusalem. Paul stresses he spent his youth among his own people, learning their customs and ways (cf. 10:22; 24:2, 10, 17). We have further and clearer confirmation Paul was brought up in Jerusalem, not Tarsus. Paul stresses it is well known that he has lived as a Pharisee since his youth, which he characterizes as the strictest sect of Judaism. In the way he presents the matter, however, Paul suggests that is how he used to live; he does so no longer. What he does still affirm from that heritage is stated clearly in v. 6: "my hope in the promise God made to our ancestors." He seems to envision the gathering of the twelve tribes at the eschaton, which is associated with the resurrection. The irony was that it was for proclaiming this very hope that Paul had been accused and seized by Jews. One of the things that is notable as one works through Acts 22–26 is that Paul is very respectful towards Agrippa, even calling him *Basileu*. This stands in contrast to the way he related to the high priest in Acts 23:3–5.

Verses 6–8 should be seen as something of a rhetorical digression which intends to foreshadow aspects of the proposition in vv. 22–23. The point is that a Jew like Agrippa not only should be well familiar with the notion of resurrection, but also since he believes in an almighty God, he should not find such a notion incredible. Verse 9 returns to the *narratio* proper with the phrase "so then," Paul candidly admits that he was convinced before his conversion that he should do many things against the name of Jesus Christ, which likely means against the Christian movement, but there could be an implication that he tried to get Jesus adherents to blaspheme that name (see 1 Cor 12:3). Paul stresses in v. 10 that he performed these acts by the authority of the high priest himself. Paul admits to being involved in the incarceration and condemnation of Christians during this period of time, though it is unlikely that he, at such a young age, was a member of the Sanhedrin. The point is the same as that of 7:58, namely Paul contributed to Christians' demise. Is Paul subtly trying to incriminate the Sanhedrin in the eyes of Festus by suggesting they took the matter of capital punishment into their own hands? It is possible. In any case, v. 11 makes clear Paul punished Christians in the synagogue, presumably using the 39 lashes and trying to get them to recant Jesus. Paul as Saul was so zealous in such activities that he pursued Christians to foreign cities. What is ironic about all these admissions is that Paul is using them to demonstrate his strong commitment to Judaism.

Verses 12–18 rehearse the by now familiar tale of Paul's conversion. The objective nature of what happened on Damascus Road is stressed, indicating that it affected Paul's companions as well as Paul. They too saw the light that was bright at midday, brighter than the sun. We learn that Jesus spoke to Saul in Aramaic and presumably he answered in Aramaic. It may be that Paul repeats this in Aramaic, in which case it is directed only to the royals, Agrippa and Bernice. Paul quotes a familiar Greek proverb at this juncture (see especially Euripides *Bacchae* 794–95; and Aeschylus *Agamemnon* 1624). The quote may be meant to reflect Paul's learning, but it could be seen as a Lukan aside to explain to Theophilus the implications of Jesus' question as to why Paul was persecuting him. The point is that it is fruitless to resist God's will. The proverb is not about

Paul's uneasy conscience when it came to the persecuting. There is no report here of Paul being blinded nor about Ananias. It is the Lord who commissions Paul, a fact possibly alluded to in Acts 22:14–15, as even there Ananias does not actually commission Paul but rather confirms and completes the conversion and healing process. Paul, in essence, indicates that he could not be disobedient to the heavenly vision and so, just as Jesus had opened his eyes about Jesus himself, so Paul's task would be to open the eyes of both Jews and especially Gentiles about Jesus so they will turn and receive forgiveness of sins and a portion among God's people through faith in Jesus (v. 18). We hear the essential Pauline message (cf., 1 Thess 1:9–10). Paul is depicted, like his master, as the fulfiller of the role of the Servant in Isaiah 49:6 (cf., Luke 4), who was called to be a light to the nations and open the eyes of the blind.

Verses 19–21 continue the *narratio* and relate what happened after the conversion. We need to bear in mind just how effective it would be to say to Agrippa and Festus that he had to be obedient to the heavenly vision, because rulers and Romans both certainly believed in paying attention to heavenly signs, warnings, visions, omens, and prophecies. Paul depicts himself as being in the line of the prophets, not only because he received a heavenly vision, but because he felt he must be obedient to it, proclaiming on the basis of that vision. He places himself in the same category as John the Baptizer by summing up his message as a call to repentance, a turning to God, and charge to do deeds indicating repentance. Paul finishes the *narratio* by stressing in v. 21 that it was because of this sort of preaching that he was seized in the Temple.

In vv. 22–23 we have the proposition clearly stated. It has been Paul's rhetorical strategy all along to convince the audience that the bone of contention between him and his accusers is religious and theological, not social and political. We have here an apt summary of the apostolic kerygma. Paul begins it by asserting that even his standing before Agrippa was a fulfillment of his divine mission to bear witness about the Gospel to one and all, from the lowest to those of highest social status, including kings. We should note the parallels with Jesus' last speech in Luke 24:44–48. In both cases Scripture is said to be fulfilled and in both cases the essential message is that it was necessary that Messiah suffer, die, and rise again from the dead so salvation would be generally available. Paul then is proposing a thesis that can be debated on the basis of the evidence in Moses and the prophets—a proper Jewish debate. Verse 23 stresses the divine necessity of the suffering of Christ (cf., Acts 2:23; 13:29; 17:3) and that he be proclaimed as a light to the world, both Jew and Gentile. At v. 24 we have the first interruption. Festus suggests that Paul's great learning and much study has led him to conclusions that seem daft, well beyond common sense. Paul rebuts the charge in v. 25 by stating he has not taken leave of his senses, but in fact what he is stating is the sober truth, attested by many witnesses.

Perhaps sensing Festus is out of his element and out of his depth, Paul once again addresses Agrippa, and in a masterful rhetorical move, he seeks to bring Agrippa in as a witness on his side about resurrection. Paul says he knows the King knows about these things, and so he feels open to speak freely about them with him. He says that since "these things" did not happen in obscurity, but were done in the open, he is sure Agrippa knows about them. In v. 27 Paul corners King Agrippa by asking, "Do you believe in the prophets?" But Paul, rather than really putting Agrippa in a tight spot, hastily answers that he knows Agrippa does believe in the prophets.

Agrippa interrupts in v. 28 asking, "In so brief a time, do you persuade me to become a Christian?" which in a rhetorical context likely means, "With so few arguments do you persuade me to become a Christian?" The complaint is that Paul has not yet offered full-fledged proofs of his views. Agrippa is incredulous not sarcastic or hostile here. We are dealing with sophisticated avoidance and perhaps slight embarrassment on the part of the King. Paul's response is that whether by few or many arguments he wishes the King was as he was, a true Christian. Paul then concludes with a wish prayer: "I would wish to God that you all were like me—except of course for these chains." This latter note interjects the proper pathos into the end of the discourse. The matter is not resolved at this juncture, but instead the King and the other recess out of the hall, neither being persuaded to act for or against Paul, but the consensus seems to have been that Paul has done nothing deserving of death or imprisonment. Indeed, v. 32 tells us that it was Agrippa's conclusion that Paul could have been set free, had he not appealed to the Emperor earlier. And so it was that Festus had to make arrangements to help Paul testify about the Gospel to an even bigger and more notable authority figure—the Emperor himself.

AND SO?

We have spent no little time in this chapter demonstrating at length the rhetorical character of the book of Acts, and especially of its speech material. We pointed out as well how rhetorical considerations shape both the narrative and the speeches, and the way that they are made to interface. We stressed that we were not merely talking about the use of micro-rhetoric, individual rhetorical devices like rhetorical questions, or personification and the like, but that rhetoric shapes the very character, structure, order of the speech summaries and the accounts. We urged that Luke goes out of his way to portray especially Paul as a man of no little learning and a considerable rhetorician. But was this only Luke's good rhetorical strategy to convince a high status Gentile that Christianity was intellectually respectable, and could even persuade the high and mighty, or did it represent the truth about Paul's life and ministry? In my view, the latter is the case, and we turn to the issue of Paul the rhetor and the rhetorical shape of his letters in the following chapters.

QUESTIONS FOR REFLECTION

1. How should knowing that we are dealing with speech summaries, and not with full speeches affect the way we evaluate this material?

2. Why do you think it is that Luke goes out of his way to portray the major Christian leaders as able rhetoricians?

3. Why do you think forensic and deliberative rhetoric predominate in the speeches in Acts?

4. In what way is the narrative in Acts driven by the speeches or their effects?

CHAPTER 5

Paul, the Rhetor and Writer

As strange as it may seem, though Luke devotes nearly half of his history of early Christianity to a person whom he highly esteemed, the Apostle to the Gentiles, he nevertheless says nothing whatsoever about Paul being a letter writer.[1] Yet on the surface of things, Paul himself offers us no other kind of documents. Thus as we analyze what we can learn about Paul from letters, we will be relying exclusively on the Pauline corpus itself. Fortunately, when we discuss Paul as a rhetor or rhetorician, one who practiced the ancient art of persuasion, we have evidence from both Paul and Acts to help us.

First, however, it will be useful to make some more general comments about orality, education, literacy, and the ancient arts of writing and speaking *as they bear* on Pauline Christianity. As well, some general remarks about Paul's own education are in order. It is my contention that Paul's literacy and his skills with rhetoric and letter writing provide significant clues to the kind of person the historical Paul really was. He was by no means an ordinary person of the first century. It also needs to be stressed at the outset that letter writing and the forming of rhetorical discourses were so interwoven in the case of Paul, who spent so much time communicating from a distance to various of his churches, that we must analyze the two phenomena together, not least because the Pauline letters are largely structured by rhetorical conventions and concerns.

---

1. This chapter appears in another and longer form in Witherington, *The Paul Quest.*

THE EDUCATIONAL AND SOCIAL MILIEU
OF THE EARLIEST CHRISTIANS

There is a renewed interest in the scholarly world in ancient literacy and education. In part this interest is a reflection of the emphasis on social history in NT studies in the last three decades. Literacy and literary ability are seen as significant clues to the social level of this or that person or group. In fact what is happening in NT studies is that the work of classicists, ancient historians, and literary scholars are finally being given due notice. For example, the older studies of ancient education by H. I. Marrou and M. L. Clarke are now regularly being cited by NT scholars.[2] Equally, we hear regularly about the importance of literacy studies by a variety of people such as W. Harris, A. D. Booth, H. C. Youtie and others.[3] Also, as we shall see later in this chapter, it is once again classics scholars who have set the stage and agenda for the rhetorical study of the NT. Nowhere has this infusion of new data from other disciplines been more welcome or helpful than in Pauline studies. Indeed, it has gotten to the point where some scholars would say that the historical Paul cannot be adequately understood or evaluated without due attention to the issue of his literacy, his literary abilities, and his rhetorical skills. Let us see where this way of approaching the historical Paul leads us.

General Considerations

To what degree were early Christians educated and literate? The two questions are not identical. There were various early Jews who had learned aurally a good deal about their faith and a variety of other subjects, yet they could not write, much less write in the lingua franca of the Empire—Greek. Some of them employed scribes or amaneuenses (or as we would call them, secretaries) to perform their writing tasks. We know, from texts like Romans 16:22 that Paul availed himself of some of these secretaries, and to judge by this verse, he used those who were already Christians. Yet it is equally clear from texts like Galatians 6:11 that Paul

2. See Marrou, *A History of Education in Antiquity*; and M. L. Clarke, *Higher Education in the Ancient World.*

3. See Harris, *Ancient Literacy*; Booth, "Elementary and Secondary Education in the Roman Empire"; Sevenster, *Do You Know Greek?*; Youtie, "Agrammatos"; and Youtie, "Upographeus."

could not only read but also write in Greek, and that like so many others, even when he used a secretary, he himself would sign the document and write a concluding postscript. The evidence then that the apostle was literate in Greek, and surely (in view of Phil 3:5) in Hebrew and probably also in Aramaic as well (see 1 Cor 16:22), is clear. Furthermore, he writes to his converts, which in turn means he expects that at least the one who delivered the letter for him could read, but presumably also some of the remote audience would have been literate in Greek as well. There was no point in writing them a postscript in one's own hand if they could not at least recognize the hand, and at least some of them could read and appreciate the postscript.

Yet answers are elusive to the question of the education and literacy level of the earliest Christians, and in any case the question is complex. As Gamble has aptly put it "the question of literacy in early Christianity is complicated by the fact that Christianity developed and spread in multi-cultural and multi-lingual settings and thus incorporated from the start a diversity that forbids the generalizations that are possible for more culturally and linguistically homogeneous groups. A Christian in first-century Palestine might have been thoroughly literate in Aramaic, largely literate in Hebrew, semiliterate in Greek, and illiterate in Latin . . . "[4]

We should not be encouraged to think of a large Christian reading and writing public in the first century AD. All of the major literacy studies of the Greco-Roman world during the Empire basically come to estimates of *at most* between ten and twenty percent of the entire population, the latter figure being an absolute upper limit.[5] In some places literacy would have been less than these estimates. There is of course the X factor that early Jews seem to have been more concerned about the education, at least the religious education, of their children than many in that portion of the Empire.[6] This does not help us much with Paul's own audience who were apparently overwhelmingly Gentiles and apparently did not grow up with the benefits of Jewish pedagogy that Paul himself may have enjoyed. What may have been of more importance was the high value early Christians placed on Scripture and the learning of and about it. Because

4. Gamble, *Books and Readers*, 3.

5. See Harris, *Ancient Literacy*, 130–45. His final conclusion about literacy in the western part of the Empire is particularly sobering—no higher than 5–10% at any point during the Empire (272).

6. See Gamble, *Books and Readers*, 7.

of Scripture, literacy could never really be a matter of indifference to the earliest Christians. Furthermore, a certain authority would clearly accrue to someone who could not merely read but could powerfully interpret the Jewish sacred books. Literacy as a criteria for Christian leadership in the early church is a factor too seldom considered.[7] Whatever else one may wish to say about the Pastoral Epistles, they surely rightly suggest that Paul wrote to his co-workers from time to time. Unless such co-workers were well off enough to afford a scribe, this likely suggests that they were literate and could read and reply to such letters.

Literacy studies are in part based on the correct conclusion that literacy is a function of education, and we know quite well that any sort of higher education, beyond the mere learning of ciphers and rudimentary writing skills for business or personal matters, was by and large for the elite in Paul world. Paul's letters were certainly not "best-sellers," and we may be sure the majority of Paul's audience was not among the elite of society (see 1 Cor 1:26).

Yet in an oral and aural culture such as the Greco-Roman world was, a culture geared far more to learning by ear than by eye, this may not have been as crucial a matter as we might think. Indeed, as we have stressed, literary documents in early Christianity were intended to be read aloud in the assemblies (Col 4:16), not least because most all ancient reading was done aloud (see Acts 8:30). In fact, letters were seen as surrogates for oral conversation, indeed as vehicles for carrying on such conversations. The living or spoken Word was primary; the written word secondary and often no more than a record of the oral.[8] In our age of millions of books, email, the internet chat rooms, and the like, it is hard for us to grasp that visible text was not primary in antiquity. It was largely a tool of oral culture. This is why the study of the rhetoric in and of Paul's letters is such a crucial matter. Paul had written his words so that they might be *heard* as persuasive, not merely seen to be persuasive.

Here would be a good place to say something about the social level of Paul's converts as this will help focus our comments about education

---

7. See Gamble, *Books and Readers,* 9.

8. Consider the famous remark of Papias, bishop of Hierapolis, in the early second century, who is quoted by Eusebius (*Ecclesiastical History* 3.39.3–4) as saying that he always inquired primarily about what the apostles had said, rather than what they had written "for I did not suppose that things from books would benefit me so much as things from a living and abiding voice."

and literacy. A recent important sociological study on earliest Christianity points out that if "the early church was like all other cult movements for which good data exist, it was not a proletarian movement but was based on the more privileged classes."[9] I would not say that early Christianity was *based* on the more privileged classes but I do think that E. A. Judge's conclusion that early Christianity was led and largely supported by an elite minority who were of the higher social strata of society is correct. Here Judge needs to be quoted at some length:

> If the common assertion that Christian groups were consti-
> tuted from the lower orders of society is meant to imply that
> they did not draw upon the upper orders of the Roman ranking
> system, the observation is correct, and pointless. In the eastern
> Mediterranean it was self-evident that members of the Roman
> aristocracy would not belong to a local cult association . . . .
> [Nevertheless] far from being a socially depressed group, . . . the
> Christians were dominated by a socially pretentious section of the
> population of big cities. Beyond that they seem to have drawn
> on a broad constituency, probably representing the household de-
> pendents of leading members . . . . But the dependent members
> of city households were by no means the most debased section
> of society. If lacking freedom, they still enjoyed security, and a
> moderate prosperity. The peasantry and persons in slavery on the
> land were the most underprivileged classes. Christianity left them
> largely untouched.[10]

9. Stark, *The Rise of Christianity*, 33. This conclusion, however, is based on cross-cultural and cross-temporal evidence. It is also based on a distinction between cult (the founding of a new faith) and sect (a schism within an existing religious group or body), which I am not sure is apt when we are discussing ancient Christianity, if we insist on calling the latter a cult. It appears to me that Christianity began as a sect or offshoot within Judaism, not as a cult. Stark eventually admits that Jesus was the leader of a sectarian movement within Judaism, but he claims that at Easter something happened to turn it into a cult (44). To be sure however, Christianity was to be seen by pagans as a cult movement within the larger Greco-Roman world.

10. Judge, *The Social Pattern of Christian Groups in the First Century*, 52, 60. A good test case is Paul's converts in Corinth. What we learn from this letter, especially for example from 1 Cor 16:15 and 19 is that there were households where Christians met that were sufficiently large for 40–50 people to have met there. We learn from 1 Corinthians 7:21–23 that there were domestic slaves among the converts. First Corinthians 16:2 and 2 Corinthians 8–9 strongly indicate that there was disposable income among the converts. There is furthermore the important case of Erastus of Romans 16:23. As I have argued elsewhere (see *Conflict and Community*, 32–35), it is highly likely that this is the same person about whom there is an inscription in the pavement in Corinth, mentioning he

Again the point of this quote is not to suggest that the majority of early Christians were among the elite in society, but rather that there was a cross-section of society in the church, and that not surprisingly the leaders seem to have been largely culled from those more nearly able to be called elite, not least because they could provide the venue for the house church meetings. What is of importance for us at this point is that Paul not only engaged in an urban strategy of ministry that would put him in contact with the more well-educated and literate in the first place (concentrating on major cities like Ephesus, Philippi, or Corinth that were along major routes), but he deliberately presented his message in a way that attracted a cross-section of society including the literate. Indeed, it attracted enough of the literate population to make letter writing a viable means of regularly nurturing distant converts in the faith. Both Paul and at least some of his audience were educated, literate, and capable of reading and appreciating a good letter, and responding to it (see 1 Cor 7:1). What then can we say about the education of Paul?

Paul's Education

We have already pointed out that Paul was both a Roman citizen and a Pharisee. The former placed him in the elite category of Greco-Roman society already; the latter potentially placed him among the elite in Jewish society. In particular, his being a Pharisee meant, quite apart from the confirmation we get from Acts, that Paul likely cut his educational teeth in Jerusalem.[11] Yet that confirmation from Acts is not unimportant, especially if, as many scholars would still say, Luke may have known about these matters from the apostle himself. Luke tells us that Paul received his essential education not in Tarsus, but rather in Jerusalem—"I am a Jew born in Tarsus in Cilicia, but brought up in this city at the feet of Gamaliel, educated strictly according to our ancestral law . . ." (Acts 22:3).[12] What did this mean?

Self-evidently it means that Paul learned to read and write not just in Greek, but also in the sacred language Hebrew and likely also Aramaic. Some of the language training and literacy may have come from Paul's

---

had performed a public service in order to obtain the office of aedile.

11. See rightly, Hengel, *The Pre-Christian Paul*, 27–30.

12. See the insights in Van Unnik, "Tarsus or Jerusalem," 259–320, especially 301–5.

instruction at home, but without doubt these skills will have been honed during his schooling outside the home. It must be remembered that through the offices of Herod the Great, Jerusalem had become a cosmopolitan and in some respects almost Hellenistic city, complete with hippodrome and Greek theater. It must have proved extremely attractive to many Greek-speaking Jews from the Diaspora, such as Paul's parents.[13] It is telling that of the inscriptions from the period in Jerusalem 33% are in Greek and another 7% are bilingual.[14] It must also be remembered that Jerusalem was the great pilgrimage site for all Jews from all over the Mediterranean crescent (cf. Acts 2), and as such this brought some of the great Jewish minds and educators to this city.

The point in time when formal education began for both pagan and Jewish boys was about six years of age.[15] I use the term boys advisedly, as girls generally did not receive the benefits of formal education outside the home in the first century. The importance of such an early start and thorough grounding in Jewish traditions was clearly impressed on the Jews in Palestine and elsewhere not least because they feared simply being amalgamated into the syncretistic Greco-Roman culture. Philo is not merely being rhetorically apt when he says, "All people are eager to preserve their own customs and laws, and the Jewish nation above all others; for looking upon theirs as oracles directly given to them by God himself, and having been instructed in this doctrine from their earliest infancy they bear in their souls the images of the commandments" (*On the Embassy to Gaius* 210; cf. Josephus *Against Apion* 2.178). Second Timothy 3:15 speaks of Timothy having been trained in the sacred writings from childhood. Thus the conclusion of Murphy-O'Connor is fully warranted that already in the context of the home but also later in school Paul would have been thoroughly grounded in the Scriptures, perhaps in the Septuagint first, and then the Hebrew Scriptures.[16] The detailed study of Paul's OT citations supports the conclusions that he regularly consulted and followed the Greek OT, and that he seems to have also known the Hebrew text as well.[17] While still at home, Paul would have also learned

13. See Hengel, *Pre-Christian Paul*, 54–60.

14. Hengel, *Pre-Christian Paul*, 55 and 136 n. 258.

15. See Marrou, *A History of Education in Antiquity*, 194–200.

16. Murphy-O'Connor, *Paul: A Critical Life*, 47.

17. See Kopf, *Die Schrift als Zeuge des Evangeliums.* It is not completely clear about Paul's knowledge of the Hebrew text because it is always possible in some cases that he

Greek from his parents, including probably the ability to read and write it. There is evidence that elite Jewish children, in addition to Torah, also learned to read some of the Greek classics such as Homer (*m. Yadayim* 4:6). Secondary studies would in fact start forthwith when someone had learned to read and write, at least as early as eleven or twelve.

So far as we know, there was no rabbinate or ordination of rabbis before AD 70. Paul's training should not be envisioned as just like that of those who go to seminary or theological college today. What we should not doubt, and what Paul's letters only confirm, is that Paul became learned in the Hebrew Scriptures, and also, as he himself suggests, in the traditions of his ancestors (Gal 1:14—though it is not completely certain that this reference means more than just the Scriptures). Unfortunately we know almost nothing about his teacher Gamaliel I, apart from what Acts says, because the rabbinic traditions regarding Gamaliel I are much later and reflect later agendas.[18] What Acts 5:33–39 suggests is that he was not among the zealots, which is to say that his pupil Saul may not at the time have learned enough from his teacher. The Pharisaic movement was not in any case a unified one from what we can tell. Though not rabbis, teachers such as Gamaliel were among those Paul would categorize as sages or wise men (*sophoi*—1 Cor 1:20); and without doubt Paul learned much about the Word from such teachers.

There would also be the matter of a way of viewing the land and Jewish life in it. Paul seems to have been among those who soaked up the eschatological as well as the theocratic and political teaching of the Pharisees.[19] It is striking that while much later Paul is still agonizing over the future fate of his ethnic kinsmen and kinswomen and is prepared to talk about "all Israel being saved" (Rom 9–11; especially 11:26–27), he says hardly a word about the future of the Temple or the Land. Surely, in his Pharisaic days he would have learned much about Torah, Temple, and Territory, but just as his conversion radically changed his view of Torah and its function, it must have also changed his views about Temple and Territory. The conversion process transformed all but the slightest trace elements of those earlier views from his thought world.

---

relied on another Greek OT text other than the LXX at certain points.

18. But see Neusner, *Rabbinic Traditions,* 341–76.

19. See Hengel, *Pre-Christian Paul,* 51–55.

Saul the persecutor of Christians surely must have had quite specific convictions about the sanctity of the Temple and the Jews' right to their own territory. These notions may well have been instilled in him while in Jerusalem, though perhaps not all of them from Gamaliel, especially if he became familiar, as is likely, with the Maccabean lore. There was, however, apparently also a dualistic and quietistic tendency among some early Pharisees, coupled with a certain amount of fatalism, that saw Rome's domination as punishment for Israel's sins and therefore not to be resisted by violence. Rather, one must concentrate on living in a Jewish fashion and pursuing ritual purity to the nth degree in hopes that God would recognize this repentance and come and cleanse the land. Saul did not subscribe to this view, which may have characterized the Hillelites as opposed to the more radical Shammaites.

Paul would surely have learned certain methods of debating or persuading, of arguing, for example, from current experience to scriptural proof in midrashic fashion (see 1 Cor 9:7–14), or of using a form of what could be called pesher or even allegory to make a point (Gal 4:21–31). This sort of creative handling of the Hebrew Scriptures should not all be put down to the inventiveness or idiosyncracies of Paul himself. At least a good measure of it came from his education.

It is believable that a Saul the persecutor, who was earnest about strictly preserving the boundaries of early Judaism, will also have been Saul the propogator of the true faith as he saw it. This would have provided considerable impetus for Saul to become conversant and literate in Greek, including rhetoric, and to gain some knowledge of Greek literature and philosophy, so that he could communicate well with Diaspora Jews coming to Jerusalem. Hengel puts it this way: "It is natural to suppose that the young Paul was at home in this environment of Pharisaic Hellenists; he studied Torah in the school on the temple mount and at the same time improved his Jewish-Greek education, since as a Greek speaking *talmid hakham* he must have felt it important to instruct Jews who came to Jerusalem from the Diaspora in the true—Pharisaic—understanding of the Law."[20]

Lest someone protest the notion of a Jew such as Paul learning Greco-Roman rhetoric in Jerusalem, we have the evidence from this pe-

---

20. Hengel, *Pre-Christian Paul,* 57–58.

riod of Nicolaus of Damascus instructing Herod in rhetoric,[21] to which we can add Josephus's remark that he himself, a Jew among the elite like Paul, and like Paul, a Pharisee well conversant with the Jerusalem scene, knew that Herod Agrippa I and his descendants also received a thorough Greek education, as had Josephus to a lesser degree (*Life* 359).[22]

It was also one of the goals of any great monarch to have a great library, and Herod the Great was one who pursued this goal with the help of Nicolaus. A fairly large Greek library would have been necessary in order to compose the historical chronicles Herod had undertaken during his reign. Furthermore the leading modern expert on these matters, B. Z. Wacholder concludes that in addition to the royal family and its circle, "certainly the leading Pharisees studied Greek."[23] We may also point to the figure of the rhetor Tertullus, who in Acts 24:1–2 was enlisted by the high priest to persuade the Romans to hand Paul over.[24] There are other small hints of the degree of Hellenization in Jerusalem even well before the time of Paul. For example, the grandson of Jesus ben Sira, who translated his grandfather's work into Greek in the second century BC, would have acquired his knowledge of Greek in Jerusalem before he moved to Egypt. Or again, someone in Jerusalem was likely responsible for the Greek translation of 1 Maccabees, a document Saul/Paul must have been well familiar with in view of his persecuting activities and commitment to zeal like the Maccabees.[25]

As Murphy-O'Connor has rightly stressed, "Oratorical skills were the key to advancement in an essentially verbal culture. The acquisition of such skills fell into three parts . . . the theory of discourse which included letter writing . . . the study of the speeches of the great masters of rhetoric . . . the writing of practice speeches."[26] Paul had the motive, the

21. See the discussion in Hengel, *The "Hellenization" of Judaea*, 35–40. A very useful parallel between very Jewish content and highly rhetorical form can be found in 4 Maccabbees. There are also some interesting content parallels between this document and Paul's letters. See Hengel, *Paul: Between Damascus and Antioch*, 191–96.

22. I agree with Nock, *St. Paul*, 235, that we should not class Paul's Greek with that of the popular letters, but also it is not at the very top level of literary Greek either. It is somewhere in between.

23. Wacholder, *Nicolaus of Damascus*, 48; see also 33–40.

24. See my discussion of this person in my *Acts of the Apostles*, 704–5; and Hengel, *Pre-Christian Paul*, 59.

25. See Hengel, *The "Hellenization" of Judaea*, 23–25.

26. Murphy-O'Connor, *Paul the Letter-Writer*, 50.

means, and the opportunity to obtain these skills, even in Jerusalem, and to some degree he is likely to have done so before he even took up formal training outside the home. As we shall see, his letters bear witness that he used these skills, both epistolary and rhetorical, to great advantage.

PAUL THE LETTER WRITER

Letter Writing in Antiquity

In a time long before printing presses, typewriters, and computers, letter writing was an arduous task, and if one did it very much, a somewhat expensive one. One needed a writing implement, one needed ink, and of course one needed something to write on. Cicero, writing in about 54 BC sums up aptly the situation: "For this letter I shall use a good pen, a well-mixed ink, and ivory polished paper too, for you write that you could hardly read my last letter . . . [because] . . . it is always my practice to use whatever pen I find in my hand as if it were a good one" (*Letters to Quintus* 2.15.1). Yet of course there was more to it than just having the implements and the ink. While throughout antiquity the reed was the pen of choice (the bird's feather appears to have been first used in the seventh century AD),[27] papyrus made from the reeds in the Nile delta was the paper, and carbon deposit or soot put into a water solution was the ink, even to begin writing one needed to prepare. There was no such thing as lined paper that one could buy, hence one also needed a lead disk to lightly line the paper and a straight ruler of sorts to keep the lining even. In addition one needed a reed sharpener, namely an abrasive stone, and of course a knife as well to cut the end of the reed if necessary to start a new point (see *Greek Anthology* 6.63–65). One also needed money, for as we have said, none of this came cheaply, especially the papyrus.[28]

27. Here and in some of what follows I am indebted to the fine study by Murphy-O'Connor, *Paul*, 2–3.

28. This is why papyri were often reused, or in desperation one might even use a potsherd or a clay tablet as had formerly been common in the ancient near east. It is highly unlikely that Paul or any of his contemporaries ever got to the point of regularly using the products of animal hides—parchment or vellum (but cf. 2 Tim. 4:13). Parchment was even more expensive and came to the fore later when the codex or book began to be more prevalent than the roll. Martial (*Epigrams* 14.184) knows of the parchment codex of many folded skins, but this was only for the wealthy. The earliest manuscript we have of the Pauline corpus is p46, the Chester Beatty Papyrus from around AD 220. Even it,

Pliny the Elder aptly describes the process of making papyrus as follows: (1) first one takes the papyrus reed and splits it with a needle into very thin and wide strips, with the center portion of the reed being the best and most durable part; (2) then these strips are laid on a board moistened with Nile water, and sometimes a sort of glue might be added to this water, made of flour; (3) the ends of the papyrus strips are then trimmed; (4) then the strips would be laid horizontally and vertically and "woven" together; (5) the papyrus is put in presses and dried in the sun; (6) finally the individual pieces might be sown together, never more than twenty sheets in any one roll (*Natural History* 13.74–77). Yet, in fact, this was not all. Prior to using papyrus for writing one would smooth the paper out with a shell or a piece of ivory (see the quote from Cicero above). Care had to be taken that one not give the paper too fine a sheen or gloss as then it would not take the ink very well. It is not surprising, in view of all that was involved in gathering the necessaries and preparing to write, that persons who did a lot of writing relied heavily on secretaries who were skilled in the whole process, except the making of the paper itself. Paul was one such person who used secretaries.

Careful study has been done on the use of secretaries for letter writing and the results are interesting.[29] In the first place, since writing material was at a premium, Greek texts were written in what was called *scriptio continua*, that is without division between words, without punctuation or accents, and without paragraphing.[30] Under these circumstances, and in view of the inordinate length of Paul's letters compared to most ancient letters (see more on this below), it would have been crucial that Paul use not only a good secretary with a fair hand but also make sure that the person who delivered the document could actually read it and probably "deliver" it orally. It would not have been sufficient to just hand it to the recipients, leaving them to puzzle out what Paul said and meant. If in fact it was possible, Paul would surely have preferred one of his co-workers who knew his mind and meaning to go and read the letter to the congregation and answer questions, though doubtless this was not always possible (cf. Col 4:7, 16—"when this letter has been read among you . . . ").

---

though in codex form, is composed of 52 papyrus sheets folded once.

29. See especially Richards, *The Secretary in the Letters of Paul.*

30. See Gamble, *Books and Readers*, 48–54.

Then as now, there were varying degrees of skill among secretaries, and there were various skills required of them. In the first place, the ancients believed that letters ought to portray the personality of the writer, and to a lesser degree of the recipients.[31] That is, the secretary had to be skilled enough to know the personality, and if possible the writing style of the author, but also to know what would communicate well with a particular audience. Furthermore, since the letter would be read aloud, clear attention had to be paid to its oral and aural features. If "the well-delivered and persuasive speech [w]as the most characteristic feature of civilized life . . . linguistic skill focused on oral speech; the written word was secondary, derived from primary rhetoric."[32] What this meant was that the rules for certain types of speeches were adapted for use in corresponding types of letters. Not surprisingly handbooks for secretaries on letter writing showed interest in rhetorical matters and topics, and already in the work of Demetrius *Style* (first century BC), *letter writing is treated with the issues and definitions of rhetoricians clearly in view.*[33] In short, a good secretary would have to know not only how to write, know the mind of his employer, know proper form for a letter, but also know rhetoric and its conventions.

There appears to have been already in the first century BC a form of Greek shorthand, which was in due course taken over by the Romans.[34] This was an important skill, called in antiquity *tachygraphy* ("fast writing"), but not a skill possessed by all secretaries. It is interesting that there has actually been found in Palestine a collection of Greek stenographic symbols from the early second century AD (*Murabba'ât* 164). *Oxyrhynchus Papyrus* 724 tells of a man who took his slave to a secretary to learn "the signs" for shorthand. Richards conclusion is surely warranted that there was already in the first century a flourishing practice of using Greek shorthand.[35] This means that it is possible that Paul's secretaries took dictation, but we cannot be sure.

It has also been shown by Richards that normally secretaries did not have license to compose letters on their own for their employer or

31. See the discussion of Theon and Nicolaus's remarks by Stowers, *Letter Writing in Greco-Roman Antiquity*, 32–33.

32. Ibid., 34.

33. Ibid., 34.

34. Murphy-O'Connor, *Paul*, 10–11.

35. Richards, *The Secretary*, 39.

master, unless one was talking about a mere formal acknowledgment of the receipt of something or submission of a simple request.[36] This makes the all too ready suggestion of epistolary pseudepigrapha for some of the later Paulines a problematic one. The moral problem of deception was a real one, even if occasionally it happened that some wrote in the name and style of another. In the case of epistolary pseudepigrapha we are not talking about secretaries occasionally composing documents in their master's or employer's name. Even when this happened it should be noted that the initiator of the process would often let the recipient know this is what had been done (see Cicero *Letters to Friends* 8.1.1). This means that the burden of proof must lie with those who wish to argue that some of the later Paulines are not ultimately by Paul. Strong evidence of differences in substance must be produced before such a conclusion can be warranted.

What about the case where the secretary was in fact a trusted co-worker? Was there such a thing as epistolary co-authorship? To judge from Cicero *Letters to Atticus* 11.5.1 such a thing was apparently rare. Yet equally rare was a mere formal mentioning in the opening line of the letter the name of someone who had nothing really to do with the document. In short, "the naming of another person in the address was anything but a meaningless convention."[37] Neither was it simply pro forma to say "we" even if one meant "I" in a letter. This means that when we are dealing with a Pauline letter where more than one person is mentioned in the address *and* one regularly finds the first person plural pronoun "we" to refer not to the author and the audience, but to the sender(s) of the letter, we should probably assume that there are collaborators in the composition of such a letter. For example, 1 and 2 Thessalonians are from Paul, Silvanus, and Timothy.

The "we" is prominent in those letters, but when we compare this for example to 1 Corinthians where we hear in the address of Paul and Sosthenes the brother, the "I" dominates throughout, giving the impression that while Sosthenes may be mentioned as the scribe who wrote the letter or as one familiar to the Corinthians who had read and agreed with the letter, here we should probably not think of co-authorship. Or again, in 2 Corinthians, Timothy is mentioned in the address, as are "all

36. Richards, *The Secretary*, 111.
37. Murphy-O'Connor, *Paul*, 18.

the brethren with me" in Galatians, but the pronoun usage that follows does not make it likely that we are dealing with multiple authors in these cases.[38] If we are concerned to look for the characteristic Pauline style or diction, we would probably do best to focus on letters when Paul seems to be the sole author, even though he had help from a secretary.

Another point needs to be noted. The evidence from Cicero (*Letters to Friends* 9.26.1) suggests that in fact it was the normal practice for the secretary to make two copies of a letter, one of which was to be retained by the sender. This has led to the plausible suggestion of Richards that the collection of Paul's letters was in fact far less difficult than we might assume. It was a matter of simply finding or having the author's copies of the various letters all in one place or in one person's possession.[39] In view of ancient practice, this suggestion should not be lightly dismissed, but we have no firm evidence this was the case. Perhaps the allusion to knowledge of "all" the Pauline corpus in 2 Peter 3:15–16 suggests that there was already in the first century known to be such a master collection, and perhaps that collection itself had been copied and circulated.

How were letters sent? There was no regular postal service before the time of Augustus, that is before about the turn of the era, and this service was only used for official business. Private persons had always to make their own arrangements. Wealthy or elite persons might well arrange a regular courier who was reliable (Cicero *Letters to Quintus* 3.1.8), but even this seems to have been rare. Cicero says of a letter he has just written, "I am thinking of giving it to the first person I meet tomorrow" (*Letters to Atticus* 2.12.4). Paul seems to have relied on the social network he built up of co-workers, converts, or fellow Christian travelers. It was a regular practice in antiquity to commend the letter bearer to the recipients in some way, and we seem to have this practice in Romans 16:1–2 and Colossians 4:7–9.[40] Paul did not likely entrust his letters into the hands of just anyone. We must at this juncture speak of Paul the letter writer more directly.

---

38. See ibid., 33–34.

39. Richards, *The Secretary*, 165 n. 169.

40. See ibid., 70–71.

Paul and His Letters

Paul in His Epistolary Context

The evidence as we have it from the first century suggests that apart from an inveterate long-winded letter writer like Cicero, Paul had few peers and no superiors in the writing of lengthy epistles. His most personal of all undisputed letters, the one written mainly to Philemon, is longer than most ancient personal letters. Paul's short letters were long by ancient standards. Indeed, even Cicero's letters generally pale in comparison to Paul's in terms of both length and strength. Paul's opponents even begrudgingly recognized "his letters are weighty and strong" (2 Cor 10:10), and his friends struggled with these letters, saying "there are some things in them hard to understand, which the ignorant and unstable twist to their own destruction" (2 Pet 3:16).[41] John Donne the great English cleric and poet was later to remark that whenever he opened one of Paul's letters he found thunder, indeed a thunder which resounded throughout the earth. How very different Paul's letters must have appeared in contrast to the ordinary epistolary fare. Consider, for example the following first-century letter written only shortly before Paul wrote 1 Corinthians:

> **Mystarion to his own Stoetis:**
>
> Greetings.
>
> I have sent you my Blastus to get forked sticks for my olive gardens.
>
> See that he does not loiter, for you know I need him every hour.
>
> Farewell. (written 13 September AD 50)

This uninspiring little document is in fact all too characteristic of ancient letters. They were, generally speaking, mostly business and very little pleasure. Cicero's and Paul's epistles are the exceptions, not the rule. Yet various of these letters are not without passion and personal interest. Consider for example the letter from an irate wife to her wandering husband, begging him to return:

---

41. For what it is worth, G. Murray and other classicists have spoken of Paul's vigorous and distinct prose style and have even called him one of the great figures of Greek literature, "a classic of Hellenism." See Murray, *Four Stages of Greek Religion*, 146.

> **Isaias to her brother Hepaestion greeting.**
>
> If you are well and other things are going right, it would accord with the prayer which I make continually to the gods. (I myself and the child and all the household are in good health and think of you always).[42] When I received your letter from Horus, in which you announce you are in detention in the Serapeum at Memphis . . . I thanked the gods, but I am disgusted that you have not come home, when all the others that have been secluded there have come. After having piloted myself and your child through such bad times and been driven to every extremity owing to the price of corn, I thought that now at least, with you at home, I should enjoy some respite, but you have not even thought of coming home nor given any regard to our circumstances, remembering how I was in need of everything while you were still here, not to mention this long lapse of time and these critical days during which you send us nothing. As moreover, Horus, who delivered the letter has brought news of your having been released, I am thoroughly displeased. Notwithstanding as your mother also is annoyed, for her sake as well as for mine please return to the city, if nothing more pressing holds you back! You will do me a favor by taking care of your bodily health. Goodbye. (*Greek Papyri in the British Museum* 42).[43]

Clearly, Paul was not the only one who could be angry in epistolary form.

In this chapter thus far, the reader will detect the fruit of recent efforts by New Testament scholars to learn more from classics scholars and experts in ancient epigraphic sources. In the 1950s through the 1970s a great deal of useful literary or form critical analysis of Paul's letters was undertaken, but not much fruitful comparison of Paul's letters with those of other writers of Paul's era. In part this was because in the latter half of this century, fewer and fewer New Testament scholars had received a classical education, which was *de rigeur* in the last century and early part of this century. The learning of the classical languages, the study of the Greek and Latin classics, and the training in ancient rhetoric were fields of study many New Testament scholars missed out on altogether in the latter half of the past century. It is part of the more recent quest for

---

42. This line was added as an afterthought, perhaps to tone down the hostile overtones of what follows. See rightly Murphy-O' Connor, *Paul,* 56 n. 1.

43. See Barrett, *The New Testament Background,* 28–29.

the historical Paul and the social context of his proclamation and letters that incorporation of lessons learned from ancient educational and letter writing practices, the classics, and other ancient sources have become common. We are especially indebted to scholars we have already been mentioning such as Gamble, Murphy-O'Connor, Richards, and a host of others for putting us on the right track in our quest for more fully orbed perspective on the historical Paul. We will have occasion to say a bit more on those who have contributed in the area of the recover of the rhetorical study of Paul's letters later in this chapter.

Not just in order to understand Paul, but in view of the fact that as many as twenty of the twenty-seven documents of the NT contain or are letters, it behooves us to consider how these sorts of documents worked and communicated in the hands of a Paul or other early Christians. First, letters in antiquity were, at least before Cicero went public, intended as private communications, much as they are today. They were generally not for public consumption and certainly not for publication. I suspect Paul would be astounded that these intense and personal communications he sent to his converts in Asia Minor, Greece, and elsewhere are now circulating to millions, being printed over and over again. Second, letters were seen as poor surrogates for face-to-face communication. This is clearly enough Paul's own feeling on the matter as well (see Rom 15:14–33; 1 Cor 4:14–21; 1 Thess 2:17–3:13; Gal 4:12–20).

Letters in antiquity, like business letters today, from about four centuries before until four centuries after Christ had by and large a rather stereotyped format or structure usually involving the following elements: (1) the name of the writer; (2) the name of the addressee; (3) the initial greeting; (4) the health wish or prayer; (5) the body of the letter; (6) conclusion usually with final greetings. Especially in business letters the style was usually simple and directly to the point with little or no chattiness, though personal letters could be more expansive and interesting.

To these bare bones of epistolary structure, Paul adds considerable flesh. Basically Paul's letters contain the following features:

1) opening, sender, addressee,
2) initial greeting
3) thanksgiving or blessing

4) body, complete with introductory formula, the body proper, eschatological or doxological conclusion, and sometimes a travelogue

5) paraenesis or ethical remarks

6) closing greetings

7) writing process and signature

8) closing benedictions

Now each of these epistolary sections can find some precedent in other ancient letters but Paul tailors these elements again and again to suit his purposes. For example, the very opening will often give a clue as to the message Paul will convey, or will prepare for that message. Thus in Philemon, Paul reminds the slave owner of Onesimus, that Paul himself is in chains for Christ. Slaves of course, especially runaway ones when caught would have such chains. In other words, Paul is identifying with the plight of Onesimus from the outset with the idea that Philemon should treat Onesmius as he treats Paul.[44]

Paul also customizes the greeting. The standard Greek greeting was *chairein*, which just happens to be from the same root as the word *charis* which we translate as "grace." The standard Jewish greeting was of course *shalom* or "peace." Paul combines the two standard greetings in order to properly greet both the Gentiles and the Jews in his audience.[45]

In a pagan letter a health wish or prayer often seems simply perfunctory, but Paul turns this portion of the letter into a major opportunity for prayer. Here especially we find a preview of coming attractions. Paul prays about the issues he will later address in the letter. For example, in 1 Corinthians 1:4–9 he gives thanks for the spiritual gifts and knowledge of the Corinthians, two issues he will have to deal with them on at length in 1 Corinthians 1–4 and 12–14. What needs to be said about this practice

---

44. See Roetzel, *The Letters of Paul.* This particular work is the best brief and readable summing up of the gains of the literary critical study of Paul's letters from the 1950s–1970s. It has rightly become the standard textbook for students beginning to study this material. It can profitably be compared to Stowers, *Letter Writing,* which focuses more on the recent gains from comparisons to letter writing in antiquity and social scientific studies of such data.

45. It is perhaps a telltale sign that his audience is mostly Gentile that he always says "peace" second rather than first in his greeting.

is that Paul is rhetorically shaping the prayer so it functions also as an *exordium* for the discourse that follows.

It is equally telling when Paul omits a standard feature of the ancient letter. Notice that among the congregational letters, Galatians is the only one without a thanksgiving section. This is likely because Paul is so upset with the Galatians that he can think of nothing to be thankful about. By contrast, in Thessalonians the thanksgiving section seems to go on and on. The situation dictates the nature of the use of the form.

Romans 1:8–17 is a clear example of how a thanksgiving section can provide a preview of coming attractions. Here we find Paul expressing four things: (1) his explicit desire to come to Rome (see 15:22–25); (2) his wish to impart to them some spiritual gift to strengthen them, namely a useful summary of some of the essence of his Gospel (see 1:18—8:39); (3) his stress that salvation is for the Jew first but also for the Gentile (see 9–11); (4) the basis of this salvation is seen to be the faithful one Christ whose gift must be accepted by faith and lived out faithfully (see 12–15).

We should remind ourselves that these are indeed ad hoc documents, written for specific situations. Paul seems to have customized his letters in one of two major ways. Some of his letters are basically problem solving letters (e.g., 1 Corinthians) with an enormous amount of time devoted to the body and ethical sections of the letter. Some of Paul's letters are basically progress-oriented letters, with a few corrective exhortations. Philippians would be a good example of the latter. The elements in the letter are tailored to suit the circumstances. More praise and thanksgiving in the progress-oriented letters, more instruction and correction in the problem-solving ones.

The body of the letter is of course where we find the bulk of the content of the document. Since the content will vary according to the situation being addressed, there is more diversity here from letter to letter than elsewhere in these documents. There are certain regular ways that Paul will signal he is beginning the body of a document:

1) with an appeal or a request—"I appeal to you brothers and sisters to agree . . . " (1 Cor 1:10);

2) with a disclosure remark—"I want you to know . . . " (Rom 1:13; 2 Cor 1:8; Phil 1:12; 1 Thess 2:1);

3) with an expression of astonishment—"I am amazed that . . . " (Gal 1:16);

4) with a remark about hearing—"I hear of your faith . . . " (Eph 1:15).

Just as the beginning of the body may be marked off by a certain kind of phrase, so there seem to be eschatological remarks that regularly crop up either at the end of the body of the letter or the end of a major section of the letter (Rom 8:31–39; 1 Cor 4:6–13; Gal 6:7–10). Travel plans also tend to be mentioned at the end of the body of the letter or the end of a particular argument in the letter (Rom 15:14–33; 2 Cor 12:14—13:13; Gal 4:12–20).

The next major section of the letter was the paraenetic or ethical section and it has become commonplace to say that here Paul is more conventional and tends to draw more on traditions than elsewhere in the letter. There is a real measure of truth in this observation, and in fact it is precisely in the ethical portions of his letters where Paul seems to allude to or cite the teaching of Jesus (cf. 1 Cor 7; Rom 14), the OT (cf. Gal 6), or Christian traditions (cf. Col 3:18—4:1). Yet of course ethical remarks are not confined by any means to this section of the letter, and in a problem-solving letter like 1 Corinthians we find ethical enjoinders throughout the body. Sometimes, too, Paul would take a particular ethical topic and give it more extended treatment such as we find in Romans 13 (relations with governing authorities) or 1 Corinthians 7 (marriage and singleness).

In his closing remarks, Paul seems least bound to the Greco-Roman epistolary conventions. Here instead we find not just the standard closing greeting or greetings but also benedictions or doxologies (Rom 16:27; Phil 4:20).

We have seen in the last few paragraphs how Paul modified and did creative things with the standard epistolary elements, but it is also true that Paul was not as original in his letters as we might sometimes think. There are various places where he makes quite clear that he is drawing on traditional confessional material (cf. 1 Cor 11:23–26; 1 Cor 15:3–11), ethical catalogues which reflect a definite indebtedness to earlier Jewish, Christian, and even Greco-Roman material (e.g., Gal. 5:19–26), particularly in his virtue and vice lists (cf. Rom 1:29–31; 13:13; 1 Cor 5:10; 6:9–10; 2 Cor 6:6–7, 14; Phil 4:8; Col 3:18–25), or hymnic material (Phil 2:6–11; Col 1:15–20). What Paul does with his autobiographical remarks is also interesting, and when we discuss Paul as a rhetorician we will say more on this subject. For now we will note that these remarks tend to have an ethical thrust, encouraging emulation or occasionally shaming the audience into proper behavior (cf. Phil 1:12–15; Gal 1:17—2:14; 1 Thess 2:1–12; 2 Cor 11–12).

Paul's letters stand out from many of his day not only in their length but also because they are group communications, and as such they are often closer to official pronouncements than private correspondence. Even the Pastoral Epistles are like official mandate letters from an authority figure. Paul, because he expects his letters to be read aloud in the congregation (Col 4:16), will only say what he wants all those present to hear. Doubtless he conveyed more private messages through the bearer of the letter who would speak personally to individuals quite apart from the reading of the letter in public. Paul's letters were but a part of a total communication effort that involved: (1) personal visits and face to face discussions; (2) the sending of oral messages by Christian courier; and (3) the sending of letters presumably with oral messages in addition. Furthermore, since Paul's letters are often parts of ongoing conversations caught in midstream, listening to them is rather like hearing one half of a phone conversation. One needs to reconstruct the other half to make complete sense of what has been said.

A humorous attempt to reconstruct what some of the letters Paul received must have been like has been undertaken by Colin Morris.[46] Consider, for example, the following imaginary reconstruction of a letter sent to Paul from Thessalonike as a result of the Thessalonians hearing his preaching about the eschaton and being converted (cf. 1 Thess 4–5; 2 Thess 2):

> My dear Paul,
>
> The followers of Jesus in this city are in receipt of your letter, which was read out in church a month ago and which appears to confirm a widely held view here that our Lord will be returning in glory at any moment to take believers such as my humble self back with him to heaven. Being a hard-headed businessman I took your words with utmost seriousness. To prepare myself and my family for the Day of the Lord, I sold my business at a knock-down price and gave the proceeds to the poor—and that, let me add, was a tidy sum, but I assume I won't need cash in heaven! So here I am with my bags packed, my property disposed of and myself, my wife, and my children taking it in shifts to scan the

46. Morris, *Epistles to the Apostle*, 13–16.

skies for something unusual to appear. In fact, every time I hear a trumpet, I nearly jump out of my skin! And what has happened? Nothing.

I can't help feeling that I've been made to look an utter fool in the eyes of my friends and business acquaintances. They all think I've gone stark, raving mad. Meanwhile, the man who bought my business, far from suffering the catastrophe reserved for the wicked, is making a handsome profit and living in my house, which is one of the finest in the city . . . .

Would you kindly tell me what I do next? The tax people are pestering me for last year's assessment, and I haven't a lead shekel to pay them with. Being a man of God you are probably unaware that disposing of one's assets in the interests of a religion which is not recognized by the state does not qualify one for retrospective tax exemption. So, I'm in a pretty pickle, let me tell you! I feel most strongly that the financial implications of the Second Coming should have been given more serious consideration by the apostles . . .

I am in a most embarrassing situation, what with a nagging wife and three children who have gotten completely out of hand because they prefer earthly pranks to what they imagine will be heavenly boredom . . . it is one thing to suffer for the faith; quite another to be made to look ridiculous. However I do not intend to move from this spot until Jesus comes to collect me. Meanwhile it would be quite dishonest of me not to express grave concern at the most unbusinesslike way in which this whole matter is being dealt with. I await an eager reply, other wise I shall be forced to turn the whole matter over to my lawyers.

Paphlos

[there followed a letter from Paphlos' lawyer telling Paul he had exactly thirty days to make good on his promise of heaven or face litigation in Thessalonike.]

Another novel fact about Paul's letters is they seem to have been geared to become part of an act of worship. For example, notice how some of Paul's letters end. In 1 Corinthians 16:20 (cf. 2 Cor 13:12), Paul tells his converts to greet one another in the assembly with a holy kiss (i.e., a gesture appropriate between Christian friends or family especially in a household setting) that in our era has become the handshake during a moment of fellowship and greeting during the service. Or again, notice how Paul tends to begin his letters with a prayer and end with a benediction (cf. 1 Cor 1:4–9 and 16:23). One would have liked to have been present at the worship service to be one of the first hearers of 1 Corinthians. It would have been a long service indeed, and apparently would have involved a fellowship meal and the Lord's Supper (1 Cor 11).

Paul was concerned about the issue of miscommunication or the suggestion that the letter delivered was not really from him. Though it was a very regular practice in antiquity, Paul was insistent on signing and post-scripting his own letters as marks of authentication (Gal 6:11; 2 Thess 3:17). What then was the particular relationship of Paul to his sécretaries and co-authors? Did Paul dictate word for word to his scribe? Did he give the scribe the gist and leave the formulation of the material to the secretary? Did he instruct a trusted literate Christian friend, such as a Timothy or Luke, to write in his name without indicating specific contents?

It is of course possible that Paul did all of these things, depending on the situation. We have reasonably clear evidence both from the personal signature remarks (see above) and from the reference to a scribe (Rom 16:22) that Paul regularly used secretaries. It is also reasonable to think of 1 and 2 Thessalonians as involving joint authorship. One would suspect that the degree of dictation by the apostle depended on how trusted and experienced a Christian friend Paul was relying on when a given letter was written. For what it is worth, however, when we read closely the capital or basically undisputed Pauline epistles (Romans, 1 and 2 Corinthians, Galatians, Philippians, 1 Thessalonians, Philemon), there is a remarkable degree of similarity between these letters in style involving not just vocabulary but also grammar and syntax. Furthermore, we find regularly indications of writer's distress, namely sentences broken off in mid-stream. Among a variety of good examples of the latter consider 1 Corinthians 9:15c. It reads literally, "For it would be better for me to die (than) . . . No one will deprive me of my boast." This and other such examples of anacoluthon (incomplete sentences) surely suggest that Paul was dictating these letters and that the scribe at various points simply could not keep up. For both of these reasons and others most scholars have rightly not doubted that we have the mind of Paul in these letters. Even in the case of co-authored documents, we must assume that Paul agreed with what was said, especially in view of the fact that in 2 Thessalonians 3:17 Paul puts his own signature and imprimatur on what the document includes.

A word of caution needs to be added at this juncture. Letter writing as a literary art, and in particular the production of letter essays like Cicero's, was just coming into vogue in the first century AD. There were no ancient schools of letter writing in Paul's day, but there were rhetorical schools all over the Empire. Furthermore, it was not an epistolary "convention" to foreshadow the contents of a letter in a thanksgiving prayer, indeed there was not even a convention in regard to a thanksgiving prayer, except for an opening health wish. Furthermore, "body middle" as an epistolary category did not exist and tells us nothing about the shape or content of the largest part of an ancient letter. My point is just this—Paul's letters are not primarily shaped or structured on the basis of pre-existing epistolary conventions. Only the opening and closing of his documents significantly reflect such conventions, but this hardly helps us when it comes to the large majority of the document and its character and purpose. We have to look to rhetorical analysis for enlightenment on that score. But this somewhat cursory discussion of epistolary matters was critical if we were going to recognize how much more indebted Paul's "letters" are to rhetorical than to epistolary conventions.

Conclusions

What then do we learn about Paul himself from his letter writing? First, we gain a clear picture of someone who cares deeply about his converts. Not just the joyful passages but also the angry one's make clear how much he loved them. We find a man prepared to go to some considerable trouble so that by some means he might continue to nurture relationships with people who are a good distance away. There is a poignancy to Paul's letters, not least because they reflect Paul's great personal desire for community, to be one with his converts and have good fellowship with them. This individual was no loner. He is far more like a parent whose children are too far beyond arms' length for the distance to be comfortable. The letters in other words belie the suggestion that Paul was much like modern individualists. Paul's chief desire was for communion and community not just with his God but also with his people—both Christians, but as Romans 9–11 makes evident, also with Jews. He reflects the collectivist mentality again and again in these letters. His social networks are crucial to him personally but also because of the shared task of spreading the Good News.

It would be a mistake not to recognize in these letters Paul the authority figure, however troubling that side of his personality may be to post-modern folk. The pastoral side of Paul of course comes through again and again, but in letters like Galatians or 1 Corinthians when Paul is nearly driven to distraction by his converts' misadventures, it is quite clear that Paul is prepared to take charge and command. Paul the apostle comes through loud and clear in passages like 1 Corinthians 4:14—5:13. Paul was not an early advocate of congregational church polity. He reflects the hierarchical bent of his society in general, including the hierarchical bent of religious communities. The difference is that Paul's hierarchy is ultimately theocratic in character. Christ is the head of the body and Paul is simply his servant and agent on earth. It is perhaps worth pondering whether this theocratic approach to his faith was not a carry over from his days as a Zealotic Pharisee.

We also learn from these letters that Paul is by ancient standards a very well educated and articulate person. He would surely have been in the top 5% of his society in literacy and education. Obviously he was primarily learned in the Hebrew Scriptures, but there are hints of considerable wider learning as well (see 1 Cor 15:32–33). We will learn more of this shortly when we reflect on Paul the rhetor. There are also other hints in a text like 1 Corinthians 9 or Philippians 3 that Paul was a person of considerable social status, stepping down to win persons for Christ.

The letters suggest that Paul attracted an important minority of people who had a similar status, people like Erastus, Stephanus, Phoebe, or Priscilla and Aquila, who could be key players in the advancement of the Gospel. House churches were a must for a religious group that had no priests, no temples, no sacrifices, and no means of support from cities or Emperors.

Paul's letters bear clear witness not only to his commitment to the conversion of households (1 Cor 1:16), but to his urban missionary strategy. Paul went to venues like Corinth, Ephesus, Philippi, and Pisidian Antioch where his Jewishness and his Roman Citizenship could provide him with open doors and opportunities and where his trade of tent-making could help him keep body and soul together and so offer the Gospel freely and without need of patronage. We have no letters from Paul's hands to non-city dwellers. Paul knew that the cities and the Roman roads that linked them were the keys to reaching the Mediterranean crescent quickly for Christ.

Finally, we learn from these letters that Paul had a profound relationship with God in Christ. One of the things that most distinguishes his letters from other ancient ones is the amount of religious and spiritual content, and the fact that it is never perfunctory in character. He would have seemed to many ancients like a great holy man or philosopher or a sage or a prophet. Ironically, the answer to the question, "Where is the wise man, where is the scribe, where is the debater of this age?" (1 Cor 1:20) is in fact right before our eyes and those of Paul's converts. This describes Paul very well. Trained as a scribe, learned in the Scriptures and Greek wisdom, always a pundit. Whatever else one may say about Paul, he can scarcely have ever been a dull or uninteresting person. His zeal and earnestness is evident on every page of his letters. But perhaps what the letters most reveal is what a powerful persuader he could be. We must turn now to Paul the persuader, Paul the rhetor.

PAUL THE RHETOR

The Rhetorical Climate and Character of Paul's World

In an oral culture, the ability to speak well is always important, and the ability to actually persuade is a required skill of any public figure. Rhetoric, though it might degenerate into the art of speaking well, was in essence the art of persuasion. So important was this ability that rhetoric was a fundamental staple of ancient education. "For the great majority of students, higher education meant taking lessons from the rhetor, learning the art of eloquence from him."[47] This education would begin ideally as soon as a young person had finished with learning the rudiments of grammar. Rhetors were everywhere in the Roman Empire. It was not as if one needed to go off to a major university town to find one. If a city like Eretria, a small city on a Greek island in the Aegean (*Sylloge inscriptionum graecarum* 714), could have one, we may be certain that a much larger cosmopolitan Hellenized city like Herod's Jerusalem surely had several.

Since powers of persuasion and eloquence, always highly admired in the Greco-Roman world, were even more important for the underdogs than the overlords if they wished to obtain what they wanted from their rulers, it is understandable how there may have been considerable desire

---

47. Marrou, *A History of Education*, 194.

and pressure for young upwardly mobile Jewish males in Jerusalem to gain rhetorical skills. The importance of these skills would certainly also have not been lost on anyone who was a Roman citizen and desired to take advantage of what that meant in the Roman Empire, or on a Pharisee who was zealous to see others become similarly Torah-true, perhaps particularly other Diaspora Jews living or staying in Jerusalem who would be like the man from Tarsus. We must reiterate here that by the time Paul was being educated, rhetoric had become the primary discipline of Roman higher education.[48] There is thus an a priori likelihood that Saul will have dedicated a considerable portion of his educational years to learning rhetoric. What then will he have learned?

As we discussed in an earlier chapter, there were three primary kinds of rhetoric, each tooled to suit a particular setting: (1) judicial or *forensic* rhetoric for use in the law courts; (2) *deliberative* rhetoric, meant to be used in the assembly; and (3) *epideictic* rhetoric, meant to be used in funeral oratory or public speeches lauding some event or person, or in oratory contests in the market place or the arena. Public speaking and the evaluation of it had become a major spectator sport, drawing crowds in all these venues well beyond the obligatory participants.

It is not surprising that with the demise of democracy, the more meaningful tasks of the public assembly (see Acts 19:35–38 and the dismissal of the crowd with reference to the proconsuls and the courts), and the rise of Empire, that the rhetoric of display, the rhetoric of pomp and circumstance, the rhetoric of entertainment came to the fore. It is also no surprise that in an agonistic culture such as existed in the Greco-Roman world of Paul's day lawyers were kept quite busy throughout the Empire (see 1 Cor 6). The main venues for deliberative rhetoric in Paul's day will have been in the royal court where one needed to persuade as an ambassador, or when interceding with a patron, or seeking votes, or interestingly enough in voluntary religious associations where people had to be persuaded to join and then to believe and behave in a specific fashion. As we shall see, Paul is capable of using all of these forms of rhetoric, but he most prefers deliberative rhetoric, not least because he sees the *ekklēsia* (now that public democratic societies had become perfunctory tools of the elite), the assembly of believers, as the ultimate place where freedom

---

48. See Bonner, *Education in Ancient Rome.*

should exist, and persuasion in the form of discourses, dialogues, debates should be used to encourage people to believe and live as they ought.[49]

Beyond the considerations of "invention" when it came to constructing the various necessary parts of a speech (the *exordium*, etc.) there was also a whole armada of rhetorical devices and tropes that could be trotted out to enhance or embellish one or another portion of a speech. In addition, any good rhetorical handbook such as Quintilian's would spend a great deal of time addressing the importance of voice, including tone and volume, gestures, appearances and the like. The art of persuasion involved more than just the art of eloquence, it involved the whole impact of the speaker on the audience and it was not uncommon for a rhetor to use a variety of kinds of rhetoric to persuade in a given speech. The end justified the variety of means. In ever so many ways, rhetors were the ancient equivalent of preachers or evangelists, and this too is yet another reason why a Paul would want to be truly adept at rhetoric, especially after his conversion to Christianity—"so that I might by all means win some for Christ" (1 Cor 9:22). But do Paul's "letters" actually reveal the patterns of rhetorical speeches? We must turn to the letters themselves to answer this question. Before that a quote from Litfin is in order:

> Rhetoric played both a powerful and pervasive role in first century Greco-Roman society. It was a commodity of which the vast majority of the population were either producers, or much more likely consumers, and not seldom avid consumers . . . [O]ratory became more prevalent than ever. In both the Roman and the Greek setting the frequency with which speakers rose to address audiences, for whatever reasons, seemed to be on the rise during the first century. The quality of oratory may have declined but the quantity had not.[50]

Paul's Rhetorical Letters

In some ways it is not surprising that the recent rebirth of the rhetorical analysis of Paul's letters has taken some scholars by surprise.[51] There is a ready explanation for this fact. The twentieth century has witnessed

49. On all of this see my discussion in *Conflict and Community*, 40–50.

50. Litfin, *St. Paul's Theology of Proclamation*, 132.

51. For a brief helpful survey on the history of rhetoric see Litfin, *St. Paul's Theology of Proclamation*, 1–134.

the demise of classical studies both in the public schools and to a lesser extent in the private schools, and to a very really extent in the universities as well. Gone are the days when rhetoric is one of the staples of North American education and yet as late as the end of the nineteenth century it was one of the three or four major subjects taught at major universities. The famous war veteran and hero of the battle of Gettysburg, Joshua Chamberlain was, prior to his enlistment, a professor of rhetoric and metaphysics (or natural and revealed religion) at a major New England college, and he was no isolated phenomenon. What has happened is that by and large, most New Testament scholars, particularly in the second half of this century have not studied the Greek and Latin classics, and rhetoric is for them like a *terra incognita*. It was not always so.

One need only read through, some of the commentaries of the early church fathers on Paul's letters, such as John Chrysostom's commentary on Galatians, to realize immediately that those who still lived in a rhetorical environment recognized Paul's letters for what they were—rhetorical speeches within an epistolary framework and with some epistolary features. After all, a letter was a surrogate for oral speech, and a good letter would seek to present as many of the best and most persuasive features of speech as possible.

I would argue that the rhetorical forms of Paul's letters are more revealing of what Paul's letters are actually about than the epistolary forms and elements. In fact, I would argue that the rhetorical forms more determine the structures of these documents than do the epistolary forms, especially if one looks beyond and between the prescript and the postscript. The proof of the pudding however is in the eating, so let us consider several samples of Paul's rhetoric.

The impetus for the renewal of the study of Paul's rhetoric may in large measure be put down to two important developments in the late seventies and early eighties: (1) H. D. Betz's landmark commentary on Paul's letter to the Galatians appeared; and (2) the work of G. A. Kennedy on rhetoric in the NT, following other key studies of his on ancient Greco-Roman rhetoric, came forth.[52] The doctoral students of these two scholars then began to carry forward the discussion until today when many others have joined the dialogue and one can say that rhetorical criticism of the

---

52. Betz, *Galatians;* Kennedy, *New Testament Interpretation through Rhetorical Criticism.*

New Testament is a major growth area in all of New Testament studies in the nineties and now in the new millennium. Since the modern discussion really began with the analysis of Galatians, we will begin there as well.

It is fair to say that Galatians is one of the most obviously rhetorical of all Paul's letters. It includes the usual epistolary framework at the beginning and at the end (1:1–5; 6:11–18), but for the most part it is pure speech material. Unlike most of Paul's other letters, in Galatians there is no thanksgiving section, no greetings to particular persons, no health wish, no mention of present or future travel plans. Galatians 1:6—6:10, being composed of mostly arguments and narrative that supports them, would surely be seen by any ancient person who was at all educated as a rhetorical tour de force—"full of sound and fury." But what sort of rhetoric was it? There are basically three major possibilities: (1) it is forensic in character (so Betz); (2) it is a mixture of forensic and deliberative rhetoric;[53] and (3) it is an example of deliberative rhetoric, but of a polemical sort (so Kennedy).[54]

One of the crucial things to be aware of in analyzing a speech or rhetorical letter is that there is a difference between the emotional tone of a letter and its argumentative substance. All three major forms of rhetoric can be polemical in tone. This does not make them apologetic in character. On close inspection, it becomes clear that all of the arguments in Galatians have one aim—to convince the Galatians to take a particular course of action in the near future as they deliberate whether or not to get themselves circumcised and submit to the Mosaic Law. As Kennedy says, the issue here is "not whether Paul had been right in what he had said or done, but what they themselves were going to believe and to do."[55] In short, even Galatians 1–2 is not an example of apologetic or forensic rhetoric, the rhetoric of attack or defense. Paul's remarks about the Gospel and his autobiography have a different function altogether than that of defending Paul's apostolic office or his message. The issue is not Paul's past, but the Galatians' future. Paul's past is brought up to provide the audience with clarity as to how they should and should not

53. So Longenecker, *Galatians*, c–cxix.

54. Hester, "The Rhetorical Structure of Galatians 1.11–14," 223–33, seems to be alone in arguing that Galatians is epideictic rhetoric.

55. Kennedy, *New Testament*, 146.

.

behave—following Paul's good example since his conversion, avoiding his pre-Christian example.

There are some very good reasons, beyond what I have just said, as to why a forensic analysis of Galatians will not work. First and foremost, forensic rhetoric has no place for exhortations such as we find in Galatians 5:1—6:10. Exhortations belong to the deliberative form of rhetoric and are part of the attempt to persuade or dissuade about a future course of action. Second, Paul calls upon his audience to imitate his behavior (4:12) something quite appropriate in a deliberative speech but not in a forensic one. Third, the major arguments in Galatians are in essence that the Galatians are foolish to listen to the agitators and wise to heed Paul. They are arguments to the effect that if the Galatians submit to the Law they will be harming themselves and losing the advantages they already have in Christ by faith. Arguments about harm or advantage are deliberative arguments. Fourth, the function of the *narratio* in chs. 1–2 is precisely what Aristotle says a deliberative *narratio* (the latter not being required in this sort of rhetoric), ought to do—speak of things past "in order that being reminded of them, the hearers may take better counsel about the future" (*Rhetorica* 3.16.11). Quintilian says it is most appropriate in a deliberative *narratio* to "begin with a reference either to ourselves or to our opponent" (*Institutio oratoria* 3.8.8–10), which is what we find in Galatians 1–2. It is true that the tone of this material is somewhat polemical and even defensive. This is because Paul must establish his ethos or character at the beginning of the speech so the audience will be ready to receive his arguments that follow. One should notice also that Paul says this is a discourse for the assemblies in Galatia (1:2), another indication that this is a deliberative act of persuasion. The following outline will show the structure of the letter of Galatians and the deliberative discourse it contains.[56]

Epistolary Opening — 1:1–2
Epistolary Greeting — 1:3–4
Doxological Conclusion to Epistolary Section — 1:5
Exordium — 1:6–10 — Two Gospels?
Narratio — 1:11—2:14 — The Origin and Character of the Gospel of Grace
        1:11–12 (transitional) — The Gospel of Grace
        1:13—2:14 — A Narrative of Surprising Developments:
        Jerusalem, Antioch, and Beyond

56. For much more along these lines see my *Grace in Galatia*, 25–35.

Propositio — 2:15–21 — By the Faithfulness of Christ, Not by Works of the Law
Probatio — 3:1—6:10

   Argument One — 3:1–18 — The Faith of Abraham and the Foolishness
   of the Galatians
      Division One — 3:1–5 — The Appeal to Spiritual Experience
      Division Two — 3:6–14 — The Appeal to Scripture
      Division Three — 3:15–18 — The Appeal to Legal Covenants
   Argument Two — 3:19—4:7 — The Goal of the Guardian,
   the Function of the Faithful One
      Division One — 3:19–22 — Why the Law was Added
      Division Two — 3:23–29 — The Guardian's Goal
      Division Three — 4:1–7 — The Heir's Apparent
   Argument Three — 4:8–20 — Shared Experience
      Division One — 4:8–11 — Déjà Vu
      Division Two — 4:12–20 — Paul's Labor Pains
   Argument Four — 4:21—5:1 — The Allegory Antipathy[57]
   Argument Five — 5:2–15 — The Unkindest Cut of All
      Division One — 5:2–6 — Testimony from the Top
      Division Two — 5:7–12 — What Cuts and What Counts
      Division Three — 5:13–15 — Freedom's Service, Love's Law
   Argument Six — 5:16–26 — Antisocial Behavior and Eschatological Fruit
      Division One — 5:16–21 — Foiling the Fulfillment of the Flesh
      Division Two — 5:22–26 — The Spirit's Fruit
   Argument Seven — 6:1–10 — Bearable Burdens and the Yoke of Christ
      Division One — 6:1–5 — The Law of Christ
      Division Two — 6:6–10 — Doing Good to Teachers and Others
Epistolary Authentication Formula — 6:11
Peroratio — 6:12–17

Galatians, however, is by no means the only example of deliberative rhetoric in the Pauline corpus. Another fine example, of a little shorter length, is the deliberative argument for concord and harmony found in Philippians.[58] Whereas Galatians sought to head off harm and enhance

57. It is perhaps possible to see this portion of the discourse as a *refutatio* if in fact it is the case that Paul is countering arguments of the agitators about Jerusalem and the Sinai covenant and Abraham at this point, but this is not certain.

58. In passing it is important to remark that there is no basis for the theory that Philippians is a combination of several Pauline letters. First, there is no textual evidence to support such a conjecture. Secondly, this conjecture is based on a complete failure

advantage for Paul's converts, Philippians deals in classic fashion (by appeal to multiple examples) with the issue of producing harmony, unity, and oneness of mind among believers in Philippi.[59] Here is a briefer outline of this rhetorical piece.

Epistolary Prescript — 1:1–2

Epistolary Thanksgiving / *Exordium* — 1:3–11

Propositio — 1:27–30

Probatio — 2:1—4:3

Peroratio — 4:4–20

Epistolary Greetings and Closing — 4:21–23

To show how much this letter focuses on positive and negative examples for the audience, following the rhetorical practice of creating a *synkrisis*, we can consider the following: (1) Paul (1:12–14, 18b–30) v. the rival preachers (1:15–18a); (2) Christ (2:5–11) and Timothy and Epaphroditus (2:19–30) v. this crooked generation (2:15); (3) Paul (3:5–17, 20–21) v. the Judaizers (3:2–6, 18–19); (4) negative examples of Euodia and Syntyche (4:2–3). The concluding *peroratio* includes a statement of the qualities or virtues one looks for in such examples (4:8–9).

I have provided elsewhere a lengthy discussion of how 1 Corinthians is also, as a whole, another excellent example of deliberative rhetoric,[60] but this particular "speech" is almost four times as long as that we find in Philippians, and if one thing was imperative in a long speech, some interesting or entertaining digressions were necessary (see Quintilian *Institutio oratoria* 3.7.1–4). Digressions would often take the form of a different kind of rhetoric, and we find this very phenomenon in 1 Corinthians 13, an excellent and poetic example of showpiece epideictic

---

to see the unifying rhetorical structure of the whole document as it presents a series of arguments from which the audience is to learn. Philippians 3:2ff. is not a piece of another letter. It provides the essential negative counterpart to the positive examples of Christ, Paul, and the Pauline co-workers already presented in Philippians 1–2. It is followed by a further example of discordant behavior in Phil 4:2–7. Against Murphy-O'Connor, *Paul*, 211ff. See my discussion in *Friendship and Finances in Philippi*, 11ff.

59. For a helpful brief analysis of Philippians as deliberative rhetoric see Watson, "A Rhetorical Analysis of Philippians," 57–87.

60. See Witherington, *Conflict and Community*, 39–41, where I am largely following the excellent study of Mitchell, *Paul and the Rhetoric of Reconciliation*. See, however, the useful critique by Pogoloff, *Logos and Sophia*.

rhetoric in praise of love. While, so far as macro-rhetoric is concerned, 1 Corinthians is deliberative in form and function, in the digression in 1 Corinthians 13 we have micro-rhetoric of an epideictic sort. Yet even ch. 13 serves the larger deliberative purposes of 1 Corinthians by showing through praising love the more excellent way that Corinthians should exercise their gifts from God. Interestingly the concept of love was often used in deliberative rhetoric in arguments for social concord such as we find in this document (see Aristotle *Nichomachean Ethics* 8.1.4).

Commentators had long noted the more eloquent and elevated style of this section of 1 Corinthians, but prior to the rhetorical analysis of the material they had no adequate explanation for why this material was in a different form than other parts of the letter. 1 Corinthians 13 functions as a sort of emotional appeal through eloquence and beauty, attempting to win the audience's heart, after many arguments directed at their minds. Epideictic rhetoric was especially useful for such purposes, and provided an opportunity to display one's skill and culture, something the Corinthians clearly sought in their teachers.[61]

Our final example of Pauline macro-rhetoric is found in 2 Corinthians. If any letter of Paul has a chance of being a combination of several Pauline letters it is this document. Usually however the division is thought to come between 2 Corinthians 1–9 and 2 Corinthians 10–13. There are problems with this assessment. First, 2 Corinthians 8–9 provides us with a different sort of material and rhetoric than what comes before and after it. Second, 2 Corinthians 6:14—7:1 seems to be of a different order or ilk as well. In short, if one is going to start petitioning this document, good arguments could be made that we have fragments of at least four letters, not just two. But in fact none of this speculation has any textual evidence to support it, and an adequate rhetorical analysis which allows for significant digressions in a lengthy rhetorical piece can explain what is going on here. In my view, 2 Corinthians is essentially a lengthy piece of forensic rhetoric with two significant deliberative digressions

---

61. See my discussion in *Conflict and Community*, 264–73; and also Holladay, "1 Corinthians 13: Paul as Apostolic Paradigm," 80–98. Holladay's argument shows that we must take the first person singular seriously in this chapter. Paul is indeed presenting himself as an example, but as part of the praise of love. Notice how the change in rhetorical mode is signaled directly at the beginning of this piece when Paul says "and now I will show or display a more excellent way . . .'" Epideictic rhetoric is the rhetoric of show or display.

in 6:14–7:1 and in 8–9, digressions which nevertheless serve the larger forensic purposes of this document.[62]

Forensic rhetoric, it will be remembered, is the rhetoric of attack and defense, and nowhere is such rhetoric so plainly evident in the Pauline corpus than in 2 Corinthians 10–13. Here Paul pulls out all the stops, using irony, sarcasm, mock boasting, a fool's discourse, and a host of other rhetorical devices to persuade his converts that he is indeed an innocent and honorable man, unlike his bogus opponents. Understanding the rhetorical function of this material is the key to understanding its character. For example, as a deflation device, meant to prick a hole in the balloon of the opponent's grandiose claims about themselves, Paul presents himself as a great ancient warrior going in reverse in 2 Corinthians 11:30–33. In antiquity a Roman soldier who was first up a wall and into a city that was conquered would win a special award called a "wall crown." Paul says he will boast of being first down the wall, in a basket, escaping his foes.[63] Paul will make himself the butt of his own joke, in order to disarm the audience and make them see the foibles of their suitors. It is a subtle way of attacking the opponents indirectly, using a kind of *insinuatio* approach, appropriate to the situation.[64] The overall structure of 2 Corinthians can be described as follows:

Epistolary Prescript — 1:1–2
Epistolary Thanksgiving / *Exordium* — 1:3–7
Narratio — 1:8—2:14 (with further thanksgiving and transitional elements
      in 2:15–16)
Propositio — 2:17, stating the basic fact under dispute
Probatio and *Refutatio* — 3:1—13:4 which includes:
  a. Paul's characerization of his ministry and of his particular rhetorical
     approach (3:1—6:13)
  b. A deliberative digression (6:14—7:1), in which Paul puts the audi-
     ence on the defensive by attacking their attendance at feasts in pagan
     temples (cf. 1 Cor 8–10)
  c. Paul's defense of the severe letter (7:2–16)

62. See my *Conflict and Community*, 355–65.

63. See ibid., 458–59.

64. The situation was that the Corinthians were favorably impressed with the "bogus apostles," and so Paul must resort to indirect means and sarcasm and irony to disengage them from such an attitude.

      d. A deliberative argument for the collection (8–9)
      e. A comparison of Paul and his rivals in Corinth, the false apostles, with
         a strong emotional appeal (10:1—13:4)
Peroratio — 13:5–10
Epistolary Greetings and Closing Remarks — 13:11–13

What 2 Corinthians shows is the degree of flexibility Paul has in the way he uses rhetoric, but it needs to be noted that Paul has not violated any rhetorical conventions in doing so. Digressions were a quite proper part of one's rhetorical strategy, especially in long speeches. The essential forensic character of the document as a whole is shown at the beginning in the long defensive *narratio*, in the further defense of the severe letter, in the attack on the continued Corinthian practice of attending idol feasts, and of course in 2 Corinthians 10–13. The other portions of the speech serve these larger forensic purposes and arguments.

How does the use of rhetorical analysis help us to understand Paul's letters and the apostle himself? For one thing, careful attention to the *propositio* and the *peroratio* provides direct clues to Paul's purposes in a given document. What is the essential proposition he will defend or advance? What is he trying to convince his audience about. It is easy to get lost in the myriad of Paul's arguments unless we know the thread which ties them together. The *propositio* and the *peroratio* provide us with the help in seeing the function and purpose of the whole, where the arguments are meant to lead us. For another thing, understanding rhetoric helps us to know when Paul is being serious and when sarcastic, when he is being ironic and when irenic. Tone is of course difficult to judge in a written document, but things become easier when one picks up the rhetorical signals that, for example, one is engaging in inoffensive self praise or *insinuatio*.

Furthermore, we discover that Paul's letters in fact are arranged quite carefully according to the patterns of ancient speeches. They were meant to be delivered orally, not just delivered by hand to the audience. The arguments that make up the bulk of the letters are carefully arranged and often build to a climax, as is clearly the case in 1 Corinthians 15 or 2 Corinthians 10–13—the former offering us the quintessence of the logical Pauline tour de force, the latter a wonderful example of a powerful emotional appeal that has real pathos. Surely few in even a slightly sympathetic audience could hear the incredible list of Paul's trials and not be moved (2 Cor 11:23–29). Paul was an excellent preacher and persuader, indeed so excellent that he was able to overcome the ethos problems created by his "thorn in the flesh" and still convert many. He knew that the heart as well as the mind had to be won, if the day was to be won. Rhetoric provided him with a powerful tool so that he might "preach for a verdict" or persuade with success. Many modern preachers would do well to study carefully ancient rhetoric—even if just by reading through Quintilian's handbook and comparing what he says to what we find in Paul's letters—if they want to understand what can and does persuade people to be and do and think things they have not been, done, or thought before.

Sometimes it is urged that Paul's rhetoric is somewhat rudimentary. This sort of critique is usually leveled by those who think that one can only find in Paul's letters micro-rhetoric, the use of simple rhetorical devices like rhetorical questions, and the like. Nothing could be further from the truth. In fact, Paul's letters reflect the use of some of the most sophisticated and complex rhetorical moves imaginable. One example of the use of more advanced rhetoric must suffice here, and so we turn to Paul's use of "impersonation" in Romans 7, where Paul retells Adam's tale for his Roman largely Gentile Christian audience

There is no more disputed text in all of ancient literature, and in fact no more commentated on text, than Romans 7. This is the stuff of which whole theologies, not to mention dissertations and scholarly careers, are made. One thing that has characterized the discussion of this text in the twentieth and into the twenty-first century is that until recently scholars have almost universally failed to apply the insights of Greco-Roman rhetoric to the analysis of this text. This is unfortunate because it provides several keys to unlocking the mysteries of this text.

Romans 7 demonstrates not only Paul's considerable skill with rhetoric, but his penchant for using even its most complex devices and techniques. This text proves beyond a reasonable doubt that Paul did not use rhetoric in some purely superficial or sparing way (e.g., using rhetorical questions).[65] To the contrary, the very warp and woof of his argument here reflects, and indeed requires an understanding of, sophisticated rhetorical techniques to make sense of the content of this passage and the

65. Against several of the essayists in Porter and Stamps, *Rhetorical Criticism and the Bible*, who continue to misjudge Paul in this regard, as has rightly also been noticed by Mitchell in several publications (e.g., *The Heavenly Trumpet*).

way it attempts to persuade the Roman audience. It will repay our close attention at this juncture.

When "Impersonation" Gets Personal

"Impersonation" or *prosopopoia* is a rhetorical technique which falls under the heading of figures of speech and is often used to illustrate or make vivid a piece of deliberative rhetoric (Quintilian *Institutio oratoria* 3.8.49; cf. Theon *Progymnasmata* 8). This rhetorical technique involves the assumption of a role; sometimes the role would be marked off from its surrounding discourse by a change in tone, inflection, accent, or form of delivery, or an introductory formula signaling a change in voice. Sometimes the speech would simply be inserted "without mentioning the speaker at all" (Quintilian *Institutio oratoria* 9.2.37).[66] Unfortunately for us, we did not get to hear Paul's discourse delivered in its original oral setting, as was Paul's intent. It is not surprising then that many have not picked up the signals, having only Paul's words left to us, that impersonation is happening in Romans 7:7–13 and also for that matter in 7:14–25.[67]

Quintilian says impersonation "is sometimes introduced even with controversial themes, which are drawn from history and involve the appearance of definite historical characters as pleaders" (*Institutio oratoria* 3.8.52). In this case, Adam is the historical figure being impersonated in Romans 7:7–13, and the theme is most certainly controversial and drawn from history. Indeed, Paul has introduced this theme already in Rom 5:12–21. One must bear in mind that this discourse would have been heard seriatim, which means the audience would have heard about Adam only a few minutes before hearing the material in Romans 7.

The most important requirement for a speech in character in the form of impersonation is that the speech be fitting, suiting the situation and character of the one speaking. "For a speech that is out of keeping with the man who delivers it is just as faulty as a speech which fails to suit the subject to which it should conform." (Quintilian *Institutio oratoria* 3.8.51). The ability to pull off a convincing impersonation is considered by Quintilian to reflect the highest skill in rhetoric, for it is often the most

---

66. For an earlier and simplified version of this discussion see Witherington and Hyatt, *Letter to the Romans*.

67. "Impersonation" was a rhetorical device used to train those learning to write letters (see Theon *Progymnasta* 2.1125.22).

difficult thing to do (*Institutio oratoria* 3.8.49). That Paul attempts it, tells us something about Paul as a rhetorician. This rhetorical technique also involves personification, sometimes of abstract qualities (like fame or virtue, or in Paul's case sin or grace; see Quintilian *Institutio oratoria* 9.2.36). Quintilian also informs us that impersonation may take the form of a dialogue or speech, but it can also take the form of a first person narrative (*Institutio oratoria* 9.2.37).

Of course since the important work of W. G. Kümmel on Romans 7, it has become commonplace, perhaps even a majority opinion in some NT circles, that the "I" of Romans 7 is not autobiographical.[68] This, however, still did not tell us what sort of literary or rhetorical use of "I" we do find in Romans 7. As S. Stowers points out, it is also no new opinion that what is going on in Romans 7 is the rhetorical technique known as "impersonation."[69] In fact, this is how some of the earliest Greek commentators on Romans, such as Origen, took this portion of the letter, and later commentators such as Jerome and Rufinus take note of this approach of Origen's.[70] Not only so, Didymus of Alexandria and Nilus of Ancyra also saw Paul using the form of speech in character or impersonation here.[71] The point to be noted is that we are talking about Church Fathers who not only knew Greek well but who understood the use of rhetoric and believed Paul is certainly availing himself of rhetorical devices.[72] Even more importantly, there is John Chrysostom (Homily 13 on Romans) who was very much in touch with the rhetorical nature and the theological substance of Paul's letters. He also does not think that Romans 7 is about Christians, much less about Paul himself as a Christian. He takes it to be talking about those who lived before the Law and those who lived outside the Law or lived under it. In other words, it is about Gentiles and Jews outside of Christ.

---

68. See Kümmel, *Römer 7 und das Bild des Menschen im Neuen Testament.*

69. Stowers, *A Rereading of Romans*, 264–69.

70. Unfortunately we have only fragments of Origen's Romans commentary. See the careful discussion by Stowers (*Rereading*, 266–67). Origen rightly notes: 1) Jews such as Paul do not speak of a time when they lived before or without the Law; and 2) what Paul says elsewhere about himself (cf. 1 Cor 6:19; Gal 3:13 and 2:20) does not fit this description of life outside Christ in Romans 7.

71. See Stowers, *Rereading*, 268–69.

72. It appears that the better commentators knew both Greek and rhetoric, the more likely they were to read Romans 7 as an example of impersonation.

But I would want to stress that since the vast majority of Paul's audience is Gentile, and Paul has as part of his rhetorical aims effecting some reconciliation between Jewish and Gentile Christians in Rome,[73] it would be singularly inept for Paul here to retell the story of Israel in a negative way, and then turn around in chs. 9–11 and try and get Gentiles to appreciate their Jewish heritage in Christ and to be understanding of Jews and their fellow Jewish Christians. No, Paul tells a more universal tale here of the progenitor of all humankind, and then the story of all those "in Adam," not focusing specifically on those "in Israel" that are within the Adamic category.[74] Even in Romans 7:14–25, Paul can be seen to be mainly echoing his discussion in 2:15 of Gentiles who had the "Law" within and struggled over its demands.[75] Because of the enormous debate about this text it will be well to rehearse a bit of the history of interpretation, as it bears on the study of Romans in general and also particularly Romans 7. It will be seen that much of the discussion of Romans 7 after Augustine was not only indebted to Augustine, it was misled by Augustine.

Father Knows Best?
Romans 7 Interpretation as Footnotes to Augustine[76]

If the measure of the importance of a text is who it has impacted in a major way, then in many regards Romans is, perhaps after one or the other of the Gospels, the most important NT book. From Augustine to Aquinas to Erasmus to Melanchthon to Luther to Calvin to Wesley, and in the modern era to Barth, Bultmann, and many others, the influence has been decisive. But what must be kept squarely in view is that the nature of the impact is in part determined by the way in which and the tradition from

---

73. See Witherington and Hyatt, *Letter to the Romans*, Introduction.

74. See Quintilian *Institutio oratoria* 2.30–31: "By this means we display the inner thoughts of our adversaries as though they were talking with themselves... or without sacrifice of credibility we may offer conversations between ourselves and others, or of others among themselves, and put words of advice, reproach, complaint, praise or pity into the mouths of appropriate persons."

75. The sensitive analysis by Aletti, "The Rhetoric of Romans 5–8," 294–308, here p. 300 deserves to be consulted. Aletti makes clear that Paul is not talking about Christians.

76. In what follows I am indebted to T. J. Deidun for pointing me in the right direction. See especially his helpful summary of the data, "Romans," 601–4. Also helpful is Godsey, "The Interpretation of Romans," 3–16.

which each of these persons has read the text, and this is especially the case with Romans.

There is of course a direct line of influence from Augustine to all these other interpreters who are in his debt. But it needs to be borne in mind that there were interpreters of Romans, and especially of Romans 7, prior to Augustine, and many of them, including luminaries among the Greek Fathers, like Origen and Chrysostom in the East and Pelagius and Ambrosiaster in the West, did not take Augustine's approach to Romans, and in particular ch. 7.

It is my view that to a real degree Augustine skewed the interpretation of this crucial Pauline text and we are still dealing with the theological fallout. Philip Melanchthon was to complain wryly: "This part of the Pauline epistle must be pondered in a particularly careful manner, because the ancients also sweated greatly in explaining these things, and few of them treated them skillfully and correctly."[77] The problem is Melanchthon thought that Augustine had it right, and the great majority of the Fathers were wrong.

The need to use Romans to dispute the Marcionites and the Gnostics preoccupied the patristic interpreters of Romans before Augustine, and as Deidun says there were emphases on very un-Augustinian themes: (1) the created goodness of human flesh and at least some human desire, and the integrity of human nature (Chrysostom); (2) free will (Pelagius); and (3) the harmony of Gospel and Law (several of the Fathers). In Pelagius's view, sin comes from human being's free imitation of Adam and can be overcome by imitating Christ. He also suggests that justification, at least final justification is through determined moral action. Augustine was to counter Pelagius by insisting on the necessity of grace for justification (see his *The Spirit and the Letter* [AD 412]).

Deidun aptly summarizes the key points of Augustine's mature interpretation of Romans, and we will turn to this in a moment, but we need to bear in mind that his interpretation immediately had enormous weight in the West and was to be, in effect, canonized for the Roman Catholic tradition at the Councils of Carthage in AD 418 and of Orange in AD 529. It was to be canonized, so to speak, for the Protestant line of interpretation by Luther and Calvin. It must be stressed that Augustine's

---

77. Melanchthon, *Commentary on Romans*, 156.

interpretation of Romans, and especially Romans 7, seems to be in various regards, an over-reaction to Pelagius.[78]

Consider now Deidun's summary of Augustine's main points on Romans:

> 1) The "works of the Law," which Paul says can never justify, mean moral actions in general without the grace of Christ, not Jewish practices as Pelagius and others maintained; 2) The "righteousness of God" . . . is not an attribute of God but the gift he confers in making people righteous; 3) Rom 5:12 now became the key text for Augustine's doctrine of original sin: all individuals (infants included) were co-involved in Adam's sin. As is well known, Augustine's exegesis of this verse largely depended on the Latin translation *in quo* ("in whom") of the Greek *eph hoi* ("in that," because) and on the omission in his manuscripts of the second mention of "death," with the result that "sin" became the subject of "spread": sin spread to all (by "generation," not by "imitation");[79] 4) Rom 7:14–25, which before the controversy Augustine had understood to be referring to humanity without Christ, he now applied to the Christian to deprive Pelagius of the opportunity of applying the positive elements in the passage (esp. v. 22) to unredeemed humanity.
>
> To do this, Augustine was obliged to water down Paul's negative statements: the apostle is describing not the bondage of sin but the bother of concupiscence; and he laments not that he cannot do good (*facere*) but that he cannot do it perfectly (*perficere*). 5) During this period Augustine came to express more boldly his teaching on predestination. It does not depend on God's advance knowledge of people's merit as Pelagius and others maintained in their interpretation of Rom 9:10ff. nor even on his advance knowledge of "the merit of faith" as Augustine himself had supposed in 394 in his remarks on the same passage: "it depends rather on God's 'most hidden judgment' whereby he graciously chooses whom he will deliver from the mass of fallen humanity. Everything is pure gift (1 Cor 4.7)."[80]

Of course all of these points of Augustine are today under dispute among interpreters of Romans, and some are clearly wrong, such as the

78. See the helpful discussion of Augustine, Luther, and Melanchthon by Meyer, "The Worm at the Core of the Apple," 66–69.

79. Erasmus, it should be noted, rejected altogether Augustine's view.

80. Deidun, "Romans," 601.

conclusions based on the Latin text of Romans 5:12. For our purposes, it is interesting to note that Augustine, having changed his mind about Romans 7:14–25 in overreacting to Pelagius, must water down the stress on the bondage of the will expressed in this text in order to apply it to Christians. Luther takes a harder and more consistent line, even though in the end he refers the text to the wrong subject—namely everyone including Christians. It is also noteworthy that Pelagius does not dispute God's destining of persons, only that God does it on the basis of his foreknowledge of the response of believers. It is also important that Augustine talks about God's gift of making people righteous. The later forensic emphasis comes as a result of the translation work of Erasmus.

It is interesting that the discussion of merit which Pelagius introduced into the conversation about Romans, resurfaces in the medieval exegetes after Augustine. Paul's doctrine of "justification" is filtered through Aristotelean thinking, so that grace becomes a *donum super additum*, something added on top of God's gift of human faculties (see Aquinas). "Divine *charis* became 'infused grace.'"[81] The nominalist school of William of Occam focused on merit, even in a Pelagian way, and it was to this repristinization of Pelagius's case that Luther, an Augustinian monk much like his founder, was to react to in his various lectures and then in his commentary on Romans. But it was not just Pelagius he was reacting to. In due course Luther came to see self-righteousness as the most fundamental of human sins (not concupiscence), and his polemics are directed against both Judaism and Catholicism which he sees as religions embodying this besetting sin, as well as being preoccupied with "merit." Luther thinks that Romans 7:14–25 is about that sin of self-righteousness.

Deidun notes, rightly, that Luther's exploration of what Augustine says about the righteousness of God, led him to criticize Augustine for not clearly explaining the imputation of righteousness. But in fact, as Deidun says, Augustine's "understanding of justification is thoroughly incompatible with the notion of imputation."[82] Luther gets this idea from Erasmus, but he is not afraid to critique Erasmus at other points. For instance, drawing on his understanding of Romans 7:14–25 as validating the notion of the Christian as being *simul justus et peccator*, he argues against Erasmus and other humanists in regard to human freedom

81. Ibid., 601.
82. Ibid., 602.

of the will. It is also noteworthy that Luther's influential two kingdom theory (spiritual and temporal) is derived from his exegesis of Romans 13. Christians are subject to earthly powers out of respect and love, but in the spiritual sphere only subject to God, not to human authorities such as the Pope. Calvin was to follow Luther's line on justification and pre-destination, except that he at least more explicitly highlights the notion of double predestination, based on a certain reading of Romans 8:29 (cf. the 1539 edition of Calvin's *Institutes*).

The English Reformation or Revival of the eighteenth century did not produce any great commentaries on Romans, not by Wesley, Coke, or Fletcher, nor later in the Wesleyan tradition by Clarke, Watson (though he offers much exposition on Romans in his *Institutes*, a rebuttal to Calvin), or Asbury. This helps explain why it is that the Protestant tradition of in-terpretation of the 19th and 20th centuries continued to be dominated by Lutheran or Calvinist interpreters including Bultmann, Barth, Kasemann, Cranfield and others of note. Even the foremost Methodist NT scholar of the last half of the 20th century, C. K. Barrett, in his Romans commen-taries (both editions), reflects primarily the influence of the Reformed tradition of interpretation, including an acknowledged indebtedness to Barth (and Bultmann).

Winds of change however have blown through NT studies since the late 1970s, and the changed views of early Judaism, and as a result of Paul and the Law, as well as a reassessment of the social setting of Romans and its rhetorical character, have led to various fresh lines of interpreta-tion that seem to be better grounded in the historical setting and matrix of Paul, rather than in the longer history of Protestant interpretation of Romans. It needs to be said that especially since Vatican II, there have also been notable contributions to the discussion of Romans by a series of Catholic scholars such as Cerfaux, Lyonnet, Kuss, Fitzmyer, and Byrne. It is interesting however that these expositors, especially Fitzmyer, seem more indebted to Augustine and Luther than to the scholastic and me-dieval Catholic traditions. Another way to measure the importance of a document is by whether it has continued to exercise the best minds in the field with fresh attempts to understand it. This Romans continues to do, for it is not only an enduring classic, and the most commented on work in human history, it is also a constant challenge to rethink the Christian faith. Since these winds of change have been sweeping through other aspects of the interpretation of Romans, it is perfectly in keeping that we make it a clean sweep by applying the rhetorical insights from the practice of "impersonation" to interpret Romans 7.

Adam's Plight Reexamined

Who is the "I" then who is speaking here in Romans 7:7–25? In my view, the "I" is Adam in vv. 7–13, and all those who are currently "in Adam" in vv. 14–25.[83] Adam, it will be remembered, is the last historical figure Paul introduced into his discourse at Romans 5:12, and we have contended that the story of Adam undergirds a good deal of the discussion from Romans 5:12 through Romans 7.[84] More will be said on this below, but suffice it to say here that the old traditional interpretations that Paul was describing his own pre-Christian experience, or alternately the experience of Christians in this text fail to grasp the rhetorical finesse and character of this material, and must be deemed very unlikely not only for that reason, but for others we will discuss in due course.[85]

I have commented on this text to some degree elsewhere,[86] but here it is important to give full attention to the narrative. There are three things that are crucial if one is to understand this text. First of all, Paul believes that Moses wrote the Pentateuch, including Genesis. Secondly, the "law" in Moses' books includes more than the Law given to Moses and with the Mosaic covenant. It would include the first commandment given to Adam and Eve.[87] Thirdly, it appears that Paul saw the "original sin" of coveting the fruit of the prohibited tree as a form of violation of the tenth commandment (cf. *Apocalypse of Moses* 19.3).

I would suggest a expansive rendering of vv. 8–11, which takes into account the Adamic story that is being retold here as follows: "But the

83. See the lengthy discussion by Theissen, *Psychological Aspects*, 177–269.

84. See Witherington and Hyatt, *Letter to the Romans*, 141–53.

85. It is telling that some of the most thorough recent treatments of Romans 7, even from the Reformed tradition, have concluded that Paul cannot be describing the Christian experience here. See Moo, *Romans*, 443–50; Wright, "Romans," 551–55 (Wright changed his mind from his earlier view that Christians were in view in Rom 7:14–25); Byrne, *Romans*, 216–26; Fitzmyer, *Romans*, 465–73; and Talbert, *Romans*, 185–209. See also Meyer, "The Worm at the Core of the Apple," 62–84; and Lambrecht, *The Wretched 'I'*.

86. See my *Paul's Narrative Thought World*, 14–15.

87. It is not surprising that some early Jews saw the commandment given to Adam and Eve as a form of one of the Ten Commandments, specifically the one having to do with coveting. See Witherington, *Paul's Narrative*, 14.

serpent [Sin], seizing an opportunity in the commandment, produced in me all sorts of covetousness . . . But I [Adam] was once alive apart from the Law, but when the commandment came, Sin sprang to life and I died, and the very commandment that promised life, proved deadly to me. For Sin [the serpent] seizing an opportunity through the commandment, deceived me and through it killed me." We have the familiar primeval tale of human life that began before the existence of the Law and apart from sin, but then the commandment entered, followed by deception, disobedience, and eventually death. We must consider the particulars of the text at this juncture.

First of all, to those who claim that there is no signal in the text that we are going into impersonation at v. 7 are simply wrong.[88] As Stowers points out:

> The section begins in v. 7 with an abrupt change in voice following a rhetorical question, that serves as a transition from Paul's authorial voice, which has previously addressed the readers explicitly . . . in 6.1—7.6. This constitutes what the grammarians and rhetoricians described as change of voice (*enallagē* or *metabolē*). These ancient readers would next look for *diaphonia*, a difference in characterization from the authorial voice. The speaker in 7.7–25 speaks with great personal pathos of coming under the Law at some point, learning about desire and sin, and being unable to do what he wants to do because of enslavement to sin or flesh.[89]

It is indeed crucial to see what we have here as not only a continuation of Paul's discussion of the Law, but a vivid retelling of the Fall in such a manner that he shows that there was a problem with commandments and the Law from the very beginning of the human story. Paul has transitioned from talking about what Christians once were in 7:5–6 before they came to Christ,[90] to talking about why they were that way and why

88. See now the very helpful treatment of Paul's rhetorical use of "I" here by Aletti, "Rom 7.7–25 encore une fois," 358–76. He is also right that Paul reflects some understanding of both Jewish and Greco-Roman anthropology in this passage.

89. Stowers, *Rereading*, 269–70.

90. As even Cranfield, *Romans*, 337, has to admit, Paul, in Romans 7:6 and in 8:8–9, uses the phrase "in the flesh" to denote a condition that for the Christian now belongs to the past. It is thus hopelessly contradictory to say on the one hand "We no longer have the basic direction of our lives controlled and determined by the flesh" (p. 337), and then turn around and maintain that Romans 7:14–25 describes the normal or even best Christian life, even though 7:14 says "we are fleshly, sold under sin," which comports

the Law had that effect on them before they became Christians, namely because of the sin of Adam. This is the outworking of and building upon what Paul says when he compares and contrasts the story of Adam and Christ in Romans 5:12–21.

Furthermore, there is a good reason not to simply lump vv. 7–13 together with vv. 14–25, as some commentators still do. In vv. 7–13 we have only past tenses of the verbs, while in vv. 14–25 we have present tenses. Either Paul is somewhat changing the subject in vv. 14–25 from vv. 7–13, or he is changing the time frame in which he is viewing the one subject. Here it will be worthwhile to consider the issue of the "I" as it has been viewed by various commentators who do not really take into account Paul's use of rhetoric and rhetorical devices, nor note the Adamic narrative subtext to Paul's discourse here.

The Pauline "I" Chart

vv. 7–13	vv. 14–25
1) the "I" is strictly autobiographical	1) the "I" is autobiographical, referring to Paul's current Christian experience
2) the "I" reflects Paul's view of a typical Jewish individual	2) the "I" is autobiographical, referring to Paul's pre-Christian experience as he viewed it then
3) the "I" reflects the experience of Jews as a whole	3) same as 2, only it is as he views his Jewish experience now
4) the "I" reflects humanity as a whole	4) the "I" presents the experience of the non-Christian Jew as seen by himself
5) the "I" is a way of speaking in general, without having a particular group of persons in mind	5) the "I" presents how Christians view Jews
	6) the "I" refers to "carnal" Christian
	7) the "I" reflects the experience of Christians in general
	8) the "I" reflects a person under conviction of sin and at the point of conversion (thus 7:14—8:1 provides a sort of narrative of a conversion)

only with the description of pre-Christian life in 7:6 and 8:8–9. This contradicts the notion that the believer has been released from "the flesh" in a moral sense.

It will be seen that there is no consensus of opinion whatsoever among scholars who do not take into account the rhetorical signals in the text, and do not recognize the echoes and allusions to the story of Adam in vv. 7–13. Sometimes too, as for instance in the case of Kasemann we have combinations of some of these views. He argues that 7:14–20 reflects the pious Jew, while 7:21–25 reflects all fallen humanity.[91] The very fact that there are so many varied conjectures about these texts counts against any of them being very likely.

The fact that many commentators through the years have thought Paul was describing Christian experience, including his own, we owe in large measure to the enormous influence of Augustine, including his influence especially on Luther, and those who have followed in Luther's exegetical footsteps. Gorday says, "This entire section of Romans 7:14–25 is absolutely omnipresent in Augustine's work, and is linked with every other passage in the epistle where the concern is to reinforce the complex interplay of grace and law that Augustine saw in Romans."[92] Furthering the impact of this view is that Augustine shared his opinions on this text in his most influential work, his *Confessions*, as well as in later works relating the text to his own experience.[93] Various important later expositors, such as Luther, resonated with this approach. This fact however does not constitute any sort of proof that this was what Paul had in mind when he wrote Romans 7. It probably says more about Augustine and Luther than it does about a rhetorically adept first-century Jewish Christian like Paul, who, K. Stendahl was later to aptly say, does not much seem to reflect the introspective consciousness of the West.[94] Paul hardly ever talks about his own personal guilt feelings or repentance, and when he does so, it a discussion of his pre-Christian period when he persecuted Christians, not about any internal moral conflict he struggled with as a Christian.[95]

91. Käsemann, *Romans*, 192–212.

92. Gorday, *Principles of Patristic Exegesis*, 164.

93. Notice that it was a Latin, rather than a Greek, Church Father who made this identification, and only after the strong influence of Manicheanism on him. It does not appear to me that Augustine was all that aware of rhetorical devices and techniques in the Greek tradition.

94. See the famous essay by Krister Stendahl with this title in *Paul among Jews and Gentiles*.

95. Note that Paul's frequent expressions of pathos in his letters, including in Romans have regularly to do with his concern for his converts, or his fellow Jews, and not with his own personal moral struggles as a Christian. The absence of expressions of guilt

Detailing Adam's Sin

What are the markers or indicators in the text of Romans 7:7–13 that the most probable way to read this text, the way Paul desired for it to be heard, is in the light of the story of Adam, with Adam speaking of his own experience?[96] Firstly, from the beginning of the passage in v. 7 there is reference to one specific commandment—"thou shalt not covet/desire." This is the tenth commandment in an abbreviated form (cf. Ex 20:17 and Deut 5:21). Some early Jewish exegesis of Genesis 3 suggested that the sin committed by Adam and Eve was a violation of the tenth commandment.[97] They coveted the fruit of the tree of the knowledge of good and evil.

Secondly, one must ask oneself, who in biblical history was only under one commandment, and one about coveting? The answer is Adam.[98] Verse 8 refers to a commandment (singular). This can hardly be a reference to the Mosaic Law in general, which Paul regularly speaks of as a collective entity. Thirdly, v. 9 says, "I was living once without/apart from the Law." The only person in the Bible said to be living before or without any law was Adam. The attempt to refer this to a person being before the time of their bar mitzvah, when one takes the yoke of the Law upon himself at 12–13 years of age, while not impossible, seems unlikely. Even a Jewish child who had not yet personally embraced the call to be a "son of the commandments" was still expected to obey the Mosaic Law, including honoring parents and God (cf. Luke 2:41–52).[99]

---

about his current conduct, unless Romans 7 is an exception, is noteworthy. Furthermore, Philippians 3:6 strongly indicates that Paul did not have a guilt-laden conscience when he was a non-Christian Jew either.

96. Some commentators, such as Barrett, *Romans*, 134–35, attempt a combination interpretation. Barrett avers the text is about Adam and also autobiographically about Paul. The rhetorical conventions suggest otherwise, but of course Paul is retelling the story of Adam because of its relevance for his audience's understanding of themselves. They are not to go back down the Adamic road.

97. See 4 Ezra 7:11; *b. Sanh.* 56b; and on the identification of Torah with the preexistent Wisdom of God see Sir 24:23; Bar 3:36–4:1.

98. See Kasemann, *Romans*, 196: "Methodologically the starting point should be that a story is told in vv. 9–11 and that the event depicted can refer strictly only to Adam . . . . There is nothing in the passage which does not fit Adam, and everything fits Adam alone."

99. But see Barrett, *Romans*, 134.

Fourthly, as numerous commentators have regularly noticed, Sin is personified in this text, especially in v. 11, as if it were like the snake in the garden. Paul says, "Sin took opportunity through the commandment to deceive me." This matches up well with the story about the snake using the commandment to deceive Eve and Adam in the garden. We can notice too how the very same verb is used to speak of this deception in 2 Corinthians 11:3 and also 1 Timothy 2:14. We know of course that physical death was said to be part of the punishment for this sin, but there was also the matter of spiritual death, due to alienation from God, and it is perhaps the latter that Paul has in view in this text.

Fifthly, notice how in v. 7 Paul says I did not know sin except through the commandment. This condition would only properly be the case with Adam, especially if "know" in this text means having personal experience of sin (cf. v. 5).[100] As we know from various earlier texts in Romans, Paul believes that all after Adam have sinned and fallen short of God's glory. The discussion in Romans 5:12–21 seems to be presupposed here. It is, however, possible to take *egnōn* to mean "recognize"—"I did not *recognize* sin for what it was except through the existence of the commandment." If this is the point, then it comports with what Paul has already said about the Law turning sin into trespass, sin being revealed as a violation of God's will for humankind. But on the whole, it seems more likely that Paul is describing Adam's awakening consciousness of the possibility of sin when the first commandment was given. All in all, the most satisfactory explanation of these verses is if we see Paul the Christian re-reading the story of Adam in the light of his Christian views about law and the Law.[101]

Certainly one of the functions of this subsection of Romans is to do something of an apologia for the Law. Paul is asking, is then the Law something evil because it not only reveals sin, but has the unintended effect of suggesting sins to commit to a human being? Is the Law's association with sin and death then a sign that the Law itself is a sinful or wicked thing? Paul's response is of course "absolutely not." Verse 7

100. Barrett, *Romans*, 132 points out the difference between here and Romans 3:20 where Paul uses the term *epignōsis* to refer to the recognition of sin. Here he simply says "know."

101. See the earlier discussion of this view at some length by Lyonnet, "L'histoire du salut selon le ch. 7 de l'epitre aux Romains," 117–51, and the helpful discussion of Elliott, *The Rhetoric of Romans*, 246–50, which comes to the same Adamic conclusion on the basis of rhetorical considerations.

suggests a parallel between *egnōn* and "know/desire," which suggests Paul has in view the experience of sin by this knower. Verse 8 says sin takes the Law as the starting point or opportunity to produce in the knower all sorts of evil desires.[102]

Stowers reads this part of the discussion in light of Greco-Roman discussions about desire and the mastery of desire, which may have been one of the things this discourse prompted in the largely Gentile audience.[103] But the story of Adam seems at the fore here. The basic argument is how sin used a good thing, the Law, to create evil desires in Adam. It is important to recognize that in chs. 5–6 Paul had already established that all humans are "in Adam," and all have sinned like him. Furthermore, Paul has spoken of the desires that plagued his largely Gentile audience prior to their conversions. The discussion here then just further links even the Gentile portion of the audience to Adam and his experience. They are to recognize themselves in this story, as the children of Adam who also have had desires, have sinned, and have died. The way Paul will illuminate the parallels will be seen in Romans 7:14–25 which I take to be a description of all those in Adam and outside of Christ.[104]

Paul then is providing a narrative in Romans 7:7–25 of the story of Adam from the past in vv. 7–13, and the story of all those in Adam in the present in vv. 14–25. In a sense what is happening here is an expansion on what Paul has already argued in Romans 5:12–21. There is a continuity in the "I" in Romans 7 by virtue of the close link between Adam and all those in Adam, a conclusion which comports with the collectivist nature of ancient thinking, including Paul's own thinking. The story of Adam is also the prototype of the story of Christ, and it is only when the person is

---

102. Barrett, *Romans*, 132 puts it vividly: "The law is not simply a reagent by which the presence of sin is detected: it is a catalyst which aids or even initiates the action of sin upon man."

103. See Stowers, *Rereading*, 271–72. Stowers suggests the tragic figure of Medea might be conjured up by what Paul says, but surely Adam is a more likely candidate to have come to Paul's mind, and his audience as well.

104. It simply complicates and confuses the matter to suggest Paul is also talking about Israel as well as Adam here. Paul is addressing a largely Gentile audience who did not identify with Israel, but could understand and identify with the progenitor of the whole human race. That Israel might be included in the discussion of those who are "in Adam" in 7:14–25 is certainly possible, but even there Paul has already described earlier in Romans 2 the dilemma of a Gentile caught between the law and a hard place. My point would be that even in vv. 14–25 he is not specifically focusing on Jewish experience, or the experience of Israel.

delivered from the body of death, it is only when a person transfers from the story of Adam into the story of Christ, that one can leave Adam and his story behind, no longer being in bondage to sin, and being empowered to resist temptation, walk in newness of life, as will be described in Rom 8. Christ starts the race of humanity over again, setting it right and in a new direction, delivering it from the bondage of sin, death, and the Law. It is not a surprise that Christ only enters the picture at the very end of the argument in ch. 7, in preparation for ch. 8, using the rhetorical technique of overlapping the end of one argument with the beginning of another. The audience which had just heard a *synkrisis* of Adam and Christ in Romans 5:12–21 only a few minutes before hearing Romans 7:7–25 would have had no difficulties in making the connections.[105]

Some have seen v. 9b as a problem for the Adam view of vv. 7–13 because the verb must be translated "renewed" or "live anew." But we should notice the contrast between "I was living" in v. 9a and "but Sin coming to life" in v. 9b. Cranfield then is right to urge that the meaning of the verb in question in v. 9b must be "sprang to life."[106] The snake/sin was lifeless until it had an opportunity to victimize some innocent victim, and had the means, namely the commandment, to do so. Sin deceived and spiritually killed the first founder of the human race. This is nearly a quotation from Genesis 3:13. One of the important corollaries of recognizing that Romans 7:7–13 is about Adam (and 7:14–25 is about those in Adam, and outside Christ), is that it becomes clear that Paul is not specifically critiquing Judaism or Jews any more than he is in Romans 7:14–25.[107]

105. This has confused those who are unaware of this rhetorical convention, and have taken the outburst "Thanks be to God in Jesus Christ" to be a cry only a Christian would make, and that therefore Romans 7:14–25 must be about Christian experience. However, if 7:14–25 is meant to be a narrative of a person in Adam who is led to the end of himself and to the point of conviction and conversion, then this outburst should be taken as Paul's interjected reply or response with the Gospel to the heartfelt cry of the lost person, a response which prepares for and signals the coming of the following argument in Romans 8 about life in Christ. On rhetorical chain-link construction see especially Longenecker, *Rhetoric at the Boundaries*.

106. Cranfield, *Romans 1–8*, 351–52.

107. As we shall see, there is also nothing in Romans 7:14–25 to suggest that his complaint is specifically with Jews. It is sin and death, and their effects on humankind, and also the Law's effect, whether on Gentiles or Jews that is critiqued. Furthermore, Paul, despite Luther's insistence, is not critiquing here the self-righteousness of Jews or others caught between a rock and a hard place when they know what they ought to do but are unable to do it. Sometimes in order to hear the text without the baggage of later interpretations, one has to deconstruct the later interpretations first.

V. 12 begins with *hōste* which should be translated 'so then' introducing Paul's conclusion about the Law that Paul has been driving toward. The commandment and for that matter the whole Law is holy, just, and good. It did not in itself produce sin or death in the founder of the human race. Rather sin/serpent/Satan used the commandment to that end. Good things, things from God, can be used for evil purposes by those with evil intent. The exceeding sinfulness of sin is revealed in that it will even use a good thing to produce an evil end—death.[108] This was not the intended end or purpose of the Law. The death of Adam was not a matter of his being killed with kindness or by something good. Verse 13 is emphatic. The Law, a good thing, did not kill Adam. But sin was indeed revealed to be sin by the Law and it produced death. This argument prepares the way for the discussion of the legacy of Adam for those who are outside of Christ. The present tense verbs reflect the ongoing legacy for those who are still in Adam and not in Christ. Romans 7:14–25 should not be seen as a further argument, but as the last stage of a four part argument which began in ch. 6, being grounded in Romans 5:12–21, and will climax Paul's discussion about sin, death, the Law, and their various effects on humankind.

Seeing Eye to "I" in Romans 7:14–25

It will not be necessary for us to go into as much depth with Romans 7:14–25 as we have with the tale of Adam in 7:7–13. Rather, we will focus on the points of rhetorical significance that should have guided the interpretation of this text all along. First, once it is realized that there is a fictive "I" being used in 7:7–13 to create a "speech in character," then it requires a change of rhetorical signals at 7:14, or thereafter, if that were to cease to be the case, in 7:14–25. We have no such compelling evidence that Paul is using "I" in a non-fictive way in these verses now under scrutiny. There is, it is true, a change in the tenses of the main verbs—here we have present tenses—signaling that Paul is talking about something that is now true of someone or some group of persons, but it must be some group that has an integral connection with the "I" of 7:7–13. Fortunately, Paul had already set up such a link in Romans 5:12–21; in particular, at the outset of that *synkrisis* or rhetorical comparison—one man sinned and death came to

108. Barrett, *Romans*, 136: "Sin in its deceitful use of the law and commandment, is revealed not merely in its true colors but in the worst possible light."

all people, not just because he sinned but also because they all sinned. The link has been forged, and we see here how it is played out as Adam's tale in 7:7–13 leads directly to the tale of all those who are in Adam in 7:14–25. Kasemann puts the matter aptly: "*Egō* [here] means [hu]mankind under the shadow of Adam: hence it does not embrace Christian existence in its ongoing temptation . . . What is being said here is already over for the Christian according to ch. 6 and ch. 8. The apostle is not even describing the content of his own experience of conversion."[109]

It is telling that most of the Church Fathers thought as well that Paul was adopting and adapting the persona of an unregenerate person, not describing his own struggles as a Christian. Most of them believed that conversion would deliver a person from the dilemma described here, deliver them from the bondage to sin or the law of sin and death, as Romans 8:1–2 puts it.[110] But what about the reference to the struggle with the "law of the mind"? Does not that suggest a person, perhaps a Jew, under the yoke of the Mosaic Law? While not an impossible interpretation of the struggle described, there is a better and more likely view if we are attentive to the rhetorical signals of the whole document. In Romans 2:15 Paul is quite explicit that Gentiles are not beholden to the Mosaic covenant or its Law; nonetheless they have the generic law of God written on their very hearts, and therefore, they do from time to time what God requires of them.

Notice that the struggle described in Romans 7:14–25 is between a law residing in one's mind and a quite different ruling principle residing in one's "flesh" or sinful inclinations. Nothing is said here about rebellion against a known external law code, nor is the book of the Law or Moses mentioned. We must remember, too, that it was said even Adam himself had a singular commandment of God to deal with, well before Moses, such that when Adam violated that one commandment sin and death reigned from Adam to Moses, even prior to the existence of the Mosaic code (Rom 5:14). The difference between Romans 7:14–25 and debates in chs. 2–3 with the Jewish teacher over the meaning of the external Law code is notable. It is thus most likely that we have here a more generic description of the condition of those who are in Adam, and are fighting

109. Kasemann, *Romans*, 200.

110. Bray, *Romans*, 189–90

but losing the battle with sin in their lives. The only way out of their dilemma is deliverance.

Paul is speaking as broadly as he can in this passage, addressing the human plight outside of Christ in general. He is not singling out Jews for special attention. That would have been rhetorically inept in any case since the great majority of his audience for Romans is likely Gentile (see Rom 11:13). We must bear in mind as well that we are dealing with a Christian interpretation of a pre-Christian condition. Paul does not assume that this is how either Gentiles or Jews themselves would view the matter if they were not also Christians. But clearly Gentiles could relate to this discussion. For example, Ovid, in his famous work *Metamorphoses*, speaks in very similar terms of the struggle with sin: "Desire persuades me one way, reason another. I see the better and approve it, but I follow the worse" (7:19–20). Even closer to Paul are the words of Epictetus: "What I wish, I do not do, and what I do not wish, I do." (*Dissertationes* 2.26.4). Paul has not traipsed into *terra incognita* for his largely Gentile audience, rather he is standing on familiar ground. The effect of law, law of any sort, on a fallen human being, whether the law of the heart, or the law in a code, is predictably the same, in Paul's view.

In the earlier parts of Romans, and especially in chs. 2–3, Paul resorts to the rhetorical device of the diatribe—a rhetorical debate with an imaginary interlocutor. Romans 7:7–25 has just a taste of that at v. 7.25a, where Paul himself, in his own and most pastoral voice responds to the heart cry of the lost person—"Who will deliver me from this body of dead?" His answer is swift and powerful—"Thanks be to God, through Jesus Christ our Lord!" What was lost on Luther is that the voice in v. 25a is not the same voice as the one that preceded it, or indeed that follows it in v. 25b.

Paul is following a well-known rhetorical technique called chain-link, or interlocking construction, which has now been described in detail, with full illustration of its use in the NT by Bruce Longenecker.[111] The basic way this technique works is that one briefly introduces the theme of the next argument or part of one's rhetorical argument, just before one concludes the argument one is presently laying out. Thus, in this case, 7:25a is the introduction to 8:1 and following, where Paul will once more speak in his own voice in the first person. Quintilian is quite

111. Longenecker, *Rhetoric at the Boundaries*.

specific about the need to use such a technique in a complex argument of many parts. He says that this sort of ABAB structure is effective when one must speak with pathos, force, energy, or pugnacity (*Institutio oratoria* 9.4.129–30). He adds, "We may compare its motion to that of men, who link hands to steady their steps, and lend each other their mutual support" (9.4.129). Failure to recognize this rhetorical device, where one introduces the next argument before concluding the previous one, has led to all sorts of misreadings of Romans 7:14–25.[112]

As Longenecker stresses, this reading of Romans 7:25a comports completely with the thrust of what has come immediately before 7:7–25 and what comes immediately thereafter. He puts it this way:

> Paul has taken great care to signal the transition from Romans 7 to Romans 8: first by contrasting the 'fleshly then' and the 'spiritual now' in 7.5–6 two verses which provide the structural foundation for the movement from 7.7ff. and 8.1ff., and second, by introducing the 'spiritual now' in 8.1 with the emphatic 'therefore now' (*ara nun*). Such structural indicators are strengthened further by the intentional inclusion of a thematic overlap in 7.25 . . . . Since in Paul's day chain-link construction was not an uncommon transitional device in assisting an audience . . . the placement of 7.25 within its surrounding context would not have been unusual or confusing. It would not have been seen as a structural anomaly requiring either textual reconstruction . . . or psychological explanation. Instead it would have been seen as a transition marker used for the benefit of Paul's audience.[113]

And So?

It is the mark of any good and correct interpretation of a complex and controverted passage that it explains not only the passage in question, but that it clears up other conundrums as well. One such conundrum for Augustine, Luther, and others who have seen Romans 7:7–25 not in the light of rhetoric, but as some sort of agonized transcript of Paul's own experience, is that there is a flat contradiction to such a reading of this

112. Longenecker, *Rhetoric at the Boundaries*, 88–93 shows in great detail how this works in Romans 7:14–25 and his argument answers every question or possible objection to this view of this passage.

113. Longenecker, *Rhetoric at the Boundaries*, 92. On the frequency of use and popularity of this rhetorical device see pp. 11–42 in this same study.

passage when one examines Philippians 3:4–6. Again we have a *synkrisis*, only here Paul is indeed contrasting his own past and his present condition and frame of mind. The key to understanding the passage is that, on the one hand, Paul says he has much to brag about "in the flesh," but, on the other hand, he says that however good those things were, he now counts them as refuse or dung because of the exceedingly great joy and glory of knowing Christ.

We need to not make the mistake of assuming that this colorful rhetorical language leads us to the wrong conclusion about Philippians 3:4–6. Paul was an outstanding and exceptionally pious Jew. On his own admission in Galatians 1:14 he was advancing in Judaism well beyond many Jews of his own age, and he was exceedingly zealous for and about his faith. Paul was no slacker.

Thus, it will come as no surprise that Paul, gets to the point of describing his rich Jewish heritage, and is even able to say that when he was a Pharisaic Jew, on the matter of keeping the Mosaic Law—he was faultless. His exact words: "as for righteousness of the Law—faultless" (Phil 3:6). I contend that the person who says this as a Christian looking back on his Jewish past, cannot also be describing his own personal experience in Romans 7:7–25, or else Paul is capable of flatly contradicting himself, even when he is talking about something he knows more intimately than any other human being—his own spiritual pilgrimage. The only thing about Paul's past, which he does indeed agonize over, is his persecuting, perhaps even to the death, of some Christians when he was a zealous Pharisee. This, as Galatians 1, 1 Corinthians 15, and also the later text 1 Timothy 1:13–15, show he did indeed regret, repent of, and have considerable remorse and anguish about. That however is very different from the described state in Romans 7:14–25 where the person knows better, but is quite unable to do better, and cries out for deliverance in his bondage.

Paul, as Krister Stendahl was to stress rightly, should not be over-psychologized, and we should not read back into his story the more tormented one of Augustine or Luther. He did not reflect the "introspective consciousness of the West" as Stendahl rightly urged.[114] I was fortunate enough to take course on Romans with Stendahl in the late 70s and hear his exposition of these crucial matters first hand. Needless to say he con-

---

114. The key essay can be found in Stendahl, *Paul among Jews and Gentiles*, but it originally was written in 1963 and caused an explosion when it first appeared in print.

vinced me. What is remarkable, however, is that he was able to come to this conclusion without fully recognizing the rhetorical character of the material and its signals.

But when one reads Paul with rhetorical spectacles, Stendahl's conclusion moves from being plausible to being by far the clearest and most convincing reading of this material in its original social and rhetorical contexts. Paul, as it turns out, was not a Lutheran before his time, nor even an Augustinian. Paul was a master rhetorician, and he fully believed that when the Christ has set a person free, they are free indeed from the bondage to sin, no longer entangled by the ruling principle of sin and death, for they have the Spirit of life within them, and they need not, indeed they must not dwell in the past. Perhaps this is why Paul also believed that Christian persons could be expected to listen to a discourse, properly evaluate its merit and be persuaded by it, without having to be ordered around by the apostle all the time. The art of persuasion is used on those that it is assumed have the capacity to respond freely and positively to something when convinced of its merits, even when the exhortation is not just about belief, but also about behavior. This presupposes an anthropological approach to Christians, in terms of their freedom from the bondage to sin, that is much different from what we find in Augustine and Luther. It also speaks volumes about how Paul views his audience, as well as himself.

What Rhetoric Tells us about Paul

But how does rhetoric help us to understand the apostle himself and what sort of person he was? First, it reminds us that we are dealing with a well-educated and articulate person. Paul was no rustic, backwoods preacher simply rattling off whatever exhortations that came to mind. To the contrary, these letters reflect significant learning, skill, organization, and preparation before one dons the mantle of the great persuader. No wonder even his opponents begrudgingly admitted his letters were powerful and weighty.

Second, Paul's use of rhetoric reminds us that he was concerned to reach his audience where he found them, which meant he had to use means of communication that worked with the largely Gentile audience with which he was dealing. He wanted his proclamation and persuasion to be a word on target, not merely a shot in the dark. This meant that Paul would seek to use all the available ancient tools of persuasion to achieve his ends, so long as basic ethical commitments and commitments to truth were not violated. Paul was a man of his time, and to a very real degree he was a successful evangelist because he knew what would and would not work with the audiences he addressed in the Greco-Roman world. He also knew enough about Mediterranean temperament to know that all the logic in the world without pathos would not likely appeal, much less persuade. As Pascal once said, "the heart has reasons that the mind knows not of," and so Paul sought to appeal to the whole person, so that by all means he might win some. To win some in an ancient, rhetorically saturated environment, one's speech needed to be winsome. It must not be forgotten how *paideia,* culture, and particularly eloquence, were a few of the great Greco-Roman cultural values of Paul's day.

Furthermore, rhetoric tells us that Paul was very much at home in the Gentile world. Though a Jew, he would not have seemed a stranger to Gentiles. He could speak their language, and he was prepared to fellowship with and even live with them, at great cost to his Jewish heritage and friendships—even his Jewish Christian friendships, as Galatians shows. It is clear that Gentiles were willing to listen to and be persuaded by such a person. Yet, it may well have taken many years in the Gentile world honing these rhetorical skills before Paul found success in Galatia, Philippi, Corinth and elsewhere. There must be a reason why the ten or more hidden years in Syria and Cilicia before Paul's time with Barnabas in Antioch still remain largely hidden.[115]

Paul's use of rhetoric also reminds us that Paul desired to be a part of a larger world than many of his Jewish Christian contemporaries who were dragged kicking and screaming into a more cosmopolitan church. It reminds us that Paul valued a good deal of Greco-Roman culture. He was not one to condemn every aspect of Greco-Roman culture. Rather he believed in sifting culture, not merely criticizing it. Paul's faith was not in a world-negating religion but rather in a world-transforming one. His was not the Amish-like enclave or withdrawal model, but rather the aggressive approach, taking every thought captive for Christ. We would do well to ponder this approach in an age where anathemas rather than engagement, critique, and persuasion seems to be the usual conservative Christian approach to society.

---

115. On the hidden years see Hengel, *Paul: Between Damascus and Antioch.*

Lastly, Paul's use of rhetoric or persuasion reminds us of Paul's commitment to freedom, to the old Greek value of democracy touted in the old assemblies. The Christian assemblies in homes could be replicas of that old assembly, if they were places of discourse, dialogue, debate, and persuasion. To be sure, Paul could and would command, if driven to it, but he would far rather "win" an audience's compliance in matters theological, ethical, and social. "For freedom Christ has set us free," is Paul's stirring cry in Galatians 5:1. Paul, as a collectivist, longed for a community that voluntarily lived in harmony and did what they ought to do to serve one another in love, and freely share Christ with the world. If love is the most important of Christian virtues, and love can never be compelled or coerced, then a community of like-minded and like-hearted persons freely interacting is the intended end product.

Rhetoric then reveals to us a Paul committed to and drawing on a great Greco-Roman heritage and working toward a great Christian community—a cosmopolitan family that embodied the best of both Jewish and Gentile worlds. We would still do well to embrace such a vision of the kingdom come on earth. "It is a consummation devoutly to be wished."

As we conclude our quest for Paul the letter writer and rhetor and what such activities tell us about the apostle, we must focus on one possible objection to this whole approach. The argument goes back to Deissmann in the early part of the last century and goes something like this:

> Paul was by no means a member of the social elite in the Greco-Roman world. Paul's sometimes awkward Greek and various aspects about his person, especially his trade of tent-making locate Paul socially several rungs below the Ciceros of the ancient world. Paul partook of the character and social level of most of his converts which is to say at best the artisan or lower class of Greco-Roman society.[116] Paul's reminder in 1 Cor 1:26 describes not only the predominant character of his audience but also himself. Most of them were likely freedmen and freedwomen, slaves, and the like.

There are a variety of problems with this assessment. Paul was a multicultural person, and while it is true that working with one's hands was considered demeaning by the Greco-Roman elite, this was certainly not

---

116. See Deissmann, *Paul*. This study actually first appeared in German in 1911.

the view of first-century Jews, nor was it the view of Greco-Roman artisans either.[117] I would agree with E. A. Judge and other social historians that in Paul we find a person deliberately stepping down the social ladder in order to reach as wide an audience for the sake of the gospel as was possible. Part of that stepping down was a deliberate taking up by Paul of his trade from time to time. It seems clear from a text like 1 Corinthians 9 that Paul admits he deserved to be remunerated for his work of sharing the gospel, but he chose not to accept the offers of money from various Corinthians because it would enmesh him in the social networks of patrons and clients. Paul did not wish to become anyone's client, because he did wish to be everyone's apostle and spiritual parent.

Ronald Hock has suggested that Paul's tent-making was right at the heart of what Paul was about, and in fact that it consumed most of his time.[118] This suggestion goes too far, as a careful evaluation of texts like 2 Corinthians 11:23–25 shows. Paul spent most of his time evangelizing and traveling, not making tents. Yet when Paul was in a city such as a Corinth, or perhaps an Ephesus or a Thessalonike, for an extended period of time, he may well have regularly practiced his trade.[119] There would have been considerable inducement to do so, for at least while Paul was in Corinth, the Isthmian Games were held and tourists who came for the games would have often been looking for a tent to rent or purchase. This provided Paul with a golden opportunity to reach all sorts of people.

Most importantly, Paul's attitude expressed in 1 Corinthians 9 about the work that he undertook does not reflect an artisan's attitude. Paul says he made a conscious decision to forego patronage. Artisans had no such luxuries; it was not a matter of choosing or not choosing to practice their trade. The Paul of the letters, be it noted, was not reluctant to accept financial aid from his converts so long as it was seen as part of a partnership in the Gospel, not a form of patronage (see Phil 4:10–13). We must assume then that Paul had specific reasons for taking up the trade he practiced for a while in Corinth.[120] The reasons, as I see them, do not

117. See MacMullen, *Roman Social Relations*, 73–83.

118. See Hock, *The Social Context of Paul's Ministry*, 67–77.

119. Acts suggests that Paul only practiced his trade in Corinth (see Acts 18), but 1 Thessalonians 2, when compared to 1 Corinthians 9, suggests Paul practiced his trade in various places.

120. It would appear likely from 1 Thessalonians 2:5–10 that Paul also practiced his trade in Thessalonike. He tells us he did so, so as not to be a burden, and perhaps so as not to appear like a money-grubbing orator or Sophist. That Paul was mainly a word-

involve the conclusion that Paul was just carrying on with his trade as he always did everywhere. To the contrary, he did it in Corinth to avoid patronage and to have ease of access through the marketplace to various of the ordinary people that would frequent the market and visit during the Isthmian games. It was part of Paul being all things to all persons so that he might by all means reach some. Paul the apostle made use of Paul the tentmaker's skills when it was useful or necessary for the sake of the gospel. Furthermore, some Cynic philosophers were known to frequent workshops, and so even when Paul did practice his trade, it would not necessarily have sent the signal that Paul was not a person of some social status.

Lastly, Martin Hengel points us to a close analogy to Paul in one named Isaac, a linen merchant from Tarsus who was an elder in the Jewish community in Jaffa. He was, in short, a person of relatively high status in his own community, and yet like Paul, he was not reluctant to practice a trade. Indeed it is proudly mentioned on his tombstone.[121] But also like Paul, this man Isaac had lived in more than one sort of world, and as with Paul while he may have had high status in the microcosmic Jewish community he was part of in Tarsus and in the Holy Land, elsewhere, he would have been seen as a Jew and an artisan, which in the anti-Semitic environment of the Roman Empire was two strikes against him. The Jewish Apostle to the Gentiles had to work in that larger Greco-Roman environment, and thus in spite of what he knew about his own social status, he obviously had to prove himself in each new place he went. He must have regularly experienced considerable status inconsistency, and we know from 2 Corinthians 11:23–24 that he often experienced treatment unbecoming of someone of his social status and education.

Having sampled the rhetoric of some of the undisputed Paulines, in our next chapter we must turn to examine the rhetoric in the Pastoral Epistles, which takes a different and less complex form. Here the enthymeme or incomplete syllogism comes into play in a major way, as we shall soon see.

---

smith meant that many would see him, especially when he just came to a town and was unknown, as suspect in the Greco-Roman world, especially if he immediately accepted patronage or lavish gifts for his oratory. His rhetoric would have been compromised and the gospel would have been viewed as just another subject speakers discoursed on to entertain or educate and so earn one's crust of bread.

121. See Hengel, *Paul: Between Damascus and Antioch*, 160–61.

QUESTIONS FOR REFLECTION

1. How significant is it that Paul's letters were meant to be heard as persuasive and not seen as such?
2. How did Paul's education influence his letter writing?
3. What was the role of secretaries in early letter writing, especially in Paul's letters?
4. How did Paul customize the standard letter structure? In what ways were these customizations significant?
5. What form of rhetoric is most prevalent in the Pauline Epistles, and why?
6. How does rhetoric help us understand Paul?

CHAPTER 6

The Elementary Rhetoric of the Pastorals

THE LUKAN FLAVOR OF THE PASTORALS

There is no dispute among NT scholars that the Pastoral Epistles look and sound different in many ways than the earlier Pauline documents. What *historically* (not just linguistically) accounts for the similarity of style between these three epistles and their differences from the earlier Paulines?

Several factors need to be considered:

1) The Pastoral Epistles are Paul's only truly personal and indeed private letters. They are not composed for oral delivery to a congregation, and so while they still reflect rhetorical devices of various sorts, Paul is engaging in encouragement and exhortation rather than offering up extended arguments and proofs, though there are simple "proofs" in 2 Timothy (alone). These arguments however are brief and largely paraenetic in character, and serve more as reminders rather than full-fledged attempts to convince, since Paul is "preaching to the choir." In Titus and 1 Timothy the form of argument is more succinct and simple, taking the form of brief rhetorical syllogisms or enthymemes, paradigms, rhetorical comparison (*synkrisis*), maxims, and using traditional or sacred materials. Full formal arguments were not required to remind two of his co-workers what they needed to preach and teach and do.

2) It is also possible, since 2 Timothy was composed later and in a different locale, that Paul took a more hands-on involvement in this letter, which explains the more developed rhetoric and the less Lukan diction in that document. In my view, we should prefer the conclusion that Luke was involved in all three documents, however—there are good historical reasons why. In the Pastorals

> the voice is the voice of Paul, but the hands are the hands of Luke,
> who wrote these documents for Paul.[1]

We are told plainly at 2 Timothy 4:11 that Luke was with Paul at the time when he spoke the things now recorded in 2 Timothy. Secondly, in my previous study of Acts, I point out that the "we" passages, which are found in Acts 16:10–17 and in the latter part of the book, do refer to the author of the document accompanying Paul on part of his second and all of his third missionary journeys, indeed accompanying him to Jerusalem and then on to Rome. I note how the "we" portions of the second missionary journey begin in Troas and end in Philippi.[2]

This is not unimportant to our discussion here, because Philippi in particular seems to be the city from which Titus and 1 Timothy were written. In my earlier Acts commentary I note it would appear that Luke was an itinerant doctor, his normal orbit being back and forth across the Aegean, between Troas and Philippi.[3] It is perfectly plausible that Paul had reconnoitered with Luke again in Philippi, Luke helped him to write these first two letters, then traveled with Paul eventually on to Rome, helping him with the final letter as well. This last letter may have been written right at the end of Paul's life and sent just before his demise. Luke of course was a trusted companion of Paul, and one who has a Hellenistic style of writing. He may well be the only Gentile among the authors of the NT, and all the evidence cited above either comports with or points in the direction of Luke as a contributor to these letters. Luke then composed 2 Timothy for Paul, based on Paul's last oral testimonies and instructions while under restricted house arrest (perhaps in the Campus Martius on the edge of Rome where military prisoners were kept until trial). Perhaps, also, Luke had before him one or the other of the previous two Pastoral letters, which he used as a model for the composition of 2 Timothy in terms of phraseology and general style, and possibly some content. Luke may have made a copy of these documents when he wrote them for Paul in Macedonia.

Finally, one factor that is strongly in favor of 1 and 2 Timothy being written to a person or persons in Ephesus is that numerous of the per-

---

1. For a detailed discussion of the similarity of style between Acts and the Pastoral Epistles see Witherington, *Letters and Homilies.*

2. See Witherington, *Acts of the Apostles,* 480–85.

3. Witherington, *Acts of the Apostles,* 480–85.

sons mentioned in these two letters have a documented connection with Ephesus, including Timothy, Titus, Prisca, Aquila, Tychichus, Erastus, and Trophimus. The personalia then favors the Ephesian destination for these documents.[4]

THE RHETORICAL CHARACTER
AND SUBSTANCE OF THE PASTORALS

Unfortunately too little study has been done thus far on the rhetoric of the Pastoral Epistles. Letters, especially personal letters, were surrogates for an oral conversation face to face, and as Demetrius was later to stress, the function of a letter was not merely to continue a conversation and further a relationship but to reveal the author's "true self" (*Style* 4.227). This is one reason why pseudepigraphical personal letters in antiquity were seen as so violating the very nature of the genre itself and were often so strongly opposed.

Cicero, one of the original architects of the rhetorically influenced personal letter, expresses the same thing when he thanks Atticus for news which made him "feel as though I was talking with you," and he goes on to add in a letter to Marcus "all of you was revealed to me in your letter" (*Letters to Atticus* 12.53; *Letters to Friends* 16.16.2). While both of these quotations are revealing, it is also important to bear in mind, as Luke Timothy Johnson says, that Greek style itself in rhetoric and in letters was "less a matter of personal expressiveness and more a matter of social presence and rhetorical craft."[5] Especially if one had some facility with language, one would adopt and adapt one's style to suit the occasion and the social context. As Johnson rightly points out, Luke himself reveals a dazzling array of styles in Luke-Acts, from more Semitic in his first volume and the first part of his second volume, to almost entirely Hellenistic by the time one gets to the accounts of Paul's missionary journeys, especially his voyage to Rome.[6] With a writer having that degree of linguistic and rhetorical skill, one has to be careful what one concludes

---

4. See W. Theissen, *Christen in Ephesus*, 251–53.

5. Johnson, *First and Second Letters to Timothy*, 60.

6. Johnson, *First and Second Letters to Timothy*, 60.

about authorship, and what was and was not within an author's scope, based on style.[7]

As T. Thatcher has rightly pointed out one can learn a good deal about the social status of the sender and receiver by the way the document opens and closes. Rhetorical modifications of standard openings and closings tell us something about the actual nature of the relationship and how such a letter further inscribes that relationship. Thus, for instance, Thatcher points out how the Pauline modifications of normal openings and closings in the Pastorals have the rhetorical effect of characterizing the author as an authority figure, but one with humility (he is the servant of God), reinscribing the intense loyalty and personal nature of the relationship between the recipient and the author. Timothy and Titus are clearly seen as under the tutelage of Paul. Stress on common concern and common faith experiences as the basis of the Christian authority come to the fore as well.[8]

Another helpful study that allows us to consider the rhetoric of the Pastoral Epistles in a general way is the work of L. Donelson. He maintains that behind all three of these letters is a coherent and consistent argumentative strategy, and upon closer inspection, I think he is correct.[9] Donelson argues, in essence, that two rhetorical forms of persuasion are pursued throughout these three letters: 1) enthymemes, and 2) inductive and illustrative paradigms. To this we could add that there is some *synkrisis* or comparisons of positive and negative examples (the false teachers vs. Paul and his co-workers; the false teaching vs. the faithful teaching), and the use of various sorts of traditional materials (Scripture texts, popular maxims, early Christian hymns, or creedal material). Enthymemes, as Aristotle pointed, out are miniature syllogisms in which usually one of

7. Johnson, *First and Second Letters to Timothy*, 63–64. Johnson also makes some very helpful comments about the methodological problems with grouping certain Pauline letters together to use as a litmus test of Pauline authorship. By this he means, for example, that if we compare the Pastorals to Philippians and 1 Thessalonians, which do not have midrash or diatribal style, they sound quite Pauline, but if we compare them to 1 Corinthians, Romans, or Galatians, they sound less Pauline because of the use of those rhetorical techniques. This is a good point and one aspect of it needs highlighting—the undisputed Pauline that the Pastorals are most like in various regards is Philippians. Is it an accident that this is the last letter Paul wrote from Rome in AD 62 not long before the Pastorals were written? I think not. Style can evolve some over time.

8. Thatcher, "The Relational Matrix," 41–45.

9. Donelson, *Pseudepigraphy*.

the elements or argumentative premises is omitted. The idea here is that the briefer syllogism prompts the audience to fill in the gap, remembering what they have been taught before. A good example which Donelson points to is 2 Timothy 3:16–17. The syllogism goes as follows: 1) the Scriptures are God-breathed; 2) therefore they are profitable for teaching, reproof, and equipping one for good works; 3) the suppressed and implied statement is "therefore, you, Timothy (and other men of God) should do good works"; and 4) the result clause states "therefore study Scripture."[10]

Enthymemes basically are a form of preaching to the choir, by which I mean they are not full-blown arguments meant to convince or persuade the undecided or even the antagonistic. Harding is right to say:

> The Pastor frames his deductive arguments in accord with his belief system. The persuasive force of the arguments thus devised would be effective only among those who shared the presuppositions of the author . . . . The author writes in such a way that the presuppositions of the audience are repeatedly affirmed and underscored in the interests of protecting the ecclesiastical vision of the author and addressees now under attack from false teachers. In effect the author is arguing about what leads to [final] salvation and what does not.[11]

This of course is a very Jewish way of arguing, grounded in Jewish wisdom teaching about the two ways (see Proverbs). But the form the argument takes here is rhetorically apt.

Sometimes it is said about the rhetoric in the Pastorals that it is of a more elementary sort than that found in the major Paulines. This is in part true, though the composer of thess documents is quite competent in what he attempts to accomplish rhetorically. The rhetoric we find there is the sort one learned first. "The list of *progymnasmata* [elementary school rhetorical exercises] was generally the same throughout Imperial times and included the following composition exercises: fable, narrative, *chreia*, aphorism, confirmation or refutation, commonplace, eulogy or censure, comparison [*synkrisis*], prosopopoeia, thesis, and discussion of the law. Each of these increased over the preceding in degree of sophistication..."[12] Enthymemes were what were used in the learning stages of doing con-

10. Donelson, *Pseudepigraphy*, 87. I have expanded his rendition of this enthymeme a bit.

11. Harding, *What are They Saying*, 87; see also Donelson, *Pseudepigraphy*, 81.

12. Young, "Whoever Has Ears to Hear," 69.

firmation and refutation, and you will notice that the use of narrative and comparison and aphorism ('this is a trustworthy saying . . . ') are all present in this list and all are found in the Pastorals. It is equally interesting that there is a warning against fable or myth in the Pastorals, which Gentiles will have learned to compose in these same elementary school exercises.

The pedagogical character and flavor of the Pastorals is undeniable and it needs to be read in the context of Greco-Roman and Hellenized Jewish educational practices. There are perhaps two good reasons the rhetoric here is of a more simple sort than in the earlier Paulines and we have already suggested one of them: 1) Paul's co-workers needed exhortation and encouragement and a little instruction on what to do, they did not need full blown acts of persuasion. The rhetorical situation dictated that Paul did not need to address these men as he would a congregation of new converts. He could speak in short hand or more telegraphic fashion, and he does so here; 2) if Luke is the composer of these wonderful letters, then it is in order to point out that his own use of rhetoric comports with what we find here. Very seldom are there full-blown speeches with proofs in Luke-Acts. The more enthymematic approach is used offering summaries of speeches and arguments or syllogisms throughout the two volumes of Luke's work.[13]

Comparison and contrast is used effectively as well in these letters, as Paul pits his own and his co-workers behavior against that of the false teachers and the apostates. As Donelson says, Paul seeks to illustrate the contrary principles (the dos and don'ts) of Christian life and lifestyle. One lifestyle leads to judgment and eschatological condemnation; the other to salvation. The goal of this instruction is not just to benefit Timothy or Titus, but to help them become paradigms for their audience—as is expected of the leaders they will be appointing in various places.[14] In fact we may note that one of the rhetorical functions of the personalia in Titus and 2 Timothy (Tit 3:12–15; 2 Tim 4:6–22) is precisely to present Paul as a model self-sacrificing pastor for his audience to emulate. These are not irrelevant or incidental details in these documents but part of the act

---

13. On Luke's rhetoric, one may consult the introduction to the forthcoming, Levine and Witherington, *The Gospel of Luke*. Also, the forthcoming doctoral thesis by one of my students at Bristol, R. Simon, on the rhetoric of Luke 1–2, will be worth consulting.

14. See Donelson, *Pseudepigraphy*, 92.

of persuasion.[15] As Donelson demonstrates, Paul has a coherent theology closely allied to an argumentative strategy in which "enthymemes link theological propositions to ethical conclusions and paradigms [and comparisons] are the vehicles for a powerful presentation of contrasting ethical lifestyles."[16]

Though there have been some attempts to figure out the rhetorical arrangement of Paul's arguments in these letters,[17] not much has been successfully accomplished on this front. This is in part because some have not recognized that we do not have full-fledged proofs in Titus and 1 Timothy and we have only brief ones in 2 Timothy.

There is also some force to C. J. Classen's reminder that we are not dealing with speeches in these letters meant to be formally delivered to a group, but rather a rhetorically shaped correspondence to individuals involving instructions and commands "supported by reasons and arguments and organized in a carefully considered manner."[18] There is a variety of rhetorical complexity in these documents, and 2 Timothy is certainly the most sophisticated of the three letters. We must turn now to examine a sampling of the enthymemes in the Pastorals, and the more complex structure of 2 Timothy, as well.

THE ENTHYMEMES OF THE PASTORALS

Sometimes there has been something of a disconnect assumed between ethical arguments and rhetoric, as if rhetoric was only interested in proving or persuading about philosophical or theological ideas. This is a mistake for as even Aristotle said in the first discussions of rhetoric, rhetoric is in a sense the offshoot of both dialectics and ethics as one is trying to influence behavior and belief by acts of persuasion (*Rhetorica* 1.2.7; 1359b 8–12). There are two sorts of reasoning, inductive and deductive,

15. See Fiore, *The Function of Personal Example*.

16. Harding, *What are They Saying*, 88.

17. See for example, Campbell, "Rhetorical Design," 190 n. 4, where he divides up 1Timothy as follows: *Exordium* (1:1–2); Proposition (1:3–7); Narration (1:8–20); Proofs (2:1—6:2)—Proof A (2:1–15); Proof B (3:1–16); Proof C (4:1–16), Proof D (5:1—6:2); Refutation (6:3–10); and Epilogue (6:11–12). There are some problems with this arrangement, not the least of which is the Epistolary Prescript here should not be seen as an *exordium*. If one wants to see an *exordium* and a narration, one should see 2 Timothy 1:3–18.

18. Classen, *Rhetorical Criticism*, 63.

and in our case what is important is that an enthymeme is an incomplete rhetorical syllogism (and so deductive) while a paradigm is a rhetorical induction (*Rhetorica* 1.2.8). Aristotle sees the former as more persuasive than the latter, and they should be more frequently used. The reason a premise is suppressed in an enthymeme is because it is odious to state the obvious, or put another way, it is an insult to the audience's intelligence. Things should be stated in a way that the hearer must reason their way to a conclusion and participate in the process of this hearing and heeding, puzzling out the missing step in the syllogism.[19]

Aristotle stressed that deliberative rhetoric is both hortatory and dissuasive (*Rhetorica* 1.3.3), focusing on what one ought to do. This certainly aptly characterizes Titus and the other Pastorals as well. One needs also to bear in mind that maxims were a regular part of deliberative rhetoric, in fact they were a regular part of an enthymeme, serving either as a premise or a conclusion (*Rhetorica* 2.21.2). Thus, for instance when we read in Titus 1:12 "all Cretans are liars," a maxim coined by a Cretan no less, we need to see it in the context of the part of the syllogism it is reinforcing. It is not an isolated saying, it is a single proposition which is either a premise or a conclusion that helps the argument. A maxim becomes an argument or a part of an argument when coupled with a conclusion or a premise. It is interesting what Aristotle goes on to say about maxims that they persuade because they hit upon opinions or famous sayings that the audience already accepts or is familiar with. Thus, he notes that a man who has bad neighbors enjoys a maxim that laments the stupidity of neighbors (*Rhetorica* 2.21.15).

Donelson reminds us that we must distinguish between the sort of traditions and literary materials used in the Pastorals (e.g., household codes, virtue and vice lists, biographical information, and personalia) and *the use made* of this material in a rhetorical way for specific purposes. Too often the study of the Pastorals has focused on isolating and identifying the sources and not on the actual way the materials are being used to persuade the audience about something. This has often led to the conclusion that the Pastorals are just examples of miscellanies, random collections of traditions with no order or organization, and having no real literary finesse. This is in fact false.[20]

19. See Donelson, *Pseudepigraphy*, 79.
20. Ibid., 67.

For one thing those sorts of formal categories are far less helpful than those identified by Donelson, who points out we have a combination of three sorts of statements in these letters: 1) salvation statements (i.e., statements about God or Jesus as actors, things that lead to salvation because God's plan works a particular way, things God wants or demands, prophecies, or prescriptions of Scripture); 2) appeals to the proper character of religious life, focusing on the social dimension of various virtues and vices and character traits; and 3) appeals to sacred traditions.[21] It is not enough to ask what formal category these traditions, maxims, or faithful sayings fall under. One must ask how they are used and how they rhetorically function to persuade the audience about something.

Furthermore, as Donelson stresses, this material in itself does not constitute an argument, they must be molded or enfolded into an argument or appeal or act of persuasion. It is interesting that nearly all the enthymemes in the Pastorals are composed out of these resources, and almost all of them take the form of cause-and-effect arguments (if you do this, then this will happen), especially in regard to what leads to or impedes salvation.[22] There are enthymemes of these ilk in all three of these letters, increasing the capacity and force of the rhetoric to persuade. To note but one example of how the rhetorical factor in analyzing these letters has been badly underestimated, Karris points out how the seemingly most artless of the three letters, Titus, in fact displays some considerable rhetorical force and skill. For example, in Titus 1:10–16 we have various catchwords and concepts playing off one another to form a coherent exhortation.[23]

What has tended to make the coherency of these letters hard to sort out is that until recently there has not been much rhetorical analysis of these letters. For another thing, it is of course true that Paul does not engage in sustained analysis, rather he moves from topic to topic rather rapidly, from enthymeme to paradigm and back again, no doubt in part because he is reminding his charges of things and elaboration is unnecessary. But it is not just the constant shifting of topics that has led to confusion and frustration in the scholarly analysis of this material. The rather dazzling ongoing shifting of kinds of resource materials used (household

21. Ibid., 80–81.

22. Ibid., 81.

23. Karris, *The Pastoral Epistles*, 108–9.

codes, virtue and vice lists, maxims, church order instructions) contributes to the bewilderment.[24]

Yet, if one can recognize that Paul's compositional goal is to highlight two competing lifestyles in the church—pleading for one, and polemicizing the other—then one can deduce that this goal is in turn what leads to the rhetorical strategy of using contrasting examples, contrasting lists, contrasting maxims (vs. trustworthy sayings):

> [Paul] counter-poses his own version of the Christian life to that of his opponents. 1 and 2 Timothy begin with inductive paradigms which provide the author with reliable principles from which he can argue, and then each shifts back and forth between positive and negative accounts of how one relates to these principles. Titus lacks the initial Pauline paradigm but it does manifest this shift from positive to negative and back. Although each letter addresses a distinct theme or a different aspect of the author's concerns, the letters do not make sustained arguments which pick up parts of the problem one at a time, but rather interlace accounts of these two life-style[s].[25]

Titus 1:10–16 provides us with a good example of both *synkrisis* and enthymeme, which serve as the sort of rhetorical one-two punch of Titus and 1 Timothy. Let us say a bit more about the former first. As rhetorical comparison or *synkrisis* became especially effective as a means of persuasion, the better one could paint the contrast between that which was to be emulated and that which was to be avoided. It is most often an example of comparison by contrast. Plutarch stressed that "it is not possible to learn better the similarity and the difference between the virtues of men and women from any other source than by putting lives beside lives and actions beside actions, like great works of art" (*Moralia* 345c–351b). Even more to the point is Aelius Theon—writing in the very same time period as the Pastorals—who says, "Comparison [*synkrisis*] is a form of speech which contrasts the better with the worse. Comparisons are drawn between people and between things . . . When one distinguishes between people, one takes into consideration their acts."[26] We may also point to the great rhetorician Quintilian who stresses that as someone begins to develop rhetorical skills one hones that ability by proceeding to "more

24. See Donelson, *Pseudepigraphy*, 109.

25. Ibid., 113.

26. See the discussion in Forbes, "Paul and Rhetorical Comparison," 143–44.

important themes such as the praise of famous men and the denunciation of the wicked. . . . It is but a step from this to practice in the comparison of the respective merits of two characters" (*Institutio oratoria* 2.4.20–21).

Suffice it to say, Paul and Luke are following these rhetorical conventions and therefore the contrasts are drawn sharply and in tandem (i.e., the description and actions of the elder who must offer sound teaching are set over against the character and actions of the false teachers who must not make a sound). This is of course a form of polemics, and it shows that there was great need in Crete for sound teachers and sound teaching. If the elders are only now being appointed, the false teachers have had a head start and so the damage must be undone and overcome.

There is some real substance to the case that has been made by R. Karris that the form of polemic here has some stock features and is like the critique that philosophers made of sophists as being rhetoricians for hire without scruple. This critique goes all the way back to Plato who called the sophistic rhetoricians "merchants in articles of knowledge for the soul" (*Sophist* 231d) a complaint echoed by both Philo from the NT era (*On the Life of Moses* 2.212) and Maximus of Tyre in the second century (*Philosophumena* 27.8de).[27] Furthermore, it can be noted that Paul himself especially in 1 and 2 Corinthians seeks to distinguish himself from the Sophists and sophistic rhetoric as has been shown at length by B. Winter.[28] It is then not a surprise that Paul might use this classical form of polemic to characterize false teachers who oppose him and his apostolic delegates.

As Karris says, this sort of rhetoric and these sorts of echoes of an earlier debate helps make the case that the Pauline teaching is genuine wisdom and truth, and that the teachings of the opponents are false wisdom, sophistry, fool's gold.[29] The implication is also that Paul and his apostolic delegates have the right to speak about the faith, whereas unauthorized teachers do not and should be silenced. This is also precisely the sort of social situation that is being dealt with in 1 Timothy 2, though in that case the unauthorized persons seeking to teach are some women who are usurping authority over some men who were already authorized to teach. The silencing of the false teachers in Titus prepares us to under-

27. See the discussion in Karris, "The Background," 549–64.

28. Winter, *Philo and Paul.*

29. Karris, "The Background," 563.

stand properly the silencing of the women in 1 Timothy—an abuse of a speaking privilege is involved in both cases.[30] We may outline the deliberative argument here as follows, recognizing that it is a continuation and contrast with what has just been said about the elders:

Primary Argument about False Teachers

1) Elders must rebuke those who oppose the right teaching,

2) because there are many who rebel against it, engaging in idle chatter and deception,

3) especially (or, *malista* can be translated "I mean") those of the circumcision (who use Jewish myths and commandments to persuade).

4) They must be silenced,

5) because they have already turned whole families in the community away from the truth, for the sake of their own profit.

6) Their own Cretan prophet warned against such teachers—"all Cretans are liars, cruel animals, lazy gluttons";

7) we can confirm this testimony is true.

8) They must be sternly rebuked also for their own good, to strengthen their own faith.

Secondary Argument about False Teachers

1) Those who have pure minds and hearts can listen to such teaching without pollution and can participate in many things without harm.

2) But to the corrupt and unbelieving, nothing but trouble comes from listening because their minds and consciences are already defiled.

3) Unfortunately, it is these same people who claim to truly know God.

4) But clearly their lifestyle makes evident this is not so.

5) Notice they are incapable of good works and instead engage in abominations.

It is perfectly clear that there is more passion in this paragraph than there was in the preceding one. Paul must expend more verbiage and

---

30. On which see pp. 172–74 below.

emotion in what he opposes than in what he positively sets forth, and in fact, he must ramp up the rhetorical finesse and force of the argument in this negative part of the *synkrisis*. In the primary argument, Paul uses the maxim as a major premise to make his case that the false teachers' mouths must be stopped because they are spreading lies and are doing it for personal gain. He backs up the force of the maxim with his own authority, confirming that what the maxim says is true, and since it is true, it provides justification for the stern rebuke, refutation, and silencing of such people. He adds that it is also for their own good, and not just because of the havoc they are wreaking in the church, leading whole families astray. The implied premise or step in the first syllogism is something like this—the false teachers are serving up Jewish myths and commandments (perhaps including the command to be circumcised).

The secondary argument provides outward and visible criteria by which the audience can tell that the false teachers do not in fact know God—you will know the tree by the fruit that it bears, and you will also know it by the effect of false teaching on the teachers themselves—they are deceived deceivers, unbelieving yet claiming to be believers. Their minds and consciences have been defiled, and they are thereby further defiled by false teaching. The evidence of their life and lifestyle make clear they do not know God and should not be teaching the things of God. In the end, the false teaching is to be judged by the effect it is having on the community, and the false teachers are to be judged by their own self-seeking and deceptive conduct. The minor and missing premise in this secondary argument is that the false teachers are neither pure nor know God, as is evident from what they say and do.

It needs to be borne in mind that this kind of arguing or persuading is only going to be persuasive for those who share certain faith premises with Paul and Luke. Donelson writes,

> His arguments are based upon special topics peculiar to a segment of early Christianity. They are, furthermore, deliberative in that they concern decisions about the future, about what is expedient and harmful and thus about what one ought to do. Of course, the data are not drawn from the dynamics of the state and the role of virtue in public life, as they are in Aristotlean deliberative rhetoric, but from the dynamics of God's plan of salvation, the needs of

the church community, and the role of virtues in their private and public ramifications.[31]

The "comparison" between elders and false teachers now being complete, we can draw up a chart of what is said:[32]

The Elder:	The False Teacher:
House manager	House wrecker
Blameless	Defiled conscience and works
Not pursuing dishonest gain	Unscrupulous teaching for gain
Not quick tempered or intemperate	Acting like a wild beast
Holding fast to sound tradition	Embracing myths and human commands
Truthful and refuting error	Liar, deceiver, embracing and teaching error

The structure of the first chapter of Titus becomes quite clear when one realizes that Paul and Luke are presenting the hearer with a clear rhetorical *synkrisis*. These are neither random nor generic remarks, but rather aids to help Titus deal with a specific problem with Jewish Christian teachers on Crete.

Having noted a careful comparison by contrast in Titus 1, when one turns to the second chapter enthymemes come into their own. For example, we have the following in Titus 2:

> The enthymematic form of the arguments is easiest to see when they are connected with a purpose clause. Here we have syllogisms with suppressed premises:
>
> 1) Younger women should submit themselves to their own husbands
>
> 2) [For outsiders will judge our faith based in their behavior]
>
> 3) So the Word of God will not be discredited by observers

31. Donelson, *Pseudepigraphy*, 80.

32. What we have not mentioned, but could be dealt with is the fact that there was a topos about traveling philosophers or sophists who did their teaching for personal gain and exploitation and so one was to be wary of them (Sophocles *Antigone* 1055–56; Dio Chrysostom *To the People of Alexandria* 10). Paul and Luke may be drawing on this widely known complaint in the critique of the false teacher. Cf. 2 Peter 2:3 and Romans 16:17–18.

Or again:

1) Titus must set a good moral example and offer teaching with
   integrity

2) [For opponents are looking for inconsistencies in our leaders]

3) so that the opponents can find nothing to criticize.

Or again:

1) Slaves must subject themselves and give evidence
   of complete reliability

2) [So that they will even be a good witness to their own
   masters]

3) For by doing so they will add honor and luster to the
   teachings of our Savior.

In each case there is a suppressed premise or key concept that must be
supplied for the syllogism to work fully. The concern about outside opinion is latent at each stage of this discussion, and shows we are not dealing with an isolationist sect that has given up any concern about public
witness.

It is interesting that these enthymemes can either be rather straightforward or more complex both in content and in form. For example, if we
turn to Titus 3 we find the following:

It is important to notice however its clear link, by means of the
word *gar* in v. 3 with the first two verses of this chapter. Here again
we find the enthymematic form of argumentation in a more extended form:

1) Remind the converts to submit and obey the governing
   authorities.

2) For we were once rebels and sinners, but now by the goodness
   and philanthropy of God we have been washed and regener-
   ated and Spirit-filled (cf. Eph 5:8).

3) [Therefore, we should be behaving differently now than before
   our conversions.]

4) The faithful saying sums up why, with gratitude, we should be
   doing good deeds and being good citizens.[33]

33. For a slightly different reading of the argumentative structure see Classen,
Rhetorical Criticism, 65.

It will be seen that this last argument in the letter is more approximately like Paul's more detailed arguments in his earlier letters, mixing profound theological and ethical remarks to produce a Christian way of thinking and lifestyle in the audience.[34] What is most striking here is that the traditions and the liturgical language of the faithful saying is used to prompt not merely adoration, but good behavior. We could continue to multiply these kinds of examples through an examination of 1 Timothy, but in fact it is the same sort of phenomena there as we find in Titus. A variety of disparate material including maxims and traditional sayings are welded into a persuasive form by using the rhetorical structure of the enthymeme. The same thing is happening with the use of a *synkrisis* rhetorical form in order to set up an ethical discourse that will persuade the audience.

THE RHETORIC OF 2 TIMOTHY

The rhetorical analysis of 2 Timothy has not been properly undertaken in full. We do have helpful remarks from Donelson and Harding, among others, but they have only really dealt with the micro-rhetoric not the macro-rhetoric of 2 Timothy. Unlike Titus and 1 Timothy, 2 Timothy, while continuing to offer a few enthymemes, paradigms, and rhetorical comparisons, takes things a step further, developing more full-fledged arguments and following the sort of rhetorical outline we see in Paul's earlier letters. I would attribute this in part to the fact that Paul may well have been more directive with Luke about this letter than about Titus and 1 Timothy. It not only has all the usual epistolary features of a Pauline letter; it has all the usual rhetorical features as an example of deliberative rhetoric, or from an epistolary point of view, one can call it a paraenetic letter.[35] That it is far closer to a paraenetic letter than a testamentary one is recognized by Karris who draws our attention to a passage from such a letter by Isocrates to one Demonicus:[36]

> So then, since I deem it fitting that those who strive for distinction and are ambitious for education should emulate the good and not the bad, I have dispatched to you this discourse . . . . Nay, if you will but recall also your father's principles, you will have

34. See Karris, *Pastoral Epistles*, 120–21 on the flow of thought here.
35. See the analysis of Johnson, *The First and Second Letters to Timothy*, 322–24.
36. Karris, *Pastoral Epistles*, 8.

> from your own house a noble example of what I am telling you
> . . . . For the present, however, I have produced a sample of the
> nature of your father Hipponicus, after whom you should pattern
> your life as an after example, regarding his conduct as your law,
> and striving to imitate and emulate your father's virtue . . . (*Ad
> Demonicum* 2, 9, and 11).

This helps us see some correspondences in content between 2 Timothy and paraenetic letters of personal exhortation to an individual who is something of an understudy, especially the appeal to imitation of an example and the stress on virtue. In such a letter we expect to find stress on memory, mimesis, maxims, and modeling, as is the case in 2 Timothy.[37] But it does not much help us with the arrangement of the material in 2 Timothy.

The rhetorical outline does a far better job of explaining the structure of this document than the purely epistolary or literary-semantic analyses do.

Epistolary Prescript and Greeting – 1:1–2

Thanksgiving Prayer/*Exordium* – 1:3–5

Propositio – 1:6–7 – Galvanize the gift; draw on the power

Argument One – 1:8–14 – Be prepared to testify, suffer, and guard the deposit

Narratio/Transitus – 1:15–18

Argument Two – 2:1–13 – Entrust, endure, remember

Argument Three – 2:14–26 – Warn the opponents; avoid quarrels

Argument Four – 3:1–9 – Apostasy and corruption of the last days

Argument Five – 3:10–17 – Continue in my teaching and the Scriptures

Peroratio – 4:1–8 – Do the work of an evangelist

Travel Plans for Timothy/Personal Remarks – 4:9–18

Closing Greetings – 4:19–21

Benediction – 4:22

Among other things, this outline recognizes the argumentative and persuasive character of the letter, which cites Paul's teaching, trustworthy

---

37. So Johnson, *The First and Second Letters to Timothy*, 323.

sayings, and Scripture as inartificial sacred proofs to back up the arguments and exhortations. The arguments are more fully developed here, beyond just offering enthymemes, paradigms, or comparisons though, these rhetorical devices are not absent, being enfolded into the larger rhetorical design. In other words, we have in 2 Timothy, more of the vintage Paul, the Paul who wants to offer one last full rhetorical salvo taking advantage of the full arsenal of macro-rhetoric. Forming careful arguments that are presaged by a thesis statement and lead up to a peroration, the rhetoric of 2 Timothy is powerful and involves the ongoing development of a full discourse. Timothy is being galvanized to change his current behavior and get on with using his gifts and doing the tasks bequeathed to him by the great Apostle. Implied in the discourse is an attempt to deal with the problems that arise as the church transitions to the post-apostolic era. Timothy and Titus are no Paul, but on the other hand, they are not merely local church elders either. The hierarchical polity remains, but its character changes in the transition, and more is required of the Pauline co-workers once Paul is off the scene. The question remained—could the co-workers become the senior leaders, stepping into the shoes of the apostle to the Gentiles? If they did not begin to do some of the things Paul insists on in these documents, the answer would be no. But these letters are written in hope and with a belief that the rhetoric will galvanize the co-workers. One must assume that the letters accomplished something, or they would not likely have been preserved for all posterity.

AND SO?

From a rhetorical point of view, what we find in the Pastoral Epistles are discourses that, while not as rhetorically elaborate as what we find in the earlier Paulines, are nonetheless just as interesting. Both comparisons and enthymemes, while more elementary forms of rhetoric, are nonetheless effective for all that, and as we said at the outset, full formal arguments were apparently not required in the opening personal letters to Titus and Timothy.

But, when we get to 2 Timothy, while the style of the Greek is much the same as in Titus and 1 Timothy, the rhetoric is more complex, and one might say, in a more familiar Pauline form, as the old master probably was more hands-on in this final rhetorical salvo of his life. It is of course not a case of non-rhetorical letters versus rhetorical ones, but rather the level of the rhetoric varies from more elementary in Titus and 1 Timothy to more developed and complex in 2 Timothy.

Lest we think it is only Paul in the NT that can be called a master rhetor, we must turn now to Hebrews, 1 John, and 1 Peter to see that the evidence of rhetorical shaping of the material of the NT is hardly an isolated or purely Pauline phenomena. Indeed, it is one of the more universally shared features of most of the NT.

QUESTIONS FOR REFLECTION

1. How does one persuade a long time co-worker to do what he or she ought to do? Is the same sort of persuasion required as when one is dealing with an ordinary congregation member?

2. What is the value of recycling familiar proverbs or maxims, or earlier Christian teaching? Is this more likely or less likely to persuade one's co-workers who are already committed to the shared core Christian values?

3. How does rhetoric serve to connect theological and ethical ideas in the Pastorals? Why is this connection important?

4. Is there a difference between dramatic rhetorical comparisons and stereotyping? How should one interpret the use of dramatic hyperbole?

CHAPTER 7

The Rhetoric of the General Epistles

THE RHETORIC OF PETER AND SILAS

Often missed in the study of 1 Peter is the fact that the author is busily constructing a rhetorical world, a world of advice and consent, of persuasion and dissuasion, where certain beliefs and behaviors are inculcated not merely for social reasons but also for theological or ideological ones as well. When we analyze 1 Peter as rhetoric, what do we learn about the aims and purposes of this document, broadly speaking? Is it meant to steel the audience for persecution by persuading them about the value of Christ-likeness? Is there some considerable rhetorical exigency or problem this discourse is meant to overcome? And what do we make of the intertextual echoes in this document, not only of the OT but of material from Jesus' rhetoric, James's rhetoric, and Paul's rhetoric as well?

Carl Holladay remarks:

> For all its Pauline echoes, however, 1 Peter also has close affinities with the synoptic tradition and to a lesser extent with the Gospel of John, Hebrews, and James. There are remarkable convergences with Peter's speeches in Acts. Since 1 Peter resonates with such a wide spectrum of early Christian witnesses, some scholars have suggested, only half jokingly, that its author knew the whole NT! . . . Part of 1 Peter's enduring appeal stems from the breadth and depth of common tradition on which it draws and its appropriation of the earlier, apostolic consensus in giving authority to its distinctive voice.[1]

Where was our author placed, geographically, socially, temporally, rhetorically that he would have known all of this material, and does such

---

1. Holladay, *Critical Introduction*, 485.

evidence provide clues to the authorship of this document? Could 1 Peter really be the masterpiece and last grand act of the great apostle who had known the persons and rhetoric of Jesus, James, and Paul, and now was making their contributions serviceable for his own audience? Was our author at the font from which the apostolic tributaries flowed forth, and so in touch with the origins of Jewish and Gentile Christianity and its leaders, or was he at the place where all those tributaries came back together at the end of the first century and the beginning of the second? All of these sorts of questions are intertwined in a study of 1 Peter, but our concern here must be with the rhetoric of 1 Peter. It is my view that this document goes back to Peter, perhaps with some help in regard to its rhetorical form from Silas/Silvanus. At the outset, I must stress that we have in 1 Peter a particular sort of ancient rhetoric—Asiatic rhetoric, which is neither surprising nor unusual in discourses that addressed Asia and the surrounding provinces of western Turkey. Indeed, it was the most popular and potent sort of rhetoric in that region, so whoever provided the rhetorical shape of 1 Peter knew well how to offer persuasion in a form that would be a word on target in that cultural setting.

About Asiatic rhetoric it can be stressed that it was noted for its emotion and even affectation. Cicero, in contrasting it with Attic rhetoric says the following: "The styles of Asiatic oratory are two—one epigrammatic and pointed, full of fine ideas which are not so weighty and serious as neat and graceful; the other with not so many sententious ideas, but voluble and hurried in its flow of language, and marked by an ornamented and elegant diction" (*Brutus* 95, 325). Both forms of the Asiatic style were also marked by the use of repetition of various sorts to hammer home the main points, just as we find in 1 Peter. It appears that Asiatic oratory was a development of the highly ornamental style cultivated by Isocrates who lived between 436–338 BC. It thus had a long history prior to NT times. It was especially prized and often practiced in western Asia Minor by sophists and rhetors of various sorts.[2] This thoroughly Hellenized region of the Empire had long been a haven for the rhetoric of advice and consent as well as the rhetoric of praise and blame, a trend only exacerbated with the rise of the Emperor cult. For our purposes, we can say that the

2. On the many sophists and rhetors in Western Asia, especially in Ephesus, Pergamum, Smyrna, and in the Lycus valley in Hierapolis, but also in the cities of Galatia, Capadoccia, and elsewhere in the region see Bowersock, *Greek Sophists in the Roman Empire*, 17–29.

influence of Asiatic style is evident in 1 Peter in several ways: 1) its long and sometimes convoluted sentences; 2) its verbosity, and use of colorful words; 3) its tendency towards repetition of both aural and cognitive features of the discourse; and 4) its strong appeals to the emotions at the outset and conclusion as suffering becomes a major theme in the discourse—not just any kind of suffering but specifically suffering for what one believes and lives out as a religious person.

When we begin to reflect more specifically on the rhetoric of 1 Peter one of the primary questions which comes to mind immediately is—is the author trying to inculcate new values and virtues, or is he simply commending and strengthening old ones? This is another way of asking is he using deliberative or epideictic rhetoric in this discourse? Is he trying to change behavior and belief in the near future, or merely praising certain extant forms of these things? Here we are helped by the detailed work of Barth L. Campbell who points out that the injunctions which introduce each major section of this discourse (1:13; 2:11; 3:14b–16b; 4:12–13) "are not for the continuation of present and acceptable behavior. Peter gives no indication whether the conduct that he enjoins is present to any degree among his readers. He writes as if it is not."[3] This document is best seen then as an example of deliberative rhetoric in an Asiatic mode.[4] He is also right that the injunctions are general in character, not surprisingly since this is a circular letter. As such it will address topics of what is advantageous, expedient, profitable, necessary, honorable and their negative counterparts, and it will do this by using *synkrisis*—rhetorical comparisons and contrasts of various sorts as well as examples in order to persuade the audience to change their beliefs and behaviors.[5]

Both Campbell and Troy Martin have rightly pointed out the major flaws in a purely epistolary analysis of 1 Peter—"it can identify basic parts of the letter (prescript; body-opening, middle and closing, and postscript) . . . but it cannot account for the composition of the letter-body. Other analytical methods must be used to explain that part of the letter . . . . According to Martin, the paraenetic genre exhibits *no fixed form and* 'therefore, the identification of 1 Peter as paraenesis does not provide an

---

3. Campbell, *Honor, Shame, and the Rhetoric of 1 Peter*, 25.

4. Campbell in fact thinks it is of mixed genre, with the *exordium* being an epideictic encomium. I will argue against this conclusion below. See pp. 181–82 below.

5. See Campbell, *Honor, Shame, and the Rhetoric of 1 Peter*, 30–31.

explanation of its compositional structure."⁶ This is as much as to admit that the majority of this document's form and structure cannot be accounted for by epistolary analysis at all. I say once more, epistolary analysis only helps us with analyzing some of the so-called epistles of the NT, and even then it mostly only helps with analyzing how they begin and end. These documents are mainly structured on the basis of rhetorical considerations, not epistolary ones, as they are oral documents—meant to be read aloud to their various audiences.

Martin is helpful in showing how various of the major images/metaphors/ideas in this discourse cohere with each other and show the author was careful about his composition of this document. Martin suggests that the Diaspora is the overarching and indeed controlling metaphor of this discourse, which results in two different sorts of supporting images, some general some specific. The author sees the audience as on an eschatological journey beginning at the new birth and climaxing when they receive final salvation at the end (1:3–5). One must then be concerned to stay on the right path on this journey hence the emphasis on the audience's conduct. One of the things seen as possibly getting the audience off track is re-assimilation to the pagan environment, resulting in apostasy from the people of God. Thus the author inculcates steadfastness, hope, and sobriety (see 1:13; 4:7; 5:8–9).

Martin stresses that there are three specific metaphor clusters which unite the discourse: 1) the *oikos* cluster, referring to the elect household of God, and not surprisingly then household codes for behavior therein (1:14—2:20); 2) the resident aliens, visiting strangers cluster (2:11—3.12); 3) the sufferers of the Diaspora cluster (3:13—5:11).⁷ We may notice then the drift of the argument. The audience, largely Jewish Christians, is alienated from both its homeland, Israel, and from its immediate environment, which is pagan. In such a situation there only "home" for now is the household of God, the community of Christ; but, of course, they can expect suffering, since association with that household makes them part of a minority sect that is both illegal and subject to persecution. Martin however does not go further to see how this development of images is being placed within a rhetorically formed discourse. For example, it would have helped his case could he have seen that, of course, the deeper emo-

6. Ibid., 20, quoting Martin, *Metaphor and Composition*, 270. Emphasis added.
7. Martin, *Metaphor and Composition*, 271–73, and also 144–61.

tions, the ones that involve pathos, love or hate, grief or euphoria are things that are appealed to at the end of the discourse and particularly in the peroration. It is not an accident that suffering, including its attendant emotions, is the major image in that segment of the discourse.

Campbell provides us with our first full-fledged rhetorical outline of 1 Peter as follows:

Epistolary prescript – 1:1–2

Exordium – 1:3–12

First Proposition – 1:13–16

First Argument – 1:17—2:10

Second Proposition – 2:11–12a

Second Argument – 2:12b—3:12

Third Proposition – 3:13–16b

Third Argument – 3:16c—4:11

Peroration – 4:12—5:14[8]

Though broadly speaking this outline is helpful and correct, there are some problems. First, Campbell wants to see the discourse as having each argument introduced by a proposition. So, for example 1:13–16, 2:11–12a and 3:13–16b are all seen as propositions. This is not normally how things would be structured in a single discourse. Normally the proposition for the whole discourse would come at the end of the *exordium* and prior to all the arguments on behalf of the proposition. Secondly, 4:12—5:14 is surely much too long and diverse to be considered the peroration of this discourse. First Peter 5:12–14 is an epistolary closing like the ones we find in Paul's letters. It is far better to see in 4:12—5:5 further deliberative arguments about suffering and leadership, and then see 5:6–9 as the peroration with a concluding doxology in 5:10–11. The peroration in 5:6–9 echoes the initial proposition in 1:13–16, where the themes of self-control and hope for the future are also brought forth. This then is a discourse which is a call to holiness which entails self-control, avoidance of old patterns of behavior and temptations, purification through obedi-

8. See Campbell, *Honor, Shame, and the Rhetoric of 1 Peter*, 58–198.

ence to the truth, endurance of suffering and following good examples like that of Christ and the author.[9]

A more exact and helpful rhetorical outline is as follows:

Epistolary Prescript – 1:1–2

Exordium – 1:3–12 – Thanksgiving for so great a salvation

Proposition – 1:13–16 – You are holy and have hope, so you should live like it.

First Argument – 1:17—2:10 – Living as redeeming resident aliens

Second Argument – 2:11—3:12 – Submission to authority figures

Third Argument – 3:13—4:11 – Suffering and self-control

Fourth Argument – 4:12–19 – Sharing the sufferings of Christ

Fifth Argument – 5:1–5 – Appeal to the elder and the youth

Peroration – 5:6–9 – Humility and self-control in suffering, with closing doxology (5:10–11)

Epistolary Postscript – 5:12–14

But whose rhetoric is this? Is Peter capable of such rhetoric? According to church tradition that goes back to Papias and is probably reliable, Mark wrote down the Petrine remembrances about Jesus in his Gospel,[10] and there is some evidence that there was an Aramaic original for some of that document.[11] If there is truth in this tradition, it suggests that Peter needed some help in communicating in Greek, at least in written form. First Peter 5:12, thus, becomes crucial.

Unlike in 1 and 2 Thessalonians, where Paul indeed is the speaker but he wants to make known that two other authority figures involved in founding the church in Thessalonike (Silvanus and Timothy) are also standing behind and are in agreement with what is said in the discourse, 1 Peter makes no such claims about the authority of Silvanus. He is not mentioned until the end of the document; at its beginning stands Peter the apostle alone. In deliberative rhetoric, the assertion of one's authority at the outset, establishing one's ethos, and indeed, the tenor of the docu-

9. See the discussion in Achtemeier, *1 Peter*, 4–8.

10. See the new study by Bauckham, *Jesus and the Eyewitnesses.*

11. See Witherington, *The Gospel of Mark.*

ment, was crucial. This discourse is presented as an authoritative word from Peter, presumably to his various converts.

What then was the role of Silvanus? It is true some scholars have attempted to see 1 Peter 5:12 as claiming that the letter was sent to these various churches through Silvanus, the letter carrier. There is a problem with this conclusion. If one diagrams the Greek sentence in question, leaving out the subordinate clauses, it reads: "through Silvanus . . . I wrote to you briefly." Silvanus may well have carried this document through the regions, just as he carried the letter from the Jerusalem Council (see Acts 15), but this sentence surely claims more. We do *not* have the verb "send/sent" in 5:12 unlike what we find in Acts 15:22–23, where it seems clear that the reference is to a letter carrier rather than a letter writer (as is also the case in Ignatius's letters to the *Philippians* 11.2 and to the *Smyrnaens* 12.1). It was the normal practice for an author who used a scribe to take up the pen towards the end of the document and add a few words of his own. We see this of course in various Pauline letters (e.g., Galatians and Romans), and there is no reason to think the situation is different in this case considering where Silvanus's name is mentioned. It is of course difficult to judge how much Silvanus contributed to what we have in 1 Peter, but since he is not claimed as an "author" *even at this juncture* (Peter says "I wrote . . ."), at most we may assume he simply played the role of scribe or amaneuenesis, so far as the composition of the document is concerned. He may have, in addition, been its deliverer and interpreter.[12]

Like Paul, Silvanus may well have received good training in Greek and rhetoric in Jerusalem, a training Peter will not have gotten growing up in Galilee prior to his conversion. Since there is some evidence of Semitic interference in 1 Peter, it may well be that Peter dictated in Aramaic and Silvanus wrote in Greek, looking at and transcribing from his own copy of the LXX when quoting the OT, or it may be that Silvanus was himself bilingual but more literate than Peter and so he framed Peter's words in better Greek and better rhetorical style. Peter's spoken Greek may well have been better than his written Greek, as is so often the case in such oral multi-lingual cultures. This being the case, we may conclude that the voice is decidedly the voice of Peter, if we trust the rhetorical claim of the document itself, even if the hands are the hands of Silvanus. The rhetoric of 1 Peter is colorful, sometimes elaborate, and certainly full of pathos.

12. On this latter point see Richards, *Paul and First-Century Letter Writing*.

It contrasts nicely with the simpler, but nonetheless effective rhetoric we find in 1 John, to which we now turn.

THE RHETORIC OF LOVE: 1 JOHN

We are in fact far better served with the Johannine Epistles than with the Pastoral Epistles when it comes to rhetorical analysis, mainly due to the work of D.F. Watson and several European scholars.[13] There is also not only detailed rhetorical analysis of these documents but clear statements can be made on their species—2–3 John are probably deliberative discourse (though 3 John could also be seen as epideictic in character), while 1 John is epideictic in character, being a sermon. This explains some of the differences between 1 John and 2–3 John, which have led those not attuned to rhetorical analysis to suggest that 1 John was by a different author.

D. L. Stamps has rightly noted that at some thirteen junctures in 1 John our author uses the verb *graphō* to signal his form of communication ("I write to you" or "I am writing to you").[14] This is clear enough and it means that 1 John is not likely just a transcript of an oral message given to the Beloved Disciple's own congregation. However, this is not the end of the story.

Written documents in antiquity were read out loud to or by the audience. They often served as surrogates for oral communication, the culture being primarily an oral culture and not a culture of the literate or of texts. Perhaps only 10–15% of the Greco-Roman world could really read or write. Thus while this document seems to have begun life as a written document, this neither means it was intended to be a letter, nor does it in any way rule out that it could be seen as a homily, meant to be effectively delivered orally to an audience.

What it does, however, mean is that this is not likely a document delivered to our author's "immediate" audience, or an audience where

---

13. As editor, I am thankful to have been able to read through Watson's forthcoming commentary on 1–3 John for the New Cambridge Bible Commentary series. It has been enormously helpful. For a good sampling of the discussion particularly as it pertains to 1 John see Watson, "Amplification Techniques"; Watson, "An Epideictic Strategy"; Watson, "1 John 2:12–14"; Klauck, "Zur rhetorischen"; Neufeld, *Reconceiving Texts*; Vouga, *Die Johannesbriefe*; and Vouga, "La réception."

14. Stamps, "The Johannine Writings," 622.

he is currently present or in residence, unless of course the author is ill. While this character of 1 John also does not necessarily make this document an encyclical, I incline to the theory that this sermon was intended to circulate in the Johannine churches, and may well have been known in the church addressed in 2 John, as some of the themes and ideas of 1 John reappear in 2 John. The content is not intended to be of a broadly generic nature, but rather of a sapiential nature, and is viewed as suitable for this cluster of churches that have interrelated problems and draw on the same Christian tradition.

Something also needs to be said about the entire paradigm of evaluation set up by Stamps, Porter, and others in an attempt to minimize the importance of rhetoric in analyzing NT documents, especially the so-called letters. Their view is that only micro-rhetoric is reflected in the NT, not the full structural outline of rhetorical discourses. In the first place rhetoric has a much longer track record than letter writing in the Greco-Roman world. This is hardly surprising, since all of these cultures in the Mediterranean crescent and beyond were essentially oral cultures. Speaking had far more influence, impact, and authority than writing, and was far more prevalent as a means of conveying information, persuading audiences, and exercising authority. Letter writing was an art that was just coming to full fruition in the first century AD, but Cicero, in the first century BC, was really the first person to write letters of considerable length and character that we find persons like Paul writing in the NT era. Cicero can be said to have popularized the notion of using the personal letter as vehicle for conveying profound ideas. Aristotle, the sophists, and the general Greek and Roman tradition of rhetoric considerably pre-date the rise to prominence of epistolary theorists and the popularity of letter writing, especially when it comes to personal letters of some substance and not just those dealing with daily affairs.

It is thus a huge mistake in analysis to assume that the letter-writing genre is the primary and controlling paradigm and that rhetoric somehow was subordinate or needed to fit into that dominant paradigm in the NT era. Most of the documents we have in the NT that we call letters and that have epistolary elements only use those elements to make up a small minority of the document, chiefly at their beginning and end. There is no such epistolary element as "the body middle," if we are talking about elements that are epistolary in character or derived from the letter genre and distinctive of that genre (such as addressor, addressee, greetings, health wish, travel plans, farewell). Furthermore, Paul's thanksgiving prayers are hardly just extensions of the initial health wish in pagan letters.[15] In other words, we need something other than epistolary categories to explain the majority of the material we find in these documents.

Anachronism also needs to be avoided in the analysis. By this I mean that later pronouncements by Pseudo-Libanius or other epistolary theorists (e.g., Pseudo-Demetrius), who were reflecting on several centuries of letter writing and trying to figure out how it fit into a rhetoric-saturated culture and carved out its own niche, should not be our primary guide for what we should think about these NT documents. It is not even clear that their works existed before the second century AD and in the case of Pseudo-Libanius not before the third century AD. Attempting to analyze largely rhetorical NT documents that have a few epistolary elements on the basis of later taxonomies of proper letter writing is rather like trying to analyze English cricket on the basis of the later rules set up for American baseball.

Stowers sets the record straight when he says:

> Greco-Roman culture regarded the well delivered and persuasive speech as the most characteristic feature of civilized life. In contrast to our own culture, linguistic skill focused on oral speech; the written word was secondary, derived from primary rhetoric. Letter writing remained only on the fringes of formal rhetorical education throughout antiquity. It was never integrated into the rhetorical systems and thus does not appear in the standard handbooks. This means *there were never any detailed systematic rules for letters, as there were for standard rhetorical forms. The rules for certain types of speeches, however were adapted for use in corresponding letter types.* So, for example, a letter of consolation written by a person with rhetorical training may more or less follow the form of the consolatory speech.
>
> The earliest extant rhetorical work that treats letter writing is the book *On Style* attributed to Demetrius of Phalerum and probably dating from the first century B.C.E. . . . The great Latin letter writers—such as Cicero, Ovid, Seneca, Pliny, Fronto—were thoroughly trained in the rhetorical schools. In the early third century C.E. Philostratus of Lemnos wrote a work on how to write letters. His now-lost book reflects controversies among rhetoricians concerning proper epistolary usage by letter writers in government

---

15. See pp. 110–20 above.

> service . . . . The handbooks of Demetrius and Libanius on letter
> writing betray close acquaintance with the issues and definitions
> of the rhetoricians.[16]

What Stowers remarks make perfectly clear is that rhetoric was the
dominant communication force in the culture, and letter writing was
influenced by that paradigm. Indeed the budding epistolary theorists
were always looking over their shoulders at the rhetoricians and examining rhetorical handbooks for guidance. We must keep this all in mind
when we read the Johannine "letters." The rhetorical analysis by Watson
of the Johannine documents is the most detailed and helpful, and so it
will be helpful to interact with his conclusions throughout the following
discussion.

It goes almost without saying that 1 John is a far more complex piece
of material than we find in 2–3 John, and it is also clear enough that we
have no obvious epistolary elements in this discourse. It begins without
an epistolary prescript, and it ends with a bang, with an exhortation about
staying away from idols. There is a similarity to and perhaps indebtedness
to John 14–17.

Watson argues that 1 John 1:1–4 is the *exordium*, 5:13–21 is the peroration, and the *probatio* involves everything in between, in essence.[17] He
sees the entire discourse as an example of epideictic rhetoric. I find very
little to quibble with either in terms of the rhetorical arrangement (or
"invention") or the species of the rhetoric, though I would suggest that
the peroration is in fact 5:18–21.

Epideictic rhetoric is the rhetoric of praise and blame, dealing
with values the audience already affirms, and is an attempt to enhance
or intensify the adherence to those values.[18] This clearly seems to be the
character of the rhetoric here as can be seen for example in 1 John 2:7
where our author says he is writing the audience not a new command
but rather an old one that they are long since familiar with and affirm. He
will draw out the new implications of that old command that they already
adhere to, for their current situation. The message throughout will have

16. Stowers, *Letter Writing*, 33–34. Emphasis added.

17. Watson, "Amplification Techniques," 118–23.

18. Rudolf Schnackenburg rightly saw what was going on in 1 John, though he does
not do a rhetorical analysis of the text. In *The Johannine Epistles*, he states "His purpose in
writing is to strengthen true faith and mutual love, and the joyful certainty of fellowships
with God (1.3) and of eternal life (5.13) which he brings" (3).

to do with love, life, and light as things to praise and treasure, and their opposites (including sin) as things to condemn. In an epideictic piece of rhetoric, neither a proposition nor a narration is required, for the author is not trying to prove some key thesis statement, nor is he mounting a series of arguments in favor of that thesis statement. Rather, he is trying to increase adherence to values already held.

Epideictic rhetoric is the rhetoric of sermons and other sorts of hortatory addresses. What we find in this particular sermon in 1 John is a series of interlocking themes or topics developed over the course of the discourse that are stated, amplified, reiterated, but not debated. Watson is absolutely right that throughout this discourse our author is using the rhetorical technique of *amplification*, ringing the changes on certain key themes over and over with slight variations in order to stress the need for the adherence to the basics. Like a musical round these themes keep coming up with slightly different permutations and combinations.

This comports with the character of epideictic rhetoric, which does not require formal proofs of some thesis statement that the audience needs to be convinced about, but rather amplification on and praise of values already affirmed, and condemnation of vices to be avoided (cf. Aristotle *Rhetorica* 1.9.36; *Rhetoric to Alexander* 3; Quintilian *Institutio oratoria* 3.7.6). The techniques used here were taught in the lower echelons of secondary education in the exercises of the *progymnasmata*.[19] How very different is the discourse here from the sort of diatribal argument patterns we find in Romans for example. We have here only the voice of the author, and he does not engage in debate with opponents or anyone else. He simply exercises his authority in the form of an epideictic discourse. But what difference does the recognition of the rhetorical species and

19. *Progymnasmata* was indeed taught to male Jewish students in Jerusalem by rhetoricians there, during and before the first century AD, showing the impact of Hellenism on Judea even well before the time of Jesus. Furthering the work of Martin Hengel, one should now consult the helpful essays in Collins and Sterling, *Hellenism in the Land of Israel*. The final conclusion of M. Goodman reaffirms Hengel's conclusion that Hellenism had considerably affected Jews in the Holy Land, and adds "No one now would want to deny that many Jews in Palestine were acculturated to some aspects of Greek language, art, commerce, philosophy, and literature by the end of the third century B.C.E." (307). By the first century AD, the impact of Greek culture had long since been recognized and taken for granted, only being rejected, and only in part, by the more sectarian groups such as those at Qumran.

tendencies of this document make when it comes to interpretation? One example must suffice.

The phrases "if we say . . . " or "if anyone says . . . " is in fact common in Greek literature in rhetorical contexts and are simply ways of advancing one's argument with an audience that already shares the speaker's worldview.[20] The phrases themselves are not polemical, nor need they be used to advance polemics. As Neufeld points out, the antithetical statements need not be seen as the slogans of the opponents at all, but rather are "rhetorical devices by which he engages the audience to consider carefully what he has to say with the hope of persuading them to accept his views."[21] In my view this antithetical rhetoric is being used to shore up the boundaries of the community now that the secessionists have left. Again, it is about damage control and healing, not about debating or refuting opponents.

Wye must turn to a more detailed discussion of the rhetoric of 1 John. Epideictic rhetoric is, by its very nature, repetitive and even hyperbolic, seeking to strengthen adherence to values already adopted or embraced by the audience and also to draw out the implications of those values. This is quite clearly the rhetoric we have in the homily we call 1 John. We hear for instance that the author is writing to "you fathers because you have known . . . to you young people because you have overcome . . . to you children because you have known . . . " (1 John 2:13). He reminds them of the message they heard and have embraced from the beginning (1 John 3:11). He writes to those who already believe in the name of the Son of God (5:13). Epideictic rhetoric is the rhetoric, for example, of funeral homilies; in a sense, our author is dealing with a post mortem situation. There has been a split in the Christian community and some members of it have been lost through departure from the community. Healing is needed, reassurance must be offered, and reasons to continue to embrace the fundamental values must be given, because eternal life for the members of the community hangs in the balance.

Epideictic rhetoric is also, by its very nature, highly emotive in character, for trust in the community's values and stronger adherence to them after a crisis requires a deeper emotional commitment. It is not surprising that various commentators, sensing the emotive character of

20. See rightly Griffith, "A Non-Polemical Reading of 1 John," 260.
21. Neufeld, *Reconceiving Texts as Speech Acts*, 89.

this homily, have assumed we were dealing with polemics against the "antichrists." There is no doubting that our author is angry with those who have departed, more because they have committed apostasy from the true faith than just because they have left the community. While our author is prepared to say that they were never "of us," it is hard to doubt that the secessionists saw themselves as part of the community, and so may have seen themselves as followers of Christ in some sense, perhaps approving of some of his teachings.

The emotive language used of the departed (antichrists, false prophets, etc.) is meant to help those remaining let them go, and focus once more on their own spiritual well being and belief system. It is meant to make sure that the community stops losing members and that none that remain are tempted to embrace the beliefs and behavior of the departed. This homily then is not about directly attacking or debating with opponents. It does not seek to delineate their views or refute them with detailed arguments. Our author assumes the audience already knows the secessionists views and feels it is sufficient to make a few salient points about their aberrant Christology, reiterating these points in various ways for emphasis and to insure adherence to them. Too much mirror-reading of 1 John has led to too much focus on the beliefs and behaviors of the departed and not enough on the beliefs and behaviors our author wants the audience to continue to embrace, an agenda furthered throughout this sermon.

Sermons were of course not uncommon in our author's time. They could be heard on a weekly basis in synagogues all across the Empire.[22] They were a particular sort of religious oration. Since Christian sermons, so far as we can tell, tended not to deal with priests, temples, and correct religious rituals (although some referred to circumcision or baptism, and some referred to the sacrifice of Christ), and since a good deal of the time they were not expositions of some OT text, they would not generally have been viewed as specifically 'religious' as opposed to philosophical in character by Gentiles who heard them. This needs to be kept in mind as we evaluate 1 John which has themes like love, truth, life, light and might sound to the casual listener like more of a philosophical discourse.

Demonstrative, or epideictic, or "ceremonial" rhetoric had a long history before the time of our author going back at least as far as Aristotle.

22. Jeal, *Integrating Theology and Ethics*, 44–45.

It was celebratory rhetoric, the rhetoric of praise and blame, and its primary temporal focus was on the present. It could be heard at festivals or funerals, or sometimes just in the market place. The audience was not a judge or an assembly, but simply interested spectators of various sorts. Epideictic oratory tended to focus on the core values of a society or some subset of a society seeking to affirm, reaffirm, or even inculcate such values (see Aristotle *Rhetorica* 2.18.1). Quintilian in our author's era simply concurs with Aristotle about the three species of rhetoric, recognizing epideictic as an important sort of discourse (*Institutio oratoria* 3.4). In summarizing what characterized epideictic rhetoric, G. A. Kennedy makes these telling remarks: "Epideictic is perhaps best regarded as including any discourse, oral or written, that *does not aim at a specific action or decision but seeks to enhance knowledge, understanding, or belief, often through praise or blame, whether of persons, things, or values. It is thus an important feature of cultural or group cohesion. Most religious preaching . . . can be viewed as epideictic*."[23] This, I would submit is a very accurate summary of what we find in 1 John, describing its character and rhetorical aims quite clearly. Certain theological and ethical truths are being reaffirmed through amplification in the wake of the shock of the loss of some community members.

Epideictic rhetoric tended to get short shrift compared to judicial or deliberative rhetoric in the standard handbooks, being deemed the least important of the three species of rhetoric. Aristotle seems to have started this trend, only giving epideictic one chapter's worth of scrutiny in his *Rhetoric*: deliberative gets four chapters, and judicial gets six. Cicero gives only a very brief treatment of epideictic in *De inventione rhetorica* at the end of book two, and Quintilian only devotes one chapter to the subject (*Institutio oratoria* 3.7). Yet the truth is, with the rise of Empire, and the demise of any sort of real democracy (except in the micro-assemblies of small groups, like church meetings, that were not official political bodies) epideictic oratory became an increasingly important feature of the culture, especially with the increase in Olympic-style games and the spread of the Emperor cult all over the Empire. There were more Roman triumphs, more festivals, more religious celebrations, more games, and hence more epideictic oratory in various venues and settings. Quintilian even speaks of an annual contest in Rome which involved creating an oration in

23. Kennedy, "The Genres of Rhetoric," 45. Emphasis added.

praise of Jupiter Capitolinus (*Institutio oratoria* 3.7.4). Christianity had to and did respond to this proliferation of the rhetoric of praise and blame. Quintilian goes on to speak about the character of epideictic rhetoric and its function during the Empire. He says, "the proper function however of panegyric is to amplify and embellish its themes" (*Institutio oratoria* 3.7.6). Quintilian stresses that this form of rhetoric is directed in the main to the praising of gods and human beings (*Institutio oratoria* 3.7.6–7), which suits 1 John very well indeed since what is praised is God in Christ. "In praising the gods our first step will be to express our veneration of the majesty of their nature in general terms, next we shall proceed to praise the special power of the individual god and the activities by which he has benefited the human race . . . Next we must record their exploits as handed down from antiquity. Even gods may derive honor from their descent" (*Institutio oratoria* 3.7.7–8). In general, humans are to be praised for their virtues and condemned for the vices, and the same applies to communities of humans as well.

At the hands of the sophists of course, epideictic rhetoric sometimes was nothing more than the art of display or speaking well, eloquence for its own sake, or for the sake of flattering a governor, or a group of citizens. But at its best, epideictic rhetoric set out the values and ideals of conduct for a society and let the audience learn and embrace them. What is especially important to note is that epideictic oratory was primarily a Greek phenomenon and thrived in settings where Hellenistic culture had taken deep roots and the overlay of Roman culture had not supplanted it. This was especially true in Asia, home of Asiatic rhetoric, which often took the form of panegyric or epideictic oratory. This sort of oratory was heard all the time even at very personal and not just at public functions, such as at weddings, or funerals, or in welcoming guests or saying farewell to friends. At the *symposion*, the after-dinner speaker would often serve up an epideictic dessert. It was often effusive in character and sometimes involved long periods. The household then was often the setting for such rhetoric, the very social setting where Johannine Christians met. It is not a surprise then if we find a good sampling of epideictic rhetoric in the NT, in this case in 1 John.

In his first rate study of the rhetoric of 1 John, D. Watson shows in detail how 1 John has as one of its major rhetorical strategies amplification.[24] As we have already noted, amplification is a rhetorical technique mainly associated with epideictic rhetoric and of course with sermons or homilies. Instead of the *probatio* being a series of arguments proving a proposition or thesis statement, it is rather dedicated to amplifying and expanding and expounding on certain key ideas and themes which are already familiar and accepted (see Aristotle *Rhetorica* 1.9.36; Quintilian *Institutio oratoria* 3.7.6). "The use of amplification indicates a careful working of the material and the need to be emphatic and clear in the face of the secessionist doctrine and practice to which his audience is subject. Far from being boringly *redundant*, the rhetor is carefully *emphatic*." [25] The very degree of emphatic repetition of key themes and ideas in 1 John shows just how concerned our author is about the need to strength the audience's embracing of these key values.

What then are the amplification techniques that our author uses: 1) the use of strong words such as "hate" and "murderers" (1 John 3:15); 2) the use of augmentation, a series of statements increasing in intensity leading to a climax (e.g., 1 John 2:2—not only is Jesus an atoning sacrifice for sins of the community but also for the sins of the whole world); 3) the use of *synkrisis* or comparison, (e.g., human testimony is good, but God's testimony is greater—1 John 5:9); 4) the use of accumulation, the piling up of words or phrases identical in meaning or all referring to the same object or subject (1:1–3—that which we have heard, seen, looked at, touched); 5) there are a panoply of figures of repetition used in 1 John, including the use of *expolitio*, which refers to the technique of saying the same thing with slight variation or with equivalent terms (*Rhetorica ad Herennium* 4.42.54; see 1 John1:7b–9b where cleansing us from all sin is later called cleansing us from all unrighteousness), or *conduplicatio* which refers to the repetition of the same word or the same phrase using the same part of speech, having the same function (1 John 2:12–14). Lest we mistake what is going on here, this need not mean our author has a very limited vocabulary. It means he is trying to be emphatic by means of repetition, and so this redundancy is a rhetorical strategy.

Clearly the rhetorical exigency that prompted the writing of this homily was the schism (2:18–19), but this starting point does not reveal the character of the rhetoric. What we find in this document is an attempt

24. Watson, "Amplification Techniques," 99–123.
25. Ibid., 122–23.

to increase the intensity of adherence to fundamental values already accepted, values that our sermonizer and his audience already hold in common, but which the audience may not see the full implications of. This is why we find the repeated use of the language of abiding (2:6, 10, 24, 28; 3:6, 24; 4:13, 16) or keeping (2:3–5; 3:22, 24).

S. Smalley has it basically right when he says, "the purpose of 1 John may therefore be summarized as *primarily* an appeal to the faithful: to strengthen the faith and resolve of true believers in the Johannine community by encouraging them to maintain the apostolic Gospel."[26] In epideictic oratory one tends to appeal to the most fundamental values and universal truths that the community adheres to, and in order to do that our author has chosen to use sapiential language about love, light, life, truth, and the like, offering up sayings that in isolation would appear to be maxims or truisms to those who were already Christians. This is not the sort of discourse one uses when one's audience is not yet convinced of the truth of the Gospel.

Finally, if we ask the vexed question about the structure of 1 John, we may say that rhetoric helps us some to decipher it. For one thing the ending of the homily need not be seen as abrupt ("little children keep yourselves from idols") when we understand the way a peroration is intended to function, in this case a peroration to make sure the audience rejects the false Christology of the secessionists. For another thing, since this is epideictic rhetoric we should not expect formal arguments carefully lain out. The author is not attempting to persuade the audience about something they do not already affirm or believe, nor is he seeking to alter their behavior in the near future, nor is he attacking or defending actions taken in the past. This homily is all about praise and blame in the present for things already believed and done. We may outline the structure of the homily as follows:

1) *exordium* – 1:1–4

2) *probatio* – 1:5—5:17

3) *peroratio* – 5:18–21[27]

26. Smalley, *1, 2, 3 John,* xxviii.

27. I differ a little with Watson in regard to where the peroration begins. It seems to me that the discussion of a sin unto death is a new topic, not a rehashing of a previously discussed matter.

The opening *exordium* establishes rapport with the audience, and makes clear the common ground they share. The *probatio* largely an exercise in amplification, rings the changes on several key topics such as love and sin and Christology, leading up to a peroration that both summarizes some of these topics one final time (5:18–20) and concludes with an emotional bang by characterizing the Christology of the secessionists as a form of idolatry. This discussion of epideictic rhetoric and the strategy of using repeated "amplification" for emphasis and reinforcement serves us in good stead as we turn to our last, and perhaps finest example of rhetoric in the NT, which is also epideictic in character and elegant as well. I am referring to the rhetoric of Hebrews, which provides us with another example of a remarkable sermon from an early Christian, probably one from the larger Pauline circle.

THE RHETORIC OF FAITH AND FAITHFULNESS—HEBREWS

Hebrews, like 1 John is a homily,[28] in fact D.J. Harrington has called it "arguably the greatest Christian sermon ever written down."[29] It does not partake of the qualities of a letter except at the very end of the document (Heb 13:22–25), and these epistolary features are added because this sermon had to be sent to the audience rather than delivered orally to them by the author. In fact, H. Thyen, after studying all the evidence for early Jewish homilies, has argued that Hebrews is the only completely preserved Jewish homily of the period, but this is overlooking 1 John, and James as well.[30]

Sermon manuscripts, ancient or modern, do not conform to the expected characteristics of the beginning of a letter. Similarly many rhetorical forms of speaking lack mention of addressor or addressee. Hebrews is a document involving rhetoric of considerable skill. It is, to use an oxymoron, an "oral document," and in fact a particular type of oral document—a homily in the form of a "word of exhortation" (Heb 13:22). It is not an accident that this is the very same phrase used to characterize

28. See rightly Hagner, *Encountering the Book of Hebrews,* 29.

29. Harrington, *What are They Saying,* 1.

30. Thyen, *Der Stil der judisch-hellenistichen Homilie,* 106. One should compare the more recent discussion in F. Siegert, *Drei hellenistisch-jüdische Predigten.* On Hebrews as a homily see Swetnam, "On the Literary Genre"; and McCullough, "Some Recent Developments."

Paul's sermon in Acts 13:15. Hebrews is not a haphazard discourse but a piece of polished rhetoric that has been variously categorized as either epideictic or deliberative rhetoric or some combination of the two (see below). The point that needs to be made is that the document's authority rests in its contents, not in its author's claims to apostolic authority. To judge from the end of ch. 13, it is assumed, but not argued, that this author has some authority over this audience, who knows very well who he is, and can anticipate a visit from him and Timothy before long. The oral and homiletical character of the document cannot be stressed enough. T. Long, a professor of homiletics, puts it as follows:

> Hebrews, like all good sermons, is a dialogical event in a mono-logical format. The Preacher does not hurl information and arguments at the readers as if they were targets. Rather, Hebrews is written to create a conversation, to evoke participation, to prod the faithful memories of the readers. Beginning with the first sentence, 'us' and 'we' language abounds. Also, the Preacher employs rhetorical questions to awaken the voice of the listener (see 1.5 and 1.14 for example); raps on the pulpit a bit when the going gets sluggish (5.11); occasionally restates the main point to insure that even the inattentive and drowsy are on board (see 8.1); doesn't bother to 'footnote' the sources the hearers already know quite well (see the familiar preacher's phrase in 2.6: "Someone has said somewhere . . . "); and keeps making explicit verbal contact with the listeners (see 3.12 and 6.9, for example) to remind them that they are not only supposed to be listening to this sermon, they are also, by their active hearing, to be a part of creating it. As soon as we experience the rise and fall of the opening words of Hebrews, the reader becomes aware that they are not simply watching a roller coaster hurtle along the rhetorical tracks; they are in the lead car. In Hebrews, the gospel is not merely an idea submitted for intellectual consideration; it is a life-embracing demand that summons to action.[31]

We are now well served in regard to the rhetorical discussion of Hebrews. The consensus of opinion is not only that this document reflects macro-rhetoric (the various divisions of a rhetorical speech) as well as micro-rhetoric but that its species is either deliberative, epideictic, or some combination of the two. In other words, there is agreement that it is

31. Long, *Hebrews*, 6.

definitely not judicial or forensic rhetoric,[32] and also that the recognition of individual rhetorical devices, which certainly are plentiful in Hebrews, does not take the full measure of the way our author uses rhetoric.

There are rather clear clues in the document itself as to what sort of rhetoric it is. Bearing in mind that paraenesis or exhortation could be found in both deliberative and epideictic rhetoric, we must consider what the author is trying to accomplish by this rhetorical masterpiece. Consider the following statements in the discourse:

1) 2:1—"we must pay more careful attention therefore to what we have [already] heard, so that we do not drift away";
2) 3:1—"therefore holy brothers and sisters who share in the heavenly calling fix your thoughts on Jesus";
3) 3:12—"see to it, brothers and sisters, that none of you . . . turns away from the living and true God";
4) 4:1—Therefore, since the promise of entering his rest still stands, let us be careful that none of you be found to have fallen short of it ;
5) 4:14—"therefore . . . let us hold firmly to the faith we profess . . . ";
6) 6:1, 11—"therefore let us leave the elementary teachings about Christ and go on to maturity . . . we want each of you to show this same diligence to the end . . . we do not want you to become lazy but to imitate those who through faith and patience inherit what has been promised";
7) 10:22–23, 35—"let us draw near to God with a sincere heart . . . . Let us hold unswervingly to the hope we profess . . . . Do not throw away your confidence . . . ";
8) 10:39—"we are not of those who shrink back and are destroyed";
9) 12:1—"let us throw off everything that hinders.. and let us run with perseverance the race marked out for us";

32. Ironically enough the first major treatment of the rhetoric of this document in the twentieth century by H. F. von Soden was in terms of forensic rhetoric. See his *Urchristliche Literaturgeschichte*, 127–28. More influential was his conclusion that Hebrews follows the pattern of a rhetorical speech with 1:1–4 being the *exordium*; 1:5—4:16 being the proposition or thematic statement; 5:1—6:20 being a statement of the plausibility of the case; 7:1—10:18 being the proof or proofs; and 10:19—13:25 being the peroration.

10) 12:14–15—"let us make every effort to live in peace . . . see to it that no one misses the grace of God";

11) 13:1—"keep on loving each other as brothers and sisters";

12) 13:22—the discourse as a whole is called a "word of exhortation" in a "brief (!) letter."

As G.H. Guthrie has rightly pointed out, the alternating back and forth between exposition and exhortation with the latter being the punch line, makes evident that this discourse exists for the sake of the exhortation which directly addresses the issue of concern. Thus one must stress that "the expositional material serves the hortatory purpose of the whole work."[33]

If we look at all of this carefully it seems very clear that this discourse is not about urging a change in direction, or a new policy, nor is the author correcting obvious new problems in belief or behavior. Further, the author is not trying to produce concord or reconciliation in the audience, he is rather trying to shore up their faith in the face of pressure, suffering, and the temptation to defect. He is trying to confirm the audience in a faith and practice they already have, urging them to stand firm against the dangers of apostasy and wandering away, and stay the course with perseverance continuing to run in the direction they are already going, and have been going since they first believed, thus going on to perfection and exhibiting their faith and perseverance. This sort of act of persuasion is surely epideictic in character, appealing to the values and virtues the audience has already embraced in the past.[34]

The focus of the rhetoric in this document is furthermore clearly in the present. Our author focuses on what Christ is now doing as the heavenly high priest, what the audience is and ought to continue to be doing in the present, and there is the appeal to continue to imitate the forbears in the faith and Christ himself. The appeal to imitation can be found in either deliberative or epideictic rhetoric, in the latter case it is

33. Guthrie, *The Structure of Hebrews,* 143.

34. See the conclusion of Lane, *Hebrews 1–8,* c: "The purpose of Hebrews is to strengthen, encourage, and exhort the tired and weary members of a house church to respond with courage and vitality to the prospect of renewed suffering in view of the gifts and resources God has lavished upon them. The writer's intention is to address the sagging faith of men and women within the group and to remind them of their responsibility to live actively in response to God's absolute claim upon their lives through the Gospel." See also Koester, "Hebrews, Rhetoric, and the Future of Humanity."

an appeal to continue to imitate the models they already know of and have looked to. When we couple all this with the doxological beginning of the discourse in ch. 1, and the worship climax in 12:18–27, it seems clear that this discourse maintains an epideictic flavor throughout. Most rhetorically adept homilies in any case fell into the category of epideictic rhetoric.

Also comporting with this conclusion is that we do not have formal arguments in this discourse, but rather one long act of persuasion that involves comparisons, enthymemes, repetition, amplification, use of catchwords, and a toggling between exposition of texts (the provide the inartificial proofs or witnesses to the truths the audience is being reminded of) and application or paraenesis. Furthermore, after the *exordium* in 1:1–4 it was not necessary to have a *narratio* or *propositio* since in effect there is only one long argument or act of persuasion in various parts throughout the discourse. The encomium of faith in Hebrews 11 does not stand out from its context as if it were some sort of digression or different type of rhetoric, or a rhetorical anomaly in the midst of a non-rhetorical document.[35] Also comporting with the conclusion that this is epideictic rhetoric is the enormous amount of honor and shame language used in this discourse to make sure that the audience will continue to be faithful in their beliefs, behavior, and life, not slipping back into pre-Christian forms of religion, in this case non-Christian Jewish ones.[36]

Most ancient commentators who were rhetorically attuned saw Hebrews as epideictic in character, and of modern commentators, Lane, Attridge, and Olbricht have all opted for seeing Hebrews as basically epideictic in character, with Olbricht concluding it most resembles a funeral encomium.[37] Koester and L. Thurén see the document as a mixture of deliberative and epideictic rhetoric as do Luke Timothy Johnson and A. T. Lincoln,[38] while W. G. Ubelacker urges that we have deliberative rhetoric

---

35. On Hebrews 11 as an encomium see Kennedy, *New Testament Interpretation through Rhetorical Criticism*, 156. See also Cosby, *The Rhetorical Composition and Function of Hebrews 11*.

36. See the detailed study of deSilva, *Despising Shame*; and now Johnson, *Hebrews*, who is much indebted to deSilva on this front.

37. See especially Olbricht, "Hebrews as Amplification."

38. For Thurén see "The General New Testament Writings." See also Lincoln, *Hebrews: A Guide*, 14–22.

here,[39] a conclusion Lindars also reached.[40] Lindars provides no justification for this conclusion at all, and Übelacker's analysis suffers, as Thurén has pointed out, from the fact that he tries to find a *narratio* and a *propositio* where there is not one. Hebrews 1:5—2:18 is no *narratio* (a narration of relevant past facts) any more than it is an *exordium*—the latter is limited to 1:1–4. In the case of Johnson and Lincoln, they are certainly right that the expositions lead to the exhortations and serve the latter, but exhortations are as common a feature of epideictic as deliberative rhetoric. It is the *nature* or *character* of the exhortation that decides the issue, and a careful analysis of all the paraenesis in this document shows that it is aiming to help the audience maintain beliefs and behaviors they have already embraced. In other words, the exhortations are epideictic in character, as are the expositions.

We also have no *propositio* in this discourse, which should have been a dead giveaway that we are dealing with epideictic rhetoric, the effusive, emotive, and often hyperbolic rhetoric of praise and blame The author is not trying to prove a thesis but rather praise some important things—Christ and faith for instance. To the contrary, at 1:5 we dive right into the first part of the discourse itself, which entails an exposition of Scripture involving a negation that God ever spoke of or to the angels in the way he spoke of Christ. This is followed by the exhortation in 2:1–4 that builds upon it. While Thurén is right that 1:5 and following amplify the *exordium*; they certainly ought not to be seen as simply part of the *exordium*.[41]

After seeing 1:1—2:4 as the *exordium*, Koester suggests that 2:5–9 is the *propositio* of the whole discourse,[42] but this simply does not work. Hebrews 2:5–9 is not a thesis statement that is then demonstrated in all the subsequent arguments. Far too much of what follows is not about Christ's superior position, condition, and nature, especially from 11:1 to the close of the discourse, but we could also point to much of chs. 4 and 6 as well. The issue is both Christology and paraenesis, or the imitation of Christ and Christ-likeness, as the author does not want the audience to commit either intellectual or moral apostasy. It comes down ultimately

39. Übelacker, *Der Hebräerbrief als Appell*, 185–92.

40. Lindars, "The Rhetorical Structure of Hebrews."

41. Vaganay ("Le plan de l'épître aux Hébreux") rightly argues that only Heb 1:1–4 should be seen as the *exordium*.

42. Koester, *Hebrews*, 84–85.

to whether they will continue to admire, emulate, and worship Jesus. Koester is, however, right that the peroration begins in ch. 12, though not at 12:28. It is best to see that in terms of macro-rhetoric we have a simple structure here:

1) *exordium* – 1:1–4. The beginning of the discourse is linked to this *exordium* through the use of hook words, preparing for the comparison with angels who are introduced in 1:4.[43]

2) the epideictic discourse composed of one long unfolding act of persuasion or sermon in many parts – 1:5—12:17. This part can, of course, be profitably divided into subsections. For example, Morna Hooker suggests a chiastic structure as follows:

   3:1—4:13 – Imagery of pilgrimage, including first warning

      4:14—5:10 – Introduction of idea of Jesus as High Priest

         5:11—6:12 – First severe warning

           6:13—10:18 – Jesus our High Priest

         10:19–32 – Second severe warning

      10:32—11:40 – The importance of faith

  12:1–29 – Imagery of pilgrimage, including final warning.

On this showing the theme of Christ as the heavenly high priest is central to the whole discourse. This makes excellent sense, and one could even talk about the imagery of placing visually Christ in the inner sanctum of the heavenly sanctuary just as he is placed at the center of the discourse verbally.

3) *peroratio* with concluding benediction – 12:18–29. The emotional climax of the argument comes with the pilgrims assembled at the holy mountain and exhorted finally to worship God acceptably.[44] This is followed, as is typical of all the expository sections, with

4) a final paraenesis – 13:1–21. Sums up some of the major exhortations of the discourse—behave responsibly, persevere steadfastly, pray fervently, and be prepared to "go outside the camp" as Jesus did. Thus, interestingly the peroration is the emotional climax of

43. See now the detailed study on the rhetorical technique of using hook words to link sections of a discourse together, Longenecker, *Rhetoric at the Boundaries*.

44. See rightly Lincoln, *Hebrews*, 17.

the theological rhetoric, whereas 13:1–21 is the emotive exhortation climaxing the ethical rhetoric.[45] This is the same sort of thing
we find in Ephesians, another example of epideictic rhetoric,
where the discourse does not stop at the peroration but offers up
some concluding exhortations that sum some things up.

5) Because this sermon is written down, there are some concluding
epistolary elements – 13:22–25 (such as the explanation of the
reason for writing, personalia, concluding greetings and a concluding grace wish).

The function of an *exordium* was to establish rapport with the audience and make them favorably disposed to hear what follows. One way
to accomplish this is to use highly elevated and eloquent language at
the outset which will immediately get the audience's attention. We certainly have this in 1:1–4 where our author unloads a variety of rhetorical
devices including a great deal of alliteration and impressive sounding
phrases ("radiance of his glory"). It was important for the style to suit
the subject matter. Thus, Koester is right to note that the "elevated style
of Hebrews' *exordium* suits the grandeur of its subject matter: the exalted
Son of God."[46] We see the same sort of exalted style in 11:1—12:3 where
the other main thing that is praised in this discourse, faith, is discoursed
on at length. As Aristotle stressed, such elevated prose can impress and
help gain the favor of the audience, appeal to their imaginations, and
make clear that an important subject is going to be dealt with here (see
Rhetorica 3.6.1–7). It was a rhetorical must that weighty matters not be
treated in an offhand matter, nor trifling things be invested with too
much dignity (*Rhetorica* 3.7.1–2). "When our audience finds [a speech]
a pleasure to listen to, their attention and their readiness to believe what
they hear are both increased" (*Institutio oratoria* 8.3.5). In an oral culture,
how something sounded had everything to do with whether it would be
listened to, much less believed. It is hard to over-estimate the importance

45. On the entire rhetorical structure I am in basic agreement with Lincoln, *Hebrews*,
24–25. The argument that ch. 13 was not originally part of this document has no textual
basis, and has been refuted at length in terms of the issues of style and content by a variety
of scholars. See Filson, '*Yesterday*'; and the summary by Lane, *Hebrews 1–8*, lxviii. From
what we can tell about the Jewish homily in the Diaspora, it normally concluded with a
final exhortation anyway. See Witherington, *Letters and Homilies*, 20–25; and Thyen, *Der
Stil*, 87–96, 106–110. See also Stegner, "The Ancient Jewish Synagogue Homily."

46. Koester, *Hebrews* , 93.

of the oral dimensions of the text in helping to persuade the audience of the content of the discourse.

As Olbricht has pointed out, in a rhetorical encomium there are standing aspects of a person's life that will be praised—his noble birth, illustrious ancestors, education, fame, offices held, titles, wealth, his physical virtues, his moral virtues, and his death. Without question many of these topics surface in the praise of Jesus in Hebrews.[47] We may also point out that the comparisons (*synkrisis*)[48] we have in this discourse (e.g., Jesus and the angels, Jesus and Melchizedek, Jesus and Moses, or the believer's current life compared to what will be the case if they commit apostasy or go in a retrograde motion toward a form of religion that will not save them) follows the conventions of epideictic rhetoric. The function of such comparisons in an epideictic discourse is to demonstrate the superiority of the one person or thing that is being praised (see Aristotle *Rhetorica* 1.9.38–39; *Rhetoric to Alexander* 1441a27–28). Lincoln ably sums up the function of "comparison" in Hebrews:

> *Synkrisis,* [is] a rhetorical form that compares representatives of a type in order to determine the superiority of one over another. It functions as a means of praise or blame by comparison and makes the comparison in terms of family, natural endowments, education, achievements and death. In Hebrews various earlier figures or types of Christ are seen as lesser by comparison with him and family relations (Christ as divine Son) education (learning perfection through suffering) and death (the achievement of Christ's sacrificial death) all feature in the comparison. This sort of argument structures the discourse because, as in an encomium, a discourse in praise of someone, the *synkrisis* is used for the purpose of moral exhortation. So in Hebrews, the comparison of angels and the Son, of Moses and Christ, of Aaron and Christ, of the Levitical priesthood and Christ, of the old covenant and the new covenant, is in each case followed by paraenesis.[49]

47. See Olbricht, "Hebrews as Amplification," 278. One of the reasons it does not work to say that we have both deliberative and epideictic in this discourse is that we do not have discrete arguments, but rather one long continuous one. There are, for instance, no deliberative digressions in this discourse, rather we have a series of topics that are praised (e.g., Christ, faith), as well as negative behavior which is "blamed" or warned against.

48. On this rhetorical device see Witherington, *Letters and Homilies,* 138–43.

49. Lincoln, *Hebrews,* 19.

In this discourse it is Christ's superiority, the superiority of faith in Christ, and following his example that is being praised. This is contrasted with falling away, defecting, avoiding shame, or suffering. Christ is the model of despising shame and maintaining one's course in life faithfully to the end, and indeed of being "perfected" through death—sent directly into the realm of the perfect.[50] While the emphasis in this discourse is mainly on that which is praiseworthy, our author does not hesitate to illustrate blameworthy behavior, for example the unfaith and apostasy of the wilderness wandering generation is pointed out (3:7–19). In fact, rhetorical comparison can be said to be the major structuring device for the whole discourse right to its climax in the peroration at the end of ch. 12. Our author exalts the better mediator, the better sacrifice, the better covenant, the better example of faith, and the better theophany, all by means of rhetorical *synkrisis*, not with something that is bad, but rather only with something that is less glorious, adequate, or able to save people.[51]

One more thing can be stressed at this point. Epideictic rhetoric characteristically would use a lot of picture language, visual rhetoric so that "you seem to see what you describe and bring it vividly before the eyes of your audience" and thus "attention is drawn from the reasoning to the enthralling effect of the imagination" (Longinus *On the Sublime* 15.1, 11). Epideictic rhetoric persuades as much by moving the audience with such images, and so enthralling them, catching them up in love, wonder, and praise. The appeal to the emotions is prominent in such rhetoric, stirred up by the visual images.

An example of this is the beginning of the peroration in 12:22, where we have the last harangue, the final appeal to the deeper emotions of these Diaspora Jewish Christians who have been pressured and persecuted, and in many cases may have never had the joy of making the pilgrimage to Mt. Zion—"But you have come to Mt. Zion, to the heavenly Jerusalem, the city of the living God. You have come to thousands upon thousands of angels in joyful assembly, to the church of the first born, whose names are written in heaven. You have come to God . . . to Jesus the mediator." These are Christians who, like the author, have likely never seen or heard Jesus in person. But now before their eyes is portrayed the climax of their faith pilgrimage, the same sort of climax that Jesus reached when he died, rose,

---

50. See deSilva, *Perseverance in Gratitude,* 34–35.

51. As is so clearly demonstrated by Evans, *The Theology of Rhetoric.*

and then ascended into heaven. The discourse ends with worshipping God with reverence and awe—clearly an epideictic topic meant to create pathos. Our author knows very well what he is doing in this epideictic discourse, and he does it eloquently and brilliantly from start to finish. He has made Jesus and true faith so attractive that it would be shameful to turn back now, shameful to defect, and stirring to carry on with the beliefs and behaviors they have already embraced.

One of the consequences of recognizing and analyzing the rhetorical species of Hebrews is that it becomes impossible to see the exhortations or paraenetic portions of the discourse as mere interruptions, digressions, after thoughts, or appendages, while the Christological discussion is seen as the essence of the discourse. To the contrary, the author chooses his OT texts carefully, gives his exposition, then offers his exhortations based on the exposition all as part of an attempt to deal with the rhetorical exigency, namely the need to stand firm and not to fall back or backslide, the need to continue on the pilgrimage already begun towards perfection, the need to continue to believe and behave in ways that comport with such commitments.

But is there some rhetorical logic to the alternations between exposition and exhortation in this homily? The answer is yes, and has been rightly discerned by T.W. Seid. Seid points out that the expositions are part of a larger effort to draw comparisons principally between Christ and others. Thus, he sees the structure as follows: comparison of Son and angels (1:1–14) and parenesis (2:1–18); comparison of Moses and Christ (3:1–6) and parenesis (3:7—4:16); comparison of Aaron and Christ (5:1–10) and parenesis (5:11—6:20); comparison of Melchizedek/Christ and the Levitical priesthood (7:1–25) and parenesis (7:26—8:3); comparison of the first covenant and new covenant (8:4—10:18) and parenesis (10:19—12:29); and epistolary appendix (13:1–25). This *synkrisis*/paraenesis alternation encourages the audience to progress in moral conduct by remaining faithful to the greater revelation in Jesus Christ and emulating the models of its scripture. The alternation also warns the audience of the greater judgment to befall those unfaithful to the greater revelation.[52]

What is praised and what is blamed in this discourse is not part of some abstruse exercise in exegesis for its own sake. It is part of a pastoral

52. See Seid "The Rhetorical Form of the Melchizedek/Christ Comparison in Hebrews 7."

effort to deal with the struggles the Jewish Christians are having in Rome
to remain true and faithful to the things they have already committed
themselves to embrace. To this end, our author's rhetorical strategy in
picking the texts that he does is not because of his intellectual curiosity
about messianism or a Christological reading of the OT; rather, Pss 8, 95,
110 (and perhaps 40), Jer 31, Hab 2, and Prov 3 are texts that are picked
and dealt with because they help make the case that the inadequacy, inef-
fectiveness, or "partial and piecemeal" character of previous revelation
and covenants is self-attested in the OT.[53] But that is only the negative
side of the persuasion going on in this rhetorical masterpiece with carefully selected inartificial proofs from the OT. Other texts are brought in as
well to support the positive side of the argument, which is that the good
things in the OT said to be yet to come are now realized only in Christ,
and faithfulness is required if these eschatological promises are also to be
realized in the lives of those who follow Christ. Thus, it can be said that
in Hebrews, "theology is the handmaiden of paraenesis in this 'word of
exhortation', as the author himself describes it."[54] With these comments in
mind it will be helpful to give a more expanded outline of the argument
of this discourse, showing the relationship of the elements in it.

Exordium – 1:1–4 – Partial revelation in the past,
full revelation in the Son

Section	Theme	OT Text	Paraenesis
Probatio			
• Part one (1:5–14)	Christ's Superiority	catena (1:5–13)	2:1–4
• Part two (2:5–18)	"You crowned him"	Ps 8 (2:6–8)	
• Part three (3:1—4:13)	"Today"	Ps 95 (3:7–11)	3:12—4:13
• Part four (4:14—7:28)	"Priest forever"	Ps 110 (5:6)	4:14–16; 5:11—6:12

---

53. Caird, "The Exegetical Method of the Epistle to the Hebrews."

54. Walters, "The Rhetorical Arrangement of Hebrews," 63. Here I have been following and am indebted to Walters's compelling argument.

Section	Theme	OT Text	Paraenesis
Probatio (cont.)			
• Part five (8:1—10:31)	"New Covenant"	Jer 31 (8:8–12)	10:19–29
• Part six (10:32—12:2)	"By faith"	Hab 2 (10:37–38)	10:32–36; 12:1–2
• Part seven (12:3–17)	"Don't lose heart"	Prov 3 (12:5–6)	12:3–16
Peroratio (12:18–29)	Pilgrim's End	Theophany at Sinai (Ex 19; Deut 4, 9, 31; Hag 2:6)	

Final Summary Paraenesis – 13:1–21[55]

Epistolary Closing – 13:22–25[56]

Several concluding remarks are in order. It is clear enough that all of these sections with the exception of Part two have paraenesis. In some cases the OT citation has preceding and following paraenesis in order to turn the exposition into exhortation or application. The paraenesis is not relegated to the end of the discourse but is rather sprinkled liberally throughout the discourse. It takes up a good deal of the verbiage of the discourse and could hardly be called a series of appendages. The problem all along has been that many scholars find the expositions more interesting and challenging than the exhortations, and therefore have tended to feature or privilege them in the ways they have thought about this discourse.

Secondly, the focus is clearly on the here and now, and what is already true, hence the emphasis on 1) "today," 2) the new covenant that is already extant and in force, 3) not losing heart but rather continuing to have faith and be faithful, persevering in the present, and 4) what Christ has accomplished and is even now doing in heaven on behalf of the be-

---

55. Spicq, *L'Epitre aux Hebreux*, 1:38, also recognizes that 1:1–4 should be seen as the *exordium* and 12:18–39 as the peroration, with the major acts of persuasion in between.

56. I am indebted to Walters, "The Rhetorical Arrangement of Hebrews," 66, which provides part of the basis for this outline, though strangely Walters does not count the first section based on the catena.

liever. The focus is on the here and now both theologically and ethically, which is appropriate in epideictic discourse.[57]

Thirdly, our author almost exclusively sticks to texts from the Pentateuch, the Psalms, and the latter prophets. There is nothing really from the historical books, which is all the more striking since he is making a salvation-historical kind of argument, and since in ch. 11 he recounts some of the adventures and misadventures of the period chronicled in 1–2 Samuel, 1–2 Kings, and 1–2 Chronicles.

Fourthly, one part of this discourse leads naturally to the next as an unfolding message develops involving both theology and ethics. Particularly striking is how the final section of the argument leads so smoothly into the peroration, with the imagery of running a race to a final destination introduced in 12:1–3, and then the pilgrim arrives at the goal as described in the peroration beginning at 12:18. There is overlap, repetition, amplification, reinforcement in the argument but this is precisely what one would expect in an epideictic discourse, as we have seen already in detail with the case of 1 John.[58] One of the interesting differences between these two sermons is that 1 John is topically driven, but not textually driven, and so is less of an expository sermon in that sense, whereas Hebrews is certainly textually oriented and is far more expository in character.

We begin to see the remarkable range of the Christian rhetoric of praise and blame in 1 John and Hebrews, and in both cases the sermons are directed in the main, if not almost exclusively, to Jewish Christians in two different major cities in the Empire (Ephesus and Rome) that were seedbeds for the early Christian movement.

We need to keep steadily in view that the function of praise and blame of any topic was to motivate the audience to continue to remember and embrace its core values (involving both ideology and praxis) and avoid slipping into blameworthy beliefs and behaviors (see Aristotle *Rhetorica* 1.9.36; Quintilian *Institutio oratoria* 3.7.28; and *Rhetorica Ad Herennium* 3.8.15). In other words, even when using complex concepts and ideas the ultimate aim of the rhetoric is practical and ethical in character.[59]

---

57. For a survey of the first twenty or so years of rhetorical analysis of Hebrews in the modern era see Watson, "Rhetorical Criticism of Hebrews."

58. On which see Witherington, *Letters and Homilies*, 325–40.

59. Here I would part company with Koester, *Hebrews*, 82, following deSilva,

Finally, something must be said about where our author could have acquired his considerable rhetorical prowess and skill, as it is sometimes doubted that Jews could have had such rhetorical skills or interests. I would suggest that there is no reason for such doubts, especially if we are talking about Jews who were educated in one of the major educational centers in the Empire.

There were of course several major centers in the Empire where one could obtain rhetorical training at a high level—Rome, Athens, Ephesus, Pergamon, Tarsus, Antioch, Jerusalem, and Alexandria provide us with a short list. Of course it was possible to obtain elementary rhetorical training in many other places as well. In elementary education (*progymnasmata*) throughout the Greco-Roman world one of the final and most important school exercises that were learned was the art of composing an encomium. Written records of speeches were copied from the great masters, and skill was acquired by copying, memorizing, and imitating. The centers of learning, which had great libraries to draw on, were at a great advantage in this regard because they had access to more source documents. All other things being equal, those who studied both elementary and advanced rhetoric in a city like Rome, Pergamon, or Alexandria had a great advantage over those who studied elsewhere. If our hypothesis that this document was likely written by Apollos from Alexandria is correct, then we ought at this juncture to say a bit more about that city and the rhetorical training available there.

Though the great library of Alexandria, which at its peak housed some 700,000 papyrus scrolls, unfortunately burned (possibly twice if one counts the torching of Alexandria when Julius Caesar's troops took the city in the first century B.C.), nevertheless, we are fortunate that many, many literary papyrus fragments have been found ranging in date from the 3rd century BC to the 5th century AD. These include a surprisingly large number of fragments of copies of famous rhetorical speeches made

---

Despising Shame, 35, and others who wants to suggest that Hebrews would function as epideictic for those continuing to hold the core values but deliberative for those tending to drift away.

by Greek orators. There are some fifty fragments from the period third century BC to first century AD, including fragments of famous speeches made or written down by Aeschines, Anaximenes, Demosthenes (especially numerous), Homer, Hyperides, Isocrates, Lysias, Adespota, and one particular Latin orator—Cicero. If we break down the evidence a bit further we discover that almost all of these fragments are examples of rhetorical speeches (Homer being the exception), and famous ones at that (for example, Demosthenes' often imitated *On the Crown* speech or Hyperides' famous Funeral Oration).[60] The concentration of the Greek tradition of rhetoric rather than the Latin tradition is not surprising since Alexandria was, since its founding by Alexander, a Greek city that prided itself on its Hellenistic culture and the promotion and preservation of that culture.

One of the aspects of the culture that had been most fully developed was the art of rhetoric. Just how important this was to the citizens of that city can be seen from the finding of *Hibeh Papyri* 26 taken from a mummy cartonage of the third century BC. The papyrus is a portion of the important rhetorical treatise *Rhetorica ad Alexandrum*. In addition to this, the most important and earliest surviving textbook for young boys enrolled in elementary rhetorical schools originated in Alexandria, being written in the first century AD by one of its citizens Aelius Theon. There is an especially telling and interesting passage from his *Progymnasmata* (145) where he complains about the children of Alexandria not being willing to do the heavy lifting of learning Greek philosophy but rather being so enamored of rhetoric that they raced right through the elementary education, skimming over the philosophical part of that training in order to get to "training in eloquence" (i.e., rhetoric), including especially the upper level training in eloquence. He bemoans, "Nowadays most young men, far from taking up philosophy before they come to the study of eloquence, do not even touch the ordinary elementary branches [of learning], and, worst of all, they attempt to handle forensic and deliberative themes before they come through the necessary preliminary training."[61] Several things are important about this remark. We might for instance aptly compare what is said in this passage to what our author says about elementary training, in which his audience ought not need a refresher

60. See the charts in the very helpful study, Smith, *The Art of Rhetoric in Alexandria*, 124–25.

61. See the discussion in Smith, *The Art of Rhetoric in Alexandria*, 134.

course (Heb 6:1–2) since they should be ready for the more advanced teaching such as our author gives them in his sermon. The second thing to be noted is that training in epideictic rhetoric (eulogies, encomiums of various sorts, rhetorical comparisons of a praise or blame nature) was a part of the final stages of elementary education, while training in deliberative and forensic rhetoric was part of the upper level of education. There were ten standard exercises in the *Progymnasmata*, of which the seventh is said by Theon to be "praise and blame" speeches, while the eighth is rhetorical *synkrisis*, which he says falls properly under the heading of encomia. Theon stresses that the good student must daily practice writing out rhetorical pieces.

Alexandria was a rare city in many regards, not least because it had not only a great library but also a famous "museum" or lecture hall where the muses inspired philosophers, teachers, and rhetoricians to speak or teach. In other words, Alexandria not only had elementary education, and the gymnasium as well, like other great cities, but it also had a world-class lecture hall providing a sort of university education to its citizens. Even if our author did not have upper level rhetorical training he could have written this epideictic sermon based on what he learned on the elementary level in Alexandria (or the other cities previously mentioned), or by imitating what he heard in the public lectures in the "museum." But this brings us to a further point.

There were over 100,000 Jewish citizens in Alexandria in the first century AD. So significant was the Jewish populace there that Emperors like Caligula, no lover of Jews, received embassies from them on important matters (one of which involved Philo being an ambassador from Alexandria), and others like Claudius issued edicts trying to keep that community in check. Many of the Jewish citizens of Alexandria were well-to-do, well-educated, Greek citizens of the city, and received a considerable education in that city. One only needs to read the writings of Philo to see just how profoundly a devout Jew could be influenced not only by his own sacred traditions in Torah (bearing in mind it was in this city that the LXX was translated and found a home), but also by Greek philosophy and rhetoric.[62] If we examine closely the description of Apollos in Acts 18:24–25, where he is described as not only have skills in eloquence (i.e., rhetoric) but as a Jew who was learned in the

62. See Winter, *Philo and Paul*.

Scriptures used in Diaspora synagogues, and compare it to what we have learned above about Alexandria and also to the scriptural and rhetorical phenomena we find in Hebrews, absolutely no social locale in the whole Roman Empire better suits what we find than Alexandria as a place of social origin and education for our author, and no known name makes better sense of all the factors and facets of Hebrews than that of Apollos of Alexandria, a sometime co-worker of Paul, Priscilla, and Aquila, in cities as diverse as Ephesus, Corinth, and finally Rome.

AND SO?

In this our final chapter that illustrates at length the types and kinds of rhetoric we find in the NT, one thing should be clear: the influence of Greco-Roman rhetoric on the writers of the vast majority of the NT was both extensive and intensive. In some cases we can speak of some NT writers becoming quite skilled in rhetoric. We see this especially in Luke-Acts, Paul's letters, and Hebrews. But most other portions of the NT do not lack rhetorical character and submit quite easily to rhetorical analysis if we use historical rhetorical criticism in that process of analysis. It has been one of the aims of this specific study to show that the analysis of the NT on the basis of its rhetoric is both helpful and essential, if we want to understand these documents and their oral and aural character. They were not meant to be read, but rather to be heard, and that as part of a larger attempt at persuading one or another Christian audience about some matter of importance. Early Christianity was an evangelistic movement in its very essence, and as such it picked up the tools of rhetoric both readily and eagerly in order to persuade the dwellers in the Roman Empire that they needed the salvation offered to them by and in Jesus Christ. That these documents were saved and treasured even unto today is silent testimony that their various acts of persuasion must not have fallen on deaf ears, indeed there is little wonder why some said—"these are the people who have turned the world upside down."

QUESTIONS FOR REFLECTION

1. While both 1 John and Hebrews reflect epideictic rhetoric, they differ in their rhetorical strategies when it comes to using source material, particularly the OT? Why do you think this is the case?

2. If you had to evaluate the educational level of the author of Hebrews, what would you say? Where in the Empire could the author have gotten training in advanced rhetoric?

3. First Peter places more emphasis on suffering and emulation of Christ than perhaps any other NT document. What rhetorical techniques does Peter use to persuade the audience to emulation or imitation of Christ? Why do you think it is that he repeats some of the key Scripture passages more than once in his discourse?

4. First John is a classic example of the use of rhetorical amplification. How does knowing this affect the way one evaluates statements that seem nearly synonymous but with slight variance of word choice? Is this an example of saying the same thing in two ways, but with stylistic variance, or something else?

CHAPTER 8

The Difference Rhetoric Makes to NT Interpretation

When I first began my academic study of the NT in college, I had already been involved in the study of the Greek and Roman classics for seven or more years, as I took Latin while I was still a young teenager. It was thus always a question in my mind as to why those studying a document like the NT, written entirely in Greek of the Empire period, would not have attempted more self-consciously to analyze these documents with the help of classics studies and studies in ancient Greek and Latin historiography. My perplexity only grew when I discovered that Professor George Kennedy at the University of North Carolina (my alma mater) was in fact pioneering studies of the NT and Greco-Roman rhetoric together in the 1970s. Why had it taken so long to recognize the connection? There are various answers to this question, and one of them has to do with the fact that we are all products of the education offered to us, and its limitations.

CURSORY REVIEW OF AMERICAN EDUCATION

A study of education in America during the end of the 19th and the beginnings of the 20th century is in fact a sobering study indeed if one cares about the liberal arts. Whereas major universities before the Civil War had required studies on the basics of 1) rhetoric; 2) logic; 3) natural and revealed religion; and 4) classics studies and ancient history, by the turn of the twentieth century any and all of these subjects had fallen by the wayside as *required* courses, even if one was doing a BA in some liberal arts field. Why had this happened? In part it was the response to the rise of required science and math curricula, which in turn was a response to the burgeoning industrial revolution. As they say, the rest is history. The remainder of the 20th century chronicled in America fewer and fewer students being trained in classics, or ancient history, much less in rhetoric and logic. This was a tragedy in many ways, and it certainly has affected biblical studies in North America.

Like the biblical story of the new Pharaoh who took over Egypt and did not know nor much care for or about the Hebrews in his midst, American education with its new pedagogy became increasingly impoverished of liberal arts, especially the study of the classics and ancient rhetoric. Unfortunately, this is true unto this very day. Many biblical scholars today have never had a course in the Greek or Latin classics, studied Greek or Roman history (whether social history or some other kind), bothered to get up to speed in the varieties of ancient Greek style (e.g., Attic and Asiatic), nor have they ever studied rhetoric. Instead, they have been trained in forms of literary and form criticism, which, while providing some insights into the text of the NT, certainly could not be claimed to be forms of literary practice that the NT writers themselves could have known or used. In other words, *much of literary criticism of the NT in my lifetime has been an essentially a-historical and sometimes even an anti-historical enterprise* (one need only consider efforts to treat the Gospels and Acts as if they were works of pure fiction, or were like modern works of fiction). No wonder many classics scholars and Greek and Roman historians end up scratching their heads when they discover the anachronistic ways which many NT scholars evaluate their particular cache of ancient literature.

This study has been intended as something of an act of persuasion in itself to urge more persons to do proper rhetorical analysis of the NT, and to stop disregarding, or belittling such a form of NT studies. It is a terra incognita still to many scholars today, and even to those who know this discipline, many have tried to minimize the sorts of rhetoric one finds in the NT to the use of rhetorical devices, what I call micro-rhetoric.

So if one is a skeptic about rhetorical criticism, this study has been an effort to ask for a suspension of disbelief and skepticism. But of course, skeptics have a right to say, So what? What difference does it really make in the interpretation of the NT if I neglect to analyze it in rhetorically adept ways? My answer must be much in every way, and so in the balance of this final chapter I wish to set out some illustrations of why I think this is the case.

ANSWERING THE SO WHAT QUESTION

Some scholars, and indeed many educated laypersons, perhaps getting lost in the minutiae of rhetorical analysis, have been prone to think that rhetoric has only to do with style or literary devices and not with the substance of a discourse. And so the cry has arisen—So what? So what if the NT writers used rhetoric? This question deserves a proper answer, and the answer involves the immediate stress on the fact that form reveals function and meaning, and indeed form and content are co-entailed. Rhetoric is not just about style or the form of a discourse, but indeed the form shapes the very substance and meaning of the discourse. A few examples must suffice.

Illustration One:
Failure to recognize a propositio (thesis statement) or peroration leads to misunderstanding of the character and themes of a document

One of the most revealing aspects of "invention" or discerning the macro-rhetorical structure of a discourse is finding its proposition statement and its peroration. Let us consider the proposition statement in Romans 1:16–17. Here Paul gives us a clear foretaste of where this whole discourse is going and what its major overarching emphasis will be. What do we learn from these verses that could have forestalled a lot of misinterpretations? First, we learn that the Gospel itself is said to be the power of God for salvation for all those believing, Jew first, but also the Greek. Salvation is not here connected to the concept of election, but rather to that of preaching and the response of believing. All those believing will be saved. There is however an *ordo salutis*, an order of salvation. The Good News, even in AD 57 or so when Paul wrote this letter, is for the Jew first, and also for the Greek. This discourse will certainly not countenance the idea that God has abandoned his first chosen people. Indeed, in the climactic theological argument in chs. 9–11, Paul will go out of his way to refute such notions, countering latent Gentile prejudices as well.

In an apocalyptic sounding statement Paul adds that the righteousness of God is being revealed from the faithful One unto faith, just as it is written "but the righteous from faith shall live." Rhetorically speaking, propositions are intended to be compact brief references to the major thesis and themes that are to follow in the discourse. They require unpacking, and the unpacking is done not just at the beginning of the discourse but in all of the succeeding arguments.

What we should conclude from this proposition is that the issues to be addressed are as follows: 1) the power of the Gospel for salvation; 2) the righteousness of God, and so the character of God (a theme which is already begun to be expounded in Romans 1:18, where we hear about one side of that righteousness, namely God's wrath); 3) the repeated reference to faith in these two verses, including the quote from Habakkuk, makes clear that too will be a major emphasis in what follows; 4) the quote from Habakkuk refers to believers as "the righteous" which in its original context referred to their piety and ethics and sanctification. This suggests that both divine and human righteousness will be focused on in the following discourse; but 5) even a righteous person should and shall live by faith, just as they have been saved through faith; 6) the cryptic, tightly packed phrase "from the faithful one unto faith" probably alludes to Christ in its first half and prepares for the use of the *pistis Christou* language later about the faithfulness of Christ, referring especially to his death on the cross.

We would expect a proposition not to be expounded on the spot, but over the whole course of the discourse, which is to say, not just in chs. 1–8, but also in chs. 9–11 (where God is said to be still interested in the salvation of Jews), and in chs. 12–16. This discourse then will not just be about theology, but also about theodicy, and not just about theodicy, but also Christian ethics that are grounded and founded on the theology earlier enunciated in the discourse.

What is not said to be the central thesis of this discourse is "justification by grace through election." Indeed, in this discourse, justification or forensic right-standing with God is at most only a subheading under the larger topic of God's and human's righteousness. A lot of endless and mostly fruitless debates about Romans could have been averted if 1:16–17 could have been seen as foreshadowing the whole discourse, including its ethics, and further had it been seen from the outset that Paul says nothing at all about salvation "by faith alone." The phrase "from the Faithful One unto faith" has quite a different rhetorical function, and Luther's translation of the Greek here is not a live possibility. Let us consider a very different example of the benefit of rhetorical analysis, this time of a peroration.

Ephesians 6:10–18 provides us with one of the most stirring conclusions in all of Paul's letters. The letter itself is an example of Asiatic and epideictic rhetoric, and not surprisingly then it finishes strong with a highly emotive exhortation full of pathos. This peroration, since it is not part of a forensic or deliberative discourse, does not reiterate or summarize a previous thesis statement, but rather reinforces the general call in this discourse to continue to stand firm in ones values, the beliefs, and behaviors already endorsed by the audience. The author is not at all urging a change of behavior. This is why the word "stand" or "continue to stand" is so prominent here. In other words, this peroration is not at all urging an attack against the powers and principalities, but it is rather reassuring the audience that they can withstand the onslaughts of evil with the weapons they already have and use, particularly the Word of truth, the Spirit, the cardinal Christian virtues faith, hope, and love, righteousness, and the practice of prayer. The language here is clearly couched in political and indeed military terms, and the Christian life is seen as an ongoing battle with the powers of darkness, the spiritual forces of evil in the heavenly realms.

How does knowledge of rhetoric help us not over- or under-interpret this passage? Firstly, since we know that perorations are the place where an orator will be highly emotive in order to assure compliance with the earlier part of the discourse it is a huge mistake to take such vituperation as revealing 'the essential problem' being addressed in the discourse, or as providing a key to what all that has gone before really was meaning and tending towards. In an epideictic piece of rhetoric the whole focus of the peroration is to do something that dramatically concludes the discourse and assures that the audience will continue to honor the values and virtues that they have honored in the past, and will continue to avoid the shameful things they have avoided in the past. The discourse was not meant to be seen as a problem-solving discourse, but rather as a progress-encouraging and reinforcement-accomplishing discourse. Attempts to relate this passage to some ongoing problem in Ephesus or Asia with Christians dabbling with the dark arts or being tempted to do so fails to recognize the generic character of the rhetoric and the emotive nature of the conclusion of the discourse, which is not meant to introduce new topics or solve old problems that have not previously been addressed in the discourse itself.

Illustration Two:
Failure to correctly identify the species of rhetoric in a discourse
leads to false conclusions

Hans Dieter Betz argues in his landmark commentary on Galatians that the discourse in Galatians is forensic in character, when in fact it is deliberative. One of the mistakes made in his analysis is mistaking polemics and strong vituperation for evidence of the forensic quality of the discourse. In fact, polemics and strong rhetoric can characterize any species of rhetoric; it is not a clear clue to what the species of the rhetoric is. There is the further problem that forensic rhetoric rarely if ever offered ethical advice, that was the provenance of deliberative, and sometimes epideictic rhetoric. When has anyone heard a prosecutor lecture the defendant, the jury, or the judge on how they should change their behavior, or avoid certain behaviors in the near future? No, they are too busy advocating for their client and demolishing the defense attorney's arguments.

Galatians attempts to head off the capitulation of the Galatian Christians to the persuasion of the Judaizers to get themselves circumcised and keep the Mosaic covenant. The arguments offered are meant to convince the audience that they ought not to take such a course of action either sooner or later.

One of the ancillary problems that arises from mis-identifying the species of rhetoric in this discourse is one will then assume the *substance* of the discourse will have a forensic cast or flavor to it. For example, one assumes that when Paul talks about righteousness here he must be focusing on some sort of legal fiction—right-standing under the Law, for instance, granted by a judge who declares one righteous. It is interesting that neither in Galatians 3, nor for that matter in Romans 4, is there any discussion about Christ's righteousness being imputed to the believer, nor is the real focus on a judge making a pronouncement of "no condemnation for sins," and thus of "not guilty." The real focus in the use of the Abraham story is on saying that Abraham's faith was *reckoned or credited* as Abraham's righteousness. This is not the language of the judge or forensic language; this is the language of a *business transaction*, or the business ledger, with columns for credits and debits. The exchange is between Abraham's faith and Abraham's righteousness. If he is the exemplar for Christians, then the imputed righteousness of Christ does not enter into the picture here.[1]

Illustration Three:
Failure to recognize "impersonation" as a rhetorical device

Because we have already dealt in some depth with Romans 7:7–25 earlier in this book,[2] we do not really need to review what was said there. Here is a case where the failure to recognize a particular rhetorical device is in play has led to whole theories about the Christian life that Paul would neither recognize nor endorse, including the *simul justus et peccator* theory (i.e., the notion that Christians are simultaneously justified and at the same time sinners caught up in the bondage and inevitability of sin). Paul speaks in the voice of Adam in Romans 7:7–13 and in the voice of those who are the descendants of Adam in the rest of the chapter, perhaps especially in the voice of those who are Jews outside of Christ. The "I" is neither autobiographical, nor is Paul speaking as a Christian or for Christians. This constant misinterpretation can be attributed in part to being unaware of the rhetorical device and the proper implications of its use.

Paul talks plainly in 7:5–6 and 8:1–2 about the Christian life and what was true before and after conversion. What is clear from the context is that Paul does not believe the Christian is in bondage to sin. This is why, of course, that he can reassure even immature Corinthian Christians that it is not inevitable they give in to sin and temptation; God can provide an adequate means of escape (1 Cor 10). Indeed, the whole ethical program of Paul presupposes that the audience can actually, by the grace of God, obey the commandments Paul, Jesus, and others have given them. They are to live a life without excuses.

It should be added that "impersonation" was one of the most difficult of rhetorical devices to pull off convincingly. In an oral presentation it would often involve changing one's voice, or tone of voice, to let the audience know someone else was speaking. It is not surprising that analyzing Romans as if it were a theological treatise or as a mute text rather than a rhetorical one has led to misunderstanding time and time again.

---

1. On which see Witherington and Hyatt, *Paul's Letter to the Romans.*
2. On which see pp. 131–50 above.

Romans is an oral text, meant to be heard, and it is a shame we have not heard it in modernity for what it is—a rhetorical masterpiece.

Illustration Four:
Failure to recognize the way a rhetorical comparison works

Rhetorical comparisons were things that even children were taught in the most elementary settings of classical education. They were taught it was like painting a Rembrandt painting, to use an anachronistic example. By this I mean, that if one wanted the exemplar to shine more brightly, then one had to paint as dark a picture of the villain as possible. The use of dramatic hyperbole was absolutely in order, and would have been understood as a normal part of such a rhetorical comparison, if the intent was comparison by contrast, and not a comparison of like individuals, both equally admirable (or equally devilish). In a comparison by contrast, irony, sarcasm, and the like were perfectly acceptable, but they were never meant to be taken literally. A rhetorical "figure" did not work that way. Let us consider one example from the NT.

Paul, in a brilliant move, devises a final theological argument based on the practice of rhetorical comparison in Galatians 4. In this case, Paul compares and contrasts two women, whom he says are allegorical figures representing two covenants. The goal is to get the Galatians to cast the Judaizers out of their churches (see Gal 4:30). In a tour de force argument meant to clinch the deal and force the Galatians to stop wavering or inclining in the wrong direction, Paul associated Hagar the slave woman with the Sinai covenant, Jerusalem, and bondage. By contrast, Sarah, the free woman, is associated with the Abrahamic covenant, the Jerusalem that is from above, and freedom. Clearly this argument is not based on pure logic, but rather on its emotional force and the element of surprise.

No one would have naturally associated the Sinai covenant or Jerusalem with Hagar. But, by the same token, freedom was universally prized over bondage. Indirectly the Judaizers were placed in the same camp with Hagar, whereas Paul was seen as being like mother Sarah in giving birth to free children who are children of the Abrahamic promise (see Gal 4:19-20).

Modern commentators have of course often approached this passage with a wry smile, often finding it an ineffective gerrymandering of OT texts and theology. But this conclusion ignores altogether the way such rhetorical comparisons were meant to work—forcing an emotional reaction and decision so that some conduct would be avoided, and other conduct embraced. The argument does not rely on pure logic or even good exegesis, but rather on painting an emotive portrait that leads to exclusion and embrace as the contrast is brought to life. And here we come to a crucial juncture in our discussion.

The fact that various arguments or acts of persuasion found in the NT do not follow the modern canons of logic, or modern notions of what is and is not persuasive is irrelevant. They were not written for 21st century minds in the first place. They were written based on the shared ancient cultural assumptions and scripts about what was rhetorically within bounds, and what was not. The fact that even modern rhetoric often works differently than ancient rhetoric worked is neither here nor there. The question must be—could this argument have been seen as persuasive in its original setting? The answer to this question is yes—absolutely. It would have been seen as exceedingly clear and clever. What it would not have been seen as is an anti-Semitic diatribe.

Illustration Five:
Failure to See the Difference between Modern and Ancient Persuasion

One of the real issues that arises from reading ancient rhetorical documents is a dawning awareness of how different ancient culture was from our own in so many ways. Most of us have had the experience of recognizing that humor is very culture specific (and sometimes sub-culture specific). What makes one audience laugh, may well lead to groans or puzzled looks in another audience and culture. The same applies to rhetoric. What might well appear manipulative in one cultural setting might appear quite normal and appropriate in another. A classic example of this can be seen in Paul's little letter to Philemon.

In the first place, Philemon is a short piece of rhetoric meant to put pressure on Philemon to set Onesimus, the slave, free. This pressure is applied in several ways. First, the letter is not a private letter, but rather written to Philemon *and to the church that met in his house.* In other words, though Paul's request of Philemon is personal, it is made in the context of a church meeting with all the other members hearing what is being asked and watching how Philemon will respond. Secondly, Paul plays on the sympathies of Philemon, reminding him from the outset that Paul himself is in chains, a prisoner of the Roman Empire. Throughout the discourse there is an attempt to apply emotional pressure on the man. Thirdly, Paul reminds Philemon of all the good he has previously done, "refreshing the hearts of the saints." Fourthly, there is rhetorical word play meant to nudge things along a little further. Onesimus is a nickname meaning "useful/beneficial," and Paul puns on this asking for some use or benefit from Philemon (v. 20), who has now become a Christian and thus truly useful to both Paul and others. Fifthly, Paul says he could be bold and order Philemon to do the right thing, but he would rather persuade him to do it, but lest we think Paul was leaving anything to chance, in v. 21 he speaks about being certain of Philemon's *obedience!* Indeed, he expects Philemon to do more than Paul asked. Sixthly, Paul pulls on the heartstrings by mentioning not only that he is in chains a second time (v. 9), but that now he is an old man. Seventhly, Paul characterizes Onesimus as his very heart, which he sends back to Philemon. The implication is that if Philemon does not send him back to Paul, Philemon will be seen to be heartless, and Paul heartbroken. Finally, the real coup de grace comes in v. 19 when Paul says that if Onesimus owes Philemon anything (which he clearly does, at the very least he owes the time he was not serving Philemon) Paul will repay, but then immediately Paul turns around and says *"not to mention you owe me your very spiritual life."*

It is safe to say that many modern persons would find this letter highly manipulative and too emotive. This would not be seen as an example of fighting fairly or persuading properly. The line between persuasion and manipulation is a moving one depending on time, culture, social and rhetorical conventions in a given culture. What I would stress is that everything Paul does in this letter is completely normal and accepted practice in his age. Nothing would be seen as unethical or over the top.[3] Paul should be evaluated on the basis of the custom and conventions of his own day, *not ours.* But then this presupposes that we *know* the differences, which requires knowledge of ancient rhetoric and what the appropriate uses of it were. In other words, a letter like Philemon cannot be properly understood or appreciated without an understanding of Greco-Roman rhetoric.

---

3. For a full discussion of this discourse see Witherington, *Letters to Philemon, the Colossians, and the Ephesians.*

Illustration Six:
Failure to recognize enthymemes (and their implied missing premise)
leads to misunderstanding NT arguments

We have discussed enthymemes at several junctures in this study, and it is fair to say that without recognizing both the form and implications of an enthymeme it becomes difficult if not impossible to see the logic of texts like Mark's Gospel, 1 John, or Titus and 1 Timothy, where we find more than a few of these compressed forms of rhetorical argument. The logical connection between statements will not be evident unless one knows to look for ways to figure out what the missing premise is. One example will have to suffice.

Enthymemes could be used for either ideological or ethical arguments. In 1 Timothy we see a good deal of the latter. For instance, some of the incomplete syllogisms in 1 Timothy are quite straightforward. We may consider for example 4:7–8: 1) You should train/discipline yourself for piety/godliness; 2) because while bodily training is helpful a little, training in piety is helpful for everything, including obtaining eternal life in the future; 3) suppressed premise—since you want eternal life, it is logical that you will pursue this spiritual discipline.

Another similarly paraenetic enthymeme can be detected in 6:17–19 with the following logic: 1) God provides for us richly not only for our enjoyment, but so we may be rich in good deeds; 2) one should not place ones hopes in earthly riches stored up in this age, but rather should be rich in good deeds; 3) this stores up riches for the future so one may obtain eternal life; 4) implied conclusion—surely even rich Christians want eternal life and so should adjust their attitude (haughtiness) and actions accordingly.

A further good example of this sort of ethical argumentation can be seen in 5:17–18: 1) those who labor in speaking and teaching are worthy of their wages; 2) because the Scripture says so, and it also says that even the ox should get some benefit from its labor; 3) unexpressed premise—elders are like laborers and therefore are worthy of the honor of being paid. Failure to see the hidden premise will inevitably lead to a misunderstanding of this or that part of the argument. Sometimes it even leads to accusations that the author is incoherent. This only shows that the critic is rhetorically uninformed.

Illustration Seven:
Overlooking the way personifications work in a rhetorical discourse

Many scholars do recognize that there are all sorts of personifications in the NT, because they accept that micro-rhetoric is part of the mostly undisputed literary devices found commonly in the NT. The problem is, they do not realize with personifications there were specific rhetorical rules on how to use them, rules that are being following by various NT writers.[4] We will take a somewhat detailed example from Titus 3:4.

Titus 3:4 in fact begins with a personification—"But when the Goodness and the Love of Humanity (*philanthropia*) of our Savior God appeared . . . ." God is depicted as a benefactor and the phrase goodness and love of humankind was a common one, almost a cliché in Paul's day used of patrons and benefactors (cf. Plutarch *Demosthenes* and *Cicero* 3; Isocrates *Evagoras* 43; Pliny the Younger *Panegyricus* 3.4). In Philo we find these terms used of God as patron as well (*On the Special Laws* 2.141; cf. *Letter of Aristeas* 208). Paul is deliberately modeling his language on the language of then extant ruler-cults in order to assert more impressively the claims of Christianity. We may compare, for example, Claudius's letter to the Alexandrians (*Greek Papyri in the British Museum* 1912.102) where he speaks of showering benefits (*philanthropa*) on the people so peace and harmony will reign in the kingdom; or Dio Cassius's reference to the Emperor's benevolence and goodness (*Roman History* 73.5.2); or Philo on Gaius Caligula (!) as *chrestos kai philanthropos* (*On the Embassy to Gaius* 67; cf. Onasander *General* 18.1 on how a general should show these two qualities on a surrendering city). What is especially striking is that Paul says this immediately *after* speaking of obedience to the governing authorities. They are to be obeyed, but they are not to be worshipped as gods, nor should one believe their rhetoric of divinity. Only in the case of God in Christ is that rhetoric apropos. This is the implication of the juxtaposition of 3:1–2 with 3:3–4.

The only God who had made a real "epiphany" in that era was Jesus. We may also contrast the tragic story of the divine Titan Prometheus who was chained to a rock and doomed to everlasting torture by pecking birds because of his way/habit of *philanthropia* to human beings (Aeschylus

4. In some ways this oversight is like the failure to recognize that in Luke's Gospel, the narrative parables, though certainly Jewish in origin and character, are set up according to the rhetorical rules of *parabolai*.

Prometheus Bound 11.28). Philo by contrast says that the God of Israel has *philanthropia* (*On the Virtues* 188). Paul is of course closer to Philo in his conception of the divine.

Personification was an important rhetorical device that one had to use cautiously without over doing it. It was known as a rhetorical figure, which involved giving a voice to things to which nature has denied it, according to Quintilian (*Institutio oratoria* 9.2.31). More specifically, it involved personifying abstract qualities and virtues such as Fame, Pleasure, Life and Death, or Virtue itself (9.2.36). The rhetorical function of this device is to highlight the importance of the quality being discussed, as is clearly the case in Titus. It is as if Paul were saying, "but when goodness and human love personified showed up in the person of our Savior, then . . . "

Sometimes however personifications are less easy to spot. Sometimes a personification could involve giving an abstract quality voice, by way of giving an animal a voice. For example, "sin" in Romans 7:7–13 is personified, and indeed the device is used in such a way that for one who knows rhetoric, it will appear reasonably clear that Paul is referring to a known story about Sin, when sin and temptation took a sentient form, namely as the snake. Once again, knowing how personifications worked in ancient discourses helps one grasp the thrust of the argument.

Illustration Eight:
Mistaking amplification for either redundancy or for saying
more than one thing

Scholars not familiar with rhetorical conventions have often complained about the sheer redundancy and lack of logical flow of some of the documents of the NT, particularly sermons like James, 1 John, or even Hebrews. Others, not wishing to accuse the NT writers of mere redundancy have instead tried to find small nuances of difference between sentences that only have slight variations of vocabulary or form. Amplification, however, is a rhetorical technique found in some abundance in the NT. Amplification quite adequately and accurately explains these issues logical flow and nuances. It will serve us well to reiterate what we said earlier in discussing the rhetoric of the sermon we call 1 John.

As we have already noted, amplification is a rhetorical technique mainly associated with epideictic rhetoric and of course with sermons or homilies. Instead of the *probatio* being a series of arguments proving a proposition or thesis statement, it is rather dedicated to amplifying, expanding, and expounding on certain key ideas and themes that are already familiar and accepted (see Aristotle *Rhetorica* 1.9.36; Quintilian *Institutio oratoria* 3.7.6). Watson notes, "The use of amplification indicates a careful working of the material and the need to be emphatic and clear in the face of the secessionist doctrine and practice to which his audience is subject. Far from being boringly *redundant*, the rhetor is carefully *emphatic*."[5] The very degree of emphatic repetition of key themes and ideas in 1 John shows just how concerned our author is about the need to strength the audience's embracing of these key values. These themes include the love of God, sin, proper behavior, and love of the brothers and sisters, to mention but a few.

What then are the amplification techniques that the author of 1 John uses?

1) The use of strong words such as "hate" and "murderers" (3:15).

2) The use of augmentation, a series of statements increasing in intensity leading to a climax (e.g., 2:2—not only is Jesus an atoning sacrifice for sins of the community but also for the sins of the whole world).

3) The use of *synkrisis* or comparison (e.g., human testimony is good, but God's testimony is greater [5:9]).

4) The use of accumulation, the piling up of words or phrases identical in meaning or all referring to the same object or subject (1:1–3—that which we have heard, seen, looked at, touched).

5) There are a panoply of figures of repetition used in 1 John, including the use of *expolito*, which refers to the technique of saying the same thing with slight variation or with equivalent terms (1:7, 9—cleansing us from all sin is later called cleansing us from all unrighteousness; on *expolito* see *Rhetorica ad Herennium* 4.42.54), or *conduplicatio*, which refers to the repetition of the same word or the same phrase, using the same part of speech, having the same function (2:12–14).

5. Watson, "Amplification Techniques," 122–23.

Lest we mistake what is going on in 1 John, none of this need mean our author has a very limited vocabulary. It means he is trying to be emphatic by means of repetition. In sum, *this redundancy is a rhetorical strategy, neither an accident, nor an invitation to over-exegete the small differences in the text, nor an excuse to accuse the author of lack of literary imagination.*

Illustration Nine:
Mistaking Asiatic rhetoric for mere verbal excess

One of the problems non-rhetorically trained scholars have, who like to see themselves as good evaluators of literary style and vocabulary, is that Asiatic rhetoric does not suit their aesthetic sensibilities. It does not fit modern literary canons like the notion that perspicuity and succinctness are chief virtues of a good style. Asiatic rhetoric, in other words is too rococo or baroque for some modern tastes. But the problem is that if one does not know Asiatic rhetoric, one will not realize 1) that this was a popular style in its day; and 2) it is deliberate, not the result of someone who cannot control their literary excesses. We can consider, for example, the case of 2 Peter.

To moderns like ourselves, on first glance, the style of 2 Peter will by and large seem to be an example of a person overcome with the exuberance of his own verbosity, loving rare words, the coining of terms, solemn, sonorous, and grandiloquent language and phrasing. Cicero tells us that in terms of "ornament," one should use rare words only occasionally, new words more frequently, and metaphors and tropes the most frequently of all (*De oratore* 3.153–55). We certainly find all of this and more in 2 Peter. There are some twenty-six metaphors in 2 Peter as identified by D. Watson, in addition to which we have a barrage of tropes—hyperbole, metonymy, synecdoche, onomatopoeia, and others.[6] This reminds us that this document was meant to be heard, not read, in the main. It is an oral document. There are several long periods that characterized Greek in the grand style—1:3–7; 2:4–10a; 2:12–14. Sometimes 1:19–20 and 3:1–4a are pointed to as well, but these latter two are not nearly as lengthy or convoluted as the first three mentioned.[7] In fact, 1:12–21 and 3:1–3 read much

---

6. Watson, *Invention, Arrangement, and Style,* 123–25.
7. See Callan, "The Style of the Second Letter of Peter," 212–13.

like the Greek of 1 Peter, which is simpler in style, though still Asiatic in tone.

Lack of a knowledge of Asiatic Greek and its great popularity in the first century and anachronistic applying of modern tastes to 2 Peter has led to the conclusion that the style is too elaborate, grandiose, baroque, or even artificial. To some extent, it should be noted, the ancients who were rhetorical experts preferred a more sedate and less florid and emotional style. Quintilian calls Asiatic style too inflated and empty (*Institutio oratoria* 12.10.16), but then he was a patrician training patricians to be orators. Cicero, having early on been trained in and being an aficionado of Asiatic style, seems to have changed his mind for pragmatic reasons. As he rose up the *cursus honorum*, and as he ingratiated himself with patricians, Cicero gradually toned down his use of the "eastern" style (see *Brutus* 13.51). Cicero was swimming against the tide of the cultural mainstream of popular rhetoric in making this stylistic adjustment in his rhetoric. But, Callan is clearly right when he stresses, "We can see that many negative assessments of style of 2 Peter are not evaluations of it according to the canons of style recognized by its author and readers. Instead, they are implicitly expressions of preference for a different style, like the criticism of Asianism in its own time."[8] Turning the matter around, Callan asks, what does the choice of the grand style tell us about our author's rhetorical purposes. He highlights several good points: 1) the use of the grand style indicates that the author sees himself as expressing powerful and important thoughts. The style suits the lofty subject matter; 2) writing in the grand style implies the author is primarily seeking to appeal to the emotions, not to inform the audience of things they do not already know. This comports well with the epideictic nature of this discourse; 3) the author wishes to arouse the audience to continue to develop their Christian virtues in light of the return of Christ.[9] In other words, a lofty subject deserved a grand style. Style was often a matter of choice, not a mere accident of one's individual vocabulary and grammar, and when one chose to use Asiatic Greek style and rhetoric on top of that, all kinds of things come into play that will not be apparent to those who do not recognize these conventions. There is no way to separate absolutely form from content when it comes to the NT, for the meaning of the words is of

8. Ibid., 223.
9. Ibid., 223–24.

course affected not only by how they are put together in a certain order, but also what conventions are being followed in forming the discourse in this or that manner.

Illustration Ten:
The importance of micro-rhetoric—recognizing a gradatio

For our last illustration of the difference knowing rhetoric makes in the interpretation of a NT text we focus on a small rhetorical device called a *sorites* or *gradatio*. Since we have not discussed this matter previously, we will deal with it in some detail, using the *gradatio* found in 2 Peter 1:5–7 as the taking off point, but referring to the examples in Romans 5 and Philippians 4 as well. This device is used to build to a climax with a stress on the last item in a list as the most important or needing most emphasis.

Without question, the rhetorical device being used in the virtue catalog in 2 Peter 1 is *sorites* or *gradatio*, providing us with an ascending chain of virtues that leads to the supreme virtue—Christian love. It is a device which involves repetition, something near to the heart of Asiatic rhetoricians. It takes the form A . . . B, B . . . C, C . . . D, and so on. Chains of virtues (and vices) were not uncommon in Hellenistic and Stoic philosophy of this era (cf. Seneca *Epistulae morales* 85.2; Maximus of Tyre *Philosophumena* 16.3b). The other example of this sort of rhetorical construction using virtues is found in Romans 5:3–5, which is similar enough to the *gradatio* in 2 Peter that one may wonder if the author of 2 Peter knew of the one in Romans. In later Christian literature, the *Acts of Peter* 2 is very similar and probably based on the *gradatio* in 2 Peter 1. We may also compare *Barnabas* 2.2.3 and *1 Clement* 62.2.

We should also especially compare this list in 2 Peter 1 to Philippians 4:8 with which it shares the characteristic of having a mixture of Hellenistic and more Christian virtues. With 2 Corinthians 8:7, it shares in common a list that begins with faith and ends with Christian love. It needs to be borne in mind that in some cases in these lists the author has taken terms that are prominent in Hellenistic lists. Interestingly "knowledge," which was often listed either first or last on the list, indicating its preeminence, here is in the middle of the pack—faith and love are more important. Words like *pistis* do occur in the pagan lists, but with the very different meaning of "loyalty" or even "faithfulness." The list in 2 Peter then has something old, something new, and something borrowed but transformed into another concept. It would have been striking to the ancients to have a list with *both* mutual affection between brothers and sisters and some other kind of love listed. There are early Jewish chain-link lists of virtues as well, the most similar in form of which is from Rabbi Phineas b. Jair (circa AD 90) which reads:

> Zeal leads to cleanliness, and cleanliness leads to purity, and purity leads to self-restraint, and self-restraint leads to sanctity, and sanctity leads to humility, and humility leads to the fear of sin, and the fear of sin leads to piety, and piety leads to the Holy Spirit, and the Holy Spirit leads to the resurrection of the dead (*m. Sotah* 9.15).[10]

To this, one may wish to compare Wisdom 6:17–20, which moves from wisdom to a kingdom.

In some ways this is just the opposite of our list, which presupposes the audience already has the Holy Spirit who is helping produce these virtues in the believer. Ritual purity is not an issue at all in our list in 2 Peter. We may also compare the near contemporary list found in *Shepherd of Hermas, Mandate* 5.2–4, but there, unlike here, it is a list of vices that have a snowballing effect with one engendering the next (e.g., from foolishness is engendered bitterness). This, however, is not the nature of the list in 2 Peter. Bauckham points to *Shepherd of Hermas, Vision* 3.8.7, which does use the *sorites* form, begins with faith, and ends with love. Hermas lists seven virtues, 2 Peter lists eight. But, in that list, once more, one virtue produces the next, which, despite Bauckham's argument, does not seem to be the case in 2 Peter.[11]

What is not at all clear is whether Bauckham is right in translating the key verb *epichorēgēsate* as "produce," indicating that each virtue is the means of producing the next. There are various problems with this view as J. B. Mayor demonstrates at length.[12] The basic idea of this verb is "one who supplies, furnishes, provides, or makes possible something originally"; it was used, for example, of a financial backer of a Greek chorus and drama. He was a provider, not a producer. Furthermore, in 1 Peter 4:11 the basic form of this verb means "supply" or "provide." God provides strength. Again, in 2 Corinthians 9:10, where we have forms of the verb

10. See the detailed discussion in Fischel, "The Uses of Sorites."
11. Bauckham, *Jude and 2 Peter,* 175–76.
12. Mayor, *The Epistle of St. Jude,* 90–91.

with and without the *epi* prefix, the idea is the same—God supplies. In 2 Corinthians 9:10 "supplies" is supplemented with "and will increase." The idea is one of providing and adding to, but not *producing*. In Theophilus *To Autolycus* 73b it means "to add further supplies" or "to provide more than was expected." In 2 Peter, to "supply" further means to "add more." In addition, it is not at all clear how some of these virtues could be said to be produced by the preceding virtue, but it is not difficult to see how they could be added to them. Thus, we may have a poetic or rhetorical use of *en de* to express addition not production.

What the author is saying is not "by virtue produce knowledge," but rather, "to virtue add knowledge." We must not confuse the interlocking rhetorical structure with a chain of dependent causes or ideas. All of these qualities are things Christians should add to their cache. There is a general progression here from faith through knowledge to affection to love, but this is not because one virtue is produced by the other, but because the author has the foundational virtue first, and the greatest or climactic virtues last. What especially makes 2 Peter 1:5–7 stand out is that even more than in the Philippian list, our author chooses to use terms that were more directly accessible to those who knew the buzzwords of Hellenistic moral philosophy—*aretē, enkrateia, eusebeia, philadelphia*. The terms more characteristic of Christian moral discourse were of course *pistis* in the sense of faith/trust, *hypomonē* in the sense of endurance/hope, and of course *agapē*

J. Daryl Charles makes the point that what the author is doing is linking the theological virtues to the natural ones, the ones admired and manifested in the wider culture.[13] He sums up as follows:

> Whereas the acquisition of virtue in pagan ethics is an absolute good and the highest human goal, for the Christian it is evidence of deeper theological realities .... Because God through Christ has made provision for the ethical life—and this *abundantly*—does not mean that there is no cooperation in the ethical enterprise. To the contrary, the readers have a necessary part to play: "For this reason make every effort to supply . . . ." Arranged in pairs and then distinguished for rhetorically stylized effect, the virtues build upon faith . . . and culminate in love . . . . The purpose of the catalog is its demarcation of exemplary—and by implication,

13. Charles, *Virtue amidst Vice*, 126–52.

unacceptable—behavior . . . . At bottom, Christians are to live a life *worthy* of their calling.[14]

A *sorites* tends to climax in the supreme virtue or vice—which here is *agapē*, and it may be implied that this virtue encompasses and crowns all the rest, being the context out of which the rest are manifested and the manner of their manifestation. "Faith" appears to be the basic trust in God through Christ or belief in the Gospel, which results in such trust, not a reference to some body of doctrines. *Aretē* is indeed a term often used in Hellenistic lists, meaning virtue, or perhaps excellence, the proper fulfillment of anything (cf. Phil 4:8). In Hellenistic thought, it involves the achievement of human excellence, not obedience to God. Knowledge is mentioned next and possibly should be distinguished from *epignōseōs* (cf. vv. 2–3), which could mean for the author "that fundamental knowledge of God in Christ which makes a person a Christian."[15]

The reason for hesitating on this point is that in Asiatic rhetoric one often, for the sake of "invention," varies the word one uses, saying the very same thing in slightly different terms. Possibly though, *gnōsis* here means practical wisdom necessary for Christian living and progressively acquired. *Egkrateian* means self-control and is another characteristic Hellenistic virtue (cf. Aristotle *Nichmachean Ethics* 7.1–11), which usually is taken to mean reason winning out over passion. Here the term is particularly appropriate in view of the apparent antinomianism or libertinism of the false teachers. *Hypomonē* means a steadfastness, and may refer to endurance under pressure, or persecution, but may be allied to endurance in a Christian way despite temptation. *Eusebeia* is yet another characteristic Hellenistic virtue—literally it means "good worship," but it normally has the broader sense of piety or godliness, and in a pagan context it means giving the gods their due in respect, in sacrifice, and perhaps also to some extent in living a life of virtue.[16] In a Christian context it refers to the godliness that necessarily entails both honoring God in worship, and also in one's behavior. *Philadelphia*, "brotherly or sisterly affection," occurs elsewhere in ethical lists only in 1 Peter 3:8; per-

14. Ibid., 157.

15. Bauckham, *Jude and 2 Peter*, 186.

16. One of the notable ways 2 Peter is like the Pastorals is in its use of Hellenistic virtue language. Our author is clearly writing at a time in which he believes it is still possible for Christians to be good citizens and model some of the widely accepted virtues of the Greco-Roman culture, while also modeling the distinctively Christ-like traits.

haps our author was led to include it here as a result of his knowledge of Petrine teaching. It is not to be confused with *agapē* a more distinctively Christian virtue.

One of the things that becomes clear from examining a text like 2 Peter 1, is that the NT writers were not afraid to "plunder the Egyptians" or "fight fire with fire." By this I mean they did not hesitate to use any and all points of contact with the larger culture as tools to help persuade non-believers to become Christians. Asiatic style, Greco-Roman rhetoric, picking and choosing from common Hellenistic virtues, and philosophical buzzwords were all fair game in the service of the faith of Jesus Christ.

We could continue to multiply illustrations of both macro- and micro-rhetoric in the NT demonstrating how a knowledge of rhetoric not merely affects the way we look at and interpret the text, but in some cases is a pre-requisite to properly understanding a particular text at all. We could talk for instance about how Paul uses inverted and ironic self-praise in 2 Corinthians 10–13 in order to shame his opponents, the "super-apostles," who are the true braggarts. We could point out how at every turn Paul is following the rhetorical rules set out by Plutarch and others about how to do "inoffensive self-praise." In other words, the apostle who regularly says "let those who boast, boast in the Lord," is not having a momentary lapse of reason and good judgment in 2 Corinthians 10–13 by letting his ego get the best of him.[17]

As we have stressed at various points, early Christianity was an evangelistic religion at heart and it would have been foolish indeed if it had not availed itself of the tools already in place that could be used to persuade a person or an audience about Jesus Christ. To be sure, the concern for truth meant that mere sophistic rhetoric or rhetoric that was mere verbal eloquence without substantive content would be eschewed. The NT writers did not say things merely because they liked the sound of this or that combination of words or were merely trying to impress some audience with their eloquence. Rhetoric in the NT is never used merely as a form of entertainment or ornamentation.

Whether simple or complex, whether elementary or advanced, we have found the use of rhetoric in the Gospels, in Acts, in the epistolary corpus of the NT, and indeed it can be found in the book of Revelation

17. See Witherington, *Conflict and Community in Corinth.*

as well.[18] There is no sort or literary type of NT literature from which Greco-Roman rhetoric is entirely absent. It even affects the most Jewish of materials in the NT, for example the way Luke presents Jesus' parables. This in turn should lead to one final and obvious conclusion.

While by no means the only essential tool for interpreting the NT, historically oriented rhetorical criticism is certainly one of the most essential tools if we are to hear and understand the NT documents as their authors intended them to be heard and understood. "Let those with two good ears, hear what the rhetorician says to the congregation."

QUESTIONS FOR REFLECTION

1. If understanding rhetoric is essential for understanding the NT, what does this imply in regard to the larger need for historical study of the NT if one is to grasp its meaning and emphases?

2. What sort of misunderstandings are possible or probable if one is not assessing a NT text in light of rhetorical conventions? Could theological or ethical errors result?

3. What goes wrong when one mis-identifies the particular rhetorical species of a Pauline discourse, such as Galatians?

4. Why is epideictic rhetoric of a more generic character? Does this make it more universally applicable or not?

18. On which see Witherington, *Revelation.*

The Rhetoric of Preaching, the Preaching of Rhetoric

In her landmark study, *Christianity and the Rhetoric of Empire*, Averil Cameron shows at length just how very much the increasingly Gentile Church over the course of the first four Christian centuries developed their own special ways of using Greco-Roman Rhetoric to their advantage, with the end result being that Christians eventually persuaded a majority of persons in the Roman Empire that being a Christian was the best of all possible religious options, especially if one wanted to have a nice afterlife. One acute reviewer on amazon.com had this to say about Cameron's crucial study:

> At the time Averil Cameron's "Christianity and the Rhetoric of Empire" came into the academic world the study of rhetoric as a historical method was still in its infancy. Much of the type of work done in ancient history ever since has changed in part due to the power of the ideas found in Cameron's insightful lectures. Any student of classical history and Christianity has to face, sooner or later, one of the greatest riddles of all history: how an eastern, small, and by all accounts marginal religion was capable not only of surviving, but ultimately of succeeding where other alternatives (and there were many) inexorably failed?
>
> Ancient Christian historians such as Eusebius had no problem with attributing the victory to God, leaving little doubt that every event was carefully coordinated and supervised by the Divine being. But what Eusebius et al. did not considered, or rather were unmoved to consider, was how much of the triumph of Christianity had to do with the way it created its own language, or, to borrow from Cameron's terminology, its own "discourse." Christianity is a faith with a message, and, if there is one thing that Christians are supposed to do well, that would be to express that message in a way that would be intelligible to all.

> The paradox, which Cameron continuously mentions, re-
> sides in that, for all its universalistic and inclusivistic features,
> Christianity could not coexist without critiquing, and ultimately
> defeating, other types of discourses. The God of the Christians is
> not one god, nor even the first god, among many; He is the only
> God or he is no god at all. How a religion that has such a exclu-
> sivist belief at its heart was able to "conquer" such a pluralistic
> culture as the Roman Empire remains one of the most fascinating
> topics any historian could possible choose to study; and among
> those who do, Cameron's work remains a must read.[1]

This is in fact a useful summary of Cameron's book. What Cameron
demonstrates at length is that early Church history, so far as its public
and private discourse was concerned, continued to be indebted to Greco-
Roman rhetoric through and through. We should not think then that
the rhetoric in the NT was an isolated phenomenon which died out after
the first century AD. To the contrary, the rhetoric of early Christianity
only increased over time, and its greatest practitioners, such as John
Chrysostom, recognized in the NT authors, their mentors, and forebears
in the use of the rhetorical arts.[2] This leads us to some important concluding observations.

First, it should have become apparent when we examined the
preaching summaries in Acts, that if we want to understand the NT as
discourse or preaching, then it is essential to understand ancient rhetoric.
This is readily apparent in the other documents that most easily can be
called sermons, such as James, 1 John, or Hebrews, but it applies to the
discourses of Paul, Peter, and others as well. It is then something of a
mystery why so many modern students of homiletics are never even told
about the ancient art of preaching and persuasion, which is to say rhetoric, *when it is the rhetorically saturated NT that they are most expected to
preach.* As the old commentator once said "these things ought not to be."
Rhetoric helps us extensively to understand not only the preaching of the
NT era, but of all the centuries leading up to the high Middle Ages, and
even beyond. As it turns out, numerous of the Reformers were rhetori-

1. Guillermo, "A thought-provoking masterpiece . . . ." I have corrected the grammar
and spelling a bit.

2. See for example the very helpful study of Mitchell, *The Heavenly Trumpet,* which
shows at length not only the rhetoric of John's preaching but also his profound reverence
for and indebtedness to Paul's rhetoric.

cians as well (e.g., Melanchthon), and knew perfectly well the rhetorical character of their NT canon.

Secondly, too often, and especially since the Protestant Reformation, a hard line has been drawn between the "apostolic" period of the first century AD, when the NT documents were written, and subsequent church history. The study of the history of the use of rhetoric by early Christians shows this is a mistake. There were important elements of continuity between apostolic and post-apostolic Christianity. One of the most obvious of these is the use of the ancient art of persuasion to aid in making converts. Cameron has opened the door to the study of this continuity, but few have as of yet walked through it.

Thirdly, in our own age, when we are increasingly made aware of the need for the critique of culture, if the Gospel is to do its leavening work in society, we could certainly use more sociological studies of how ancient Christian rhetoric worked. To what degree was it world-affirming and to what degree world-denying? We have seen strong elements of adopting and adapting Hellenistic virtue lists and "Christianizing" them in some of the rhetoric of the NT. We could also note the anti-Imperial rhetoric that is not so subtle at places in the NT (e.g., 2 Thess 2; Revelation). Clearly there was a tension between being a good citizen in the world, and not being "of the world" in terms of its idolatries and immorality that led to a delicate balancing in both the discourse and the praxis of the early church.

Fourthly, it would be useful if modern homileticians were well schooled in ancient rhetoric and its handbooks, for example, Quintilian's classic *Institutio oratoria*. Here they would find clues as to why the NT material looks like it does, why early Christians preferred certain types of rhetoric, what sort of gestures and voicings were deemed appropriate, and a host of other useful information. The modern rhetoric of preaching would do well to learn much from the ancient preaching of rhetoric.

Lastly, though human nature is perhaps much the same over the course of time and history, human psychology and what one culture deems appropriate and persuasive certainly changes over time and across cultures. The study of ancient rhetoric shows that ancient orators knew that for a word to be a word on target, it most often needed to be audience-specific. This is why some NT documents reflect Asiatic rhetoric and some do not. Some NT documents offer complex rhetorical arguments, and some do not. But, it needs to be asked before the NT is preached—*do these sorts of arguments and discourses have the same effect on modern audiences as they did on ancient ones? If one simply repeats the patterns found in the NT, are they equally or less likely to persuade a modern audience as they did ancient ones? How do modern pluralistic culture and its biases and assumptions differ from the pluralistic cultures of the NT era?* In other words, the more indigenous the rhetoric is seen to be in the NT, the more it raises the questions about how that message can be proclaimed in a very different culture and time today.

Throughout the NT we hear reverberating the basic conviction that the proclamation of the Gospel, of God's living Word, is an unleashing of the power of God for salvation (see Rom 1:16–17 and cf. 1 Thess 2:13—"when you received the Word of God . . . you accepted it not as a human word, but as it actually is, the Word of God"). According to Paul and others, it was not mere rhetorical skill that persuaded people but the divine content of the message; even so, the content needed the assistance of the Spirit to convince dulled and sinful human minds. This in turn reminds us that even when we have plumbed the depths of NT rhetoric we will not have fully grasped the mystery of why so many persons became Christians in the first four centuries of the Christian era. Perhaps after all it is still true today as it has been in the past, that "the truth will set you free."

Annotated Bibliography

There are now several useful guidebooks one can consult on rhetorical criticism. The following can be especially recommended:

Kennedy, George A. *New Testament Interpretation through Rhetorical Criticism.* Chapel Hill, NC: University of North Carolina Press, 1984. [holds pride of place because it really helped to get the ball rolling in the discussion, especially in the US]

Mack, Burton L., and Vernon K. Robbins. *Patterns of Persuasion in the Gospels.* Sonoma, CA: Polebridge, 1989. [somewhat less helpful, though still pushing us in the right direction at least in regard to the use of rhetorical *chreia* in the Gospels]

More recently we have the work of Carl Joachim Classen, *Rhetorical Criticism of the New Testament* (Boston: Brill Academic, 2002), which has various helpful chapters but spends more time on the history of rhetorical interpretation of the NT from Melanchthon forwards than on the actual analysis of the rhetoric of the NT. There are, however, a couple of useful chapters on Paul and the Gospels and rhetoric, and an interesting rhetorical reading of Titus is included. The problem however is that Classen does not seem to understand the flexible nature of the form of a discourse in any of the three rhetorical species (forensic, epideictic, and deliberative), and therefore fails to come to grips with the use of what I call "macro-rhetoric" in Paul's letters, including Titus.

That the discussion has burgeoned and been fruitful can be seen from even a cursory examination of the very helpful volume from Duane F. Watson, *The Rhetoric of the New Testament: A Bibliographic Survey* (Tools for Biblical Study 8; Blandford Forum: Deo, 2006), which lays before us almost every useful article, monograph, or book on the subject published during the first twenty or so years of the discussion.

There is now a collection of essays edited by Stanley E. Porter and Dennis L. Stamps, *Rhetorical Criticism and the Bible* (Journal for the Study of the New Testament, Supplement Series 195; Sheffield: Sheffield Academic, 2002). Like all collections of essays, some are more helpful than others. Duane Watson in this volume in an essay entitled "Why We Need Socio-Rhetorical Commentary and What It Might Look Like," (pp. 129–57) calls for us to do commentaries following Vernon Robbin's rubric of organizing materials under the headings Introduction, Inner Texture, Intertexture, Social and Cultural Texture, Ideological Texture, and Sacred Texture (see Robbin's influential *The Tapestry of Early Christian Discourse: Rhetoric, Society and Ideology* [London: Routledge, 1996]). While I do not have a problem with approaching the NT text in this manner and it can certainly produce some helpful insights, from a historical point of view, this approach is problematic. It involves imposing modern analytical categories on the text that the NT writers neither knew nor used. A prior exercise should be examining the NT in light of rhetorical methodologies the authors could actually have known and used. A further problem with this approach is its dependency on certain modern theories of meaning, epistemology (how we know what we know), and the role of the reader in the process of forming meaning (not unlike some of the things said in reader-response criticism). In other words, this methodology is indebted to the school of New Rhetoric, which, while drawing on ancient rhetoric, goes well beyond it in various directions, *and most problematically goes against the theories and assertions about meaning that the NT writers both assumed and articulated.* Most particularly it involves an implicit denial of the theory or theology of revelation that the NT writers assumed and on the basis of which they operated (see Ben Witherington III, *The Living Word of God: Rethinking the Theology of the Bible* [Waco: Baylor University Press, 2007]).

Two massive handbooks bear witness not only to the influence of 'new rhetoric' on the discussion, but also to the methodological confusion created by drawing on it without asking and seeking to answer the proper historical questions first:

Lausberg, Heinrich. *Handbook of Literary Rhetoric: A Foundation for Literary Study.* Edited by David E. Orton and R. Dean Anderson. Leiden: Brill, 1997. [a translation of the 1973 2nd German edition]

Porter, Stanley E., editor. *Handbook of Classical Rhetoric in the Hellenistic Period, 330 B.C.–A.D. 400.* Leiden: Brill, 1997.

Shall we approach rhetorical criticism as a subset of modern literary criticism of the Bible or as a form of historical criticism and historical analysis? If these are the choices, this companion can be said to follow the latter approach, which is also used by Hans Dieter Betz and Margaret M. Mitchell (see especially the introductory discussion about historical rhetorical criticism in Mitchell's *Paul and the Rhetoric of Reconciliation: An Exegetical Investigation of the Language and Composition of 1 Corinthians* [Louisville: Westminster John Knox, 1993]).

In this particular guide book, we discussed the NT in light of ancient Greco-Roman rhetoric and its categories. In addition, when we dealt in passing with social phenomena (since the use of rhetoric is indeed an ancient social phenomenon), we focused on social history, not various modern sociological theories and their categories. The phrase socio-rhetorical criticism referred to the use of these approaches and methods, not to the inter-disciplinary and complex modern approach of Vernon Robbins and those who have followed him. A very fine introductory guide to the distinction and discussions can be found in David E. Aune, *The Westminster Dictionary of New Testament and Early Christian Literature and Rhetoric* (Louisville: Westminster John Knox, 2003; see especially 414–25 and the bibliographical materials there).

The present bibliography is not meant to be comprehensive. Duane Watson has already provided us with such a bibliography (see above). Rather, the following are selected studies to help the reader further explore rhetoric in the NT.

For those looking for helpful introductions to the rhetoric of whole NT books, I would commend the Eerdmans socio-rhetorical commentary series, which I have been instigating for the last fifteen years. In addition to the published volumes listed below, there are now volumes under contract on Philippians (Duane F. Watson), 1 Peter (Todd Still), Gospel of John (John Painter), and Revelation (David A. deSilva).

deSilva, David A. *Perseverance in Gratitude: A Socio-Rhetorical Commentary on the Epistle "to the Hebrews."* Grand Rapids: Eerdmans, 2000.

Witherington, Ben III. *Conflict and Community in Corinth: A Socio-Rhetorical Commentary on 1 and 2 Corinthians.* Grand Rapids: Eerdmans, 1995.

———. *The Acts of the Apostles: A Socio-Rhetorical Commentary.* Grand Rapids: Eerdmans, 1997.

———. *The Gospel of Mark: A Socio-Rhetorical Commentary.* Grand Rapids: Eerdmans, 2001.

———. *Paul's Letter to the Romans: A Socio-Rhetorical Commentary*. With Darlene Hyatt. Grand Rapids: Eerdmans, 2004.

———. *1 and 2 Thessalonians: A Socio-Rhetorical Commentary*. Grand Rapids: Eerdmans, 2006.

———. *The Letters to Philemon, the Colossians, and the Ephesians: A Socio-Rhetorical Commentary on the Captivity Epistles*. Grand Rapids: Eerdmans, 2007.

One should also see the three-volume series I have produced for InterVarsity Press:

Witherington, Ben III. *Letters and Homilies for Hellenized Christians*. Vol. 1, *A Socio-Rhetorical Commentary on Titus, 1–2 Timothy, and 1–3 John*. Downers Grove, IL: InterVarsity, 2006.

———. *Letters and Homilies for Jewish Christians: A Socio-Rhetorical Commentary on Hebrews, James and Jude*. Downers Grove, IL: InterVarsity, 2007.

———. *Letters and Homilies for Hellenized Christians*. Vol. 2, *A Socio-Rhetorical Commentary on 1–2 Peter*. Downers Grove, IL: InterVarsity, 2008.

There are, in addition, individual commentaries in "non-rhetorical" series that, nonetheless, do some or much rhetorical analysis. Here is a brief list:

Achtemeier, Paul J. *1 Peter: A Commentary on First Peter*. Hermeneia. Minneapolis: Fortress, 1996.

Aletti, Jean-Noël. *Saint Paul: Épître aux Colossiens*. Etudes bibliques 20. Paris: Gabalda, 1993.

Attridge, Harold W. *The Epistle to the Hebrews*. Hermeneia: A Critical and Historical Commentary on the Bible. Philadelphia: Fortress, 1989.

Betz, Hans Dieter. *Galatians: A Commentary on Paul's Letter to the Churches in Galatia*. Philadelphia: Fortress, 1979. [This is the commentary that really began the modern attempts to read whole NT documents rhetorically]

Bockmuehl, Markus. *The Epistle to the Philippians*. Black's New Testament Commentary. Peabody, MA: Hendrickson, 1998.

Brosend II, William F. *James and Jude*. New Cambridge Bible Commentary. Cambridge: Cambridge University Press, 2004.

Hays, Richard B. *First Corinthians*. Interpretation, a Bible Commentary for Teaching and Preaching. Louisville: Westminster John Knox, 1997.

Jewett, R. *Romans: A Commentary*. Hermeneia. Minneapolis: Fortress, 2006.

Johnson, Luke Timothy. "James." In *The New Interpreter's Bible*, edited by Leander E. Keck, 12:175–225. Nashville: Abingdon, 1998. [This is a simplified form of Johnson's much more useful volume, *The Letter of James*. Anchor Bible 37A. NY: Doubleday, 1995.]

Lincoln, Andrew T. *Ephesians*. Word Biblical Commentary 42. Waco: Word, 1990.

———. *The Gospel according to Saint John.* Black's New Testament Commentary. Peabody, MA: Hendrickson, 2005.

Longenecker, Richard N. *Galatians.* Word Biblical Commentary 41. Waco: Word, 1990.

Martyn, James Louis. *Galatians.* Anchor Bible 33A. NY: Doubleday, 1997.

Menken, Maarten J.J. *2 Thessalonians: Facing the End with Sobriety.* New Testament Readings. New York: Routledge, 1994.

Neyrey, J. H. *2 Peter, Jude.* Anchor Bible 37c. NY: Doubleday, 1993.

Pokorný, Petr. *Colossians: A Commentary.* Peabody, MA: Hendrickson, 1990.

Thiselton, Anthony C. *The First Epistle to the Corinthians.* New International Greek Testament Commentary. Grand Rapids: Eerdmans, 2000.

Wanamaker, Charles A. *The Epistles to the Thessalonians.* New International Greek Testament Commentary. Grand Rapids: Eerdmans, 1990.

Watson, Duane F. "The Second Letter of Peter." In *The New Interpreter's Bible,* edited by Leander E. Keck, 12:321–61. Nashville: Abingdon, 1998.

Witherington, Ben III. *Friendship and Finances in Philippi: The Letter of Paul to the Philippians.* New Testament in Context. Valley Forge, PA: Trinity, 1994.

———. *Revelation.* Cambridge: Cambridge U. Press, 2001. [D. F. Watson's rhetorical commentary on 1–3 John will be in this series, which I edit].

There are frankly far too many excellent monographs and articles on the rhetoric of this or that part of the NT to list in full. Watson has listed the articles in full. Here we list some of the most influential rhetorical monographs:

Campbell, Barth L. *Honor, Shame and the Rhetoric of 1 Peter.* SBL Dissertations Series 160. Atlanta: Scholars, 1998.

Cosby, Michael R. *The Rhetorical Composition of Function of Hebrews 11: In Light of Example Lists in Antiquity.* Macon, GA: Mercer University Press, 1988.

Donelson, Lewis R. *Pseudepigraphy and Ethical Argument in the Pastoral Epistles.* Hermeneutische Untersuchungen zur Theologie 22. Tübingen: Mohr Siebeck, 1984.

Duff, Paul B. *Who Rides the Beast?: Prophetic Rivalry and the Rhetoric of Crisis in the Churches of the Apocalypse.* Oxford: Oxford University Press, 2001.

Harding, Mark. *Tradition and Rhetoric in the Pastoral Epistles.* Studies in Biblical Literature 3. New York: Lang, 1998.

Jeal, Roy R. *Integrating Theology and Ethics in Ephesians: Ethos of Communication.* Studies in Bible and Early Christianity 43. Lewiston, NY: Mellen, 2000.

Litfin, A. Duane. *St. Paul's Theology of Proclamation: 1 Corinthians 1–4 and Greco-Roman Rhetoric.* Society of New Testament Studies Monograph Series 79. Cambridge: Cambridge University Press, 1994. [One of the best introductions to the history of rhetoric and its relevance for NT, and especially Pauline studies]

Long, Frederick J. *Ancient Rhetoric and Paul's Apology: The Compositional Unity of 2 Corinthians.* Society of New Testament Studies Monograph Series 131. Cambridge: Cambridge University Press, 2004.

Longenecker, Bruce W. *Rhetoric at the Boundaries: The Art and Theology of New Testament Chain-Link Transitions.* Waco: Baylor University Press, 2005. [One of the best volumes that introduces us to how rhetoric helps shape narrative in the NT]

Lyons, George. *Pauline Autobiography: Toward a New Understanding.* SBL Dissertation Series 73. Atlanta: Scholars Press, 1985. [Another outstanding monograph involving several of Paul's letters]

Mitchell, Margaret M. *Paul and the Rhetoric of Reconciliation: An Exegetical Investigation of the Language and Composition of 1 Corinthians.* Louisville: Westminster John Knox, 1993. [In my view this is the best and most thorough of all the scholarly monographs on rhetoric in the NT]

Puskas, Charles B. *The Letters of Paul: An Introduction.* Good News Studies 25. Collegeville, MN: Liturgical, 1993. [includes an introduction to the rhetoric of each of Paul's letters]

Rothschild, Clare K. *Luke-Acts and the Rhetoric of History: An Investigation of Early Christian Historiography.* WUNT 2/175. Tübingen: Mohr Siebeck, 2004. [first-rate thesis on Luke's rhetorical historiography]

Thurén, Lauri. *Argument and Theology in 1 Peter: The Origins of Christian Paraenesis.* Journal for the Study of the New Testament Supplement Series 114. Sheffield: Sheffield Academic, 1995.

Watson, Duane F. *Invention, Arrangment, and Style: Rhetorical Criticism of Jude and 2 Peter.* SBL Dissertation Series 104. Atlanta: Scholars, 1988.

There have been numerous conferences on rhetoric with published papers of varying quality and even some *festschriften* of note on the subject, for example the volume edited by D. F. Watson, *Persuasive Artistry: Studies in New Testament Rhetoric in Honor of George A Kennedy,* (Sheffield: JSOT Press, 1991). The conference papers have tended to be edited by those most involved in the field such as Watson or Stanley Porter and can be readily found in Watson's extensive bibliographical volume, *The Rhetoric of the New Testament* (Blandford Forum: Deo, 2006).

The field continues to expand with an increasing number of doctoral dissertations that further the discussion. One of note is the first class work of David Michael Young, "Whoever has Ears to Hear: The Discourses of Jesus in Mark as Primary Rhetoric of the Greco-Roman Period" (PhD diss., Vanderbilt University, 1994), which should have been published long ago. Even more recently there is the dissertation of R. Simon who demonstrates at length the rhetorical devices and strategies in Luke's birth narrative. This has recently been completed at Bristol under my and John Nolland's supervision.

Works Cited

Achtemeier, Paul J. *1 Peter: A Commentary on First Peter*. Hermeneia. Minneapolis: Fortress, 1996.

Aletti, Jean-Noël. "Rm 7.7-25 encore une fois: enjeux et propositions." *New Testament Studies* 48 (2002) 358-76.

———. "The Rhetoric of Romans 5-8." In *The Rhetorical Analysis of Scripture: Essays from the 1995 London Conference*, edited by Stanley E. Porter and Thomas H. Olbricht, 294-308. Journal for the Study of the New Testament Supplements 146. Sheffield: Sheffield Academic, 1997.

Aune, David E. *The New Testament in its Literary Environment*. Library of Early Christianity 8. Philadelphia: Westminster John Knox, 1987.

Barrett, C. K. *The Epistle to the Romans*. Rev. ed. Black's New Testament Commentary. Peabody, MA: Hendrickson, 1991.

———. *The New Testament Background: Selected Documents*. Rev. ed. San Francisco: Harper, 1989.

Bauckham, Richard J. "James and the Gentiles (Acts 15.13-21)." In *History, Literature, and Society in the Book of Acts*, edited by Ben Witherington III, 154-84. Cambridge: Cambridge University Press, 1996.

———. *Jesus and the Eyewitnesses: The Gospels as Eyewitness Testimony*. Grand Rapids: Eerdmans, 2006.

———. *2 Peter and Jude*. Word Biblical Commentary 50. Waco: Word, 1983.

Betz, Hans Dieter. *Galatians: A Commentary on Paul's Letter to the Churches in Galatia*. Hermeneia. Philadelphia: Fortress, 1979.

Black, C. Clifton. "The Rhetorical Form of the Hellenistic Jewish and Early Christian Sermon." *Harvard Theological Review* 81 (1988) 1-18.

Bonner, Stanley F. *Education in Ancient Rome: From the Elder Cato to the Younger Pliny*. Berkeley: University of California Press, 1977.

Booth, A. D. "Elementary and Secondary Education in the Roman Empire." *Florilegium* 1 (1979) 1-14.

Bowersock, G. W. *Greek Sophists in the Roman Empire*. Oxford: Clarendon, 1969.

Bray, Gerald, editor. *Romans*. Ancient Christian Commentary on Scripture 6. Downers Grove, IL: InterVarsity, 1998.

Burridge, Richard A. *What Are the Gospels?: A Comparison with Graeco-Roman Biography*. Cambridge: Cambridge University Press, 1992.

Byrne, Brendan. *Romans*. Sacra Pagina 6. Collegeville, MN: Liturgical, 1996.

Cadbury, H. J. "Four Features of Lukan Style." In *Studies in Luke-Acts: Essays Presented in Honor of Paul Schubert*, edited by Leander Keck and J. Louis Martyn, 87–102. London: SPCK, 1968.

————. *Style and Literary Method of Luke*. Cambridge: Harvard University Press, 1920. Reprint, Eugene, OR: Wipf and Stock, 2001.

Caird, George B. "The Exegetical Method of the Epistle to the Hebrews." *Canadian Journal of Theology* 5 (1959) 44–51.

Callan, Terrance. "The Style of the Second Letter of Peter." *Biblica* 84 (2003) 202–24.

Cameron, Averil. *Christianity and the Rhetoric of Empire: The Development of Christian Discourse*. Sather Classical Lectures 55. Berkeley: University of California Press, 1991.

Campbell, Barth L. *Honor, Shame, and the Rhetoric of 1 Peter*. SBL Dissertation Series 160. Atlanta: Scholars, 1998.

————. "Rhetorical Design in 1 Timothy 4." *Bibliotheca Sacra* 154 (1997) 189–204.

Cantarella, Eva. *Pandora's Daughters: The Role and Status of Women in Greek and Roman Antiquity*. Translated by Maureen B. Fant. Baltimore: John Hopkins University Press, 1987.

Charles, J. Daryl. *Virtue amidst Vice: The Catalog of Virtues in 2 Peter 1*. Journal for the Study of the New Testament Supplement Series 150. Sheffield: Sheffield Academic, 1997.

Clark, Donald Lemen. *Rhetoric in Greco-Roman Education*. New York: Columbia University Press, 1957.

Clarke, M. L. *Higher Education in the Ancient World*. Albuquerque: University of New Mexico Press, 1971.

Classen, Carl Joachim. *Rhetorical Criticism of the New Testament*. Reprint, Boston: Brill Academic, 2002.

Collins, John J., and Gregory E. Sterling, editors. *Hellenism in the Land of Israel*. Christianity and Judaism in Antiquity. South Bend, IN: Notre Dame University Press, 2001.

Cosby, Michael R. *The Rhetorical Composition and Function of Hebrews 11: In Light of Example Lists in Antiquity*. Macon: Mercer University Press, 1988.

Cranfield, C. E. B. *Romans 1–8*. International Critical Commentary. Edinburgh: T. & T. Clark, 1975.

Deidun, T. J. "Romans." In *A Dictionary of Biblical Interpretation*, edited by R. J. Coggins and J. L. Houlden, 601–4. Philadelphia: Trinity, 1990.

Deissmann, Adolf. *Paul: A Study of Social and Religious History*. New York: Harper, 1957.

deSilva, David A. *Despising Shame: Honor Discourse and Community Maintenance in the Epistle to the Hebrews*. SBL Dissertation Series 152. Atlanta: Scholars, 1995.

———. *Honor, Patronage, Kinship & Purity: Unlocking New Testament Culture*. Downers Grove, IL: InterVarsity, 2000.

Sylva, Dennis. "Meaning and Function of Acts 7.46–50," *Journal of Biblical Literature* 106 (1987) 261–75.

———. *Perseverance in Gratitude: A Socio-Rhetorical Commentary on the Epistle "To the Hebrews."* Grand Rapids: Eerdmans, 2000.

Donelson, Lewis R. *Pseudepigraphy and Ethical Argument in the Pastoral Epistles*. Hermeneutische Untersuchungen zur Theologie 22. Tübingen: Mohr Siebeck, 1984.

Dupont, J. "La structure oratoire du discourse d'Etienne (Actes 7)." *Biblica* 66 (1985) 153–67.

Elliott, Neil. *The Rhetoric of Romans: Argumentative Constraint and Strategy, and Paul's Dialogue with Judaism*. Journal for the Study of the New Testament Supplement Series 45. Sheffield: JSOT Press, 1990.

Evans, Christopher Francis. *The Theology of Rhetoric. The Epistle to the Hebrews*. London: Dr. William's Trust, 1988.

Filson, Floyd V. *'Yesterday': A Study of Hebrews in the Light of Chapter 13*. Studies in Biblical Theology 2/4. Naperville, IL: Allenson, 1967.

Fiore, Benjamin. *The Function of Personal Example in the Socratic and Pastoral Epistles*. Analecta Biblica 105. Rome: Biblical Institute Press, 1986.

Fischel, Henry Albert. "The Uses of Sorites (Climax, Gradatio) in the Tannaitic Period." *Hebrew University College Annual* 44 (1973) 119–51.

Fitzmyer, Joseph A. *Romans: A New Translation with Introduction and Commentary*. Anchor Bible 33. New York: Doubleday, 1992.

Foakes-Jackson, F. J. *The Acts of the Apostles*. New York: Harper, 1931.

Forbes, Christopher. "Paul and Rhetorical Comparison." In *Paul in the Greco-Roman World*, edited by J. Paul Sampley, 134–71. Harrisburg, PA: Trinity, 2003.

Fornara, Charles W. *The Nature of History in Ancient Greece and Rome*. Eidos. Berkeley: University of California Press, 1983.

Fowler, Robert M. *Let the Reader Understand: Reader-Response Criticism and the Gospel of Mark*. Minneapolis: Fortress, 1991.

Gamble, Harry Y. *Books and Readers in the Early Church*. New Haven: Yale University Press, 1995.

Griffith, Terry. "A Non-Polemical Reading of 1 John: Sin, Christology and the Limits of Johannine Christology." *Tyndale Bulletin* 49 (1998) 253–76.

Godsey, J. D. "The Interpretation of Romans in the History of the Christian Faith." *Interpretation* 34 (1980) 3–16.

Gorday, Peter. *Principles of Patristic Exegesis: Romans 9–11 in Origen, John Chrysostom, and Augustine*. Studies in the Bible and Early Christianity 4. New York: Mellen, 1983.

Guillermo. "A thought-provoking masterpiece . . . ." Review of *Christianity and the Rhetoric of Empire: The Development of Christian Discourse*, by Averil Cameron. http://www.amazon.com/review/RRO6WoWFHULDF/ref=cm_cr_rdp_perm (May 30, 2005; accessed July 14, 2008).

Guthrie, George H. *The Structure of Hebrews: A Text-Linguistic Analysis*. Biblical Studies Library. Grand Rapids: Baker Academic, 1998.

Hagner, Donald A. *Encountering the Book of Hebrews: An Exposition*. Encountering Biblical Studies. Grand Rapids: Baker, 2002.

Harding, Mark. *What Are They Saying about the Pastoral Epistles?* New York: Paulist, 2001.

Harrington, Daniel J. *What Are They Saying about The Letter to the Hebrews?* Mahwah, NJ: Paulist, 2005.

Harris, William V. *Ancient Literacy*. Cambridge: Harvard University Press, 1989.

Harrington, *What Are They Saying about The Letter to the Hebrews?* New York: Paulist, 2005.

Hemer, Colin. *The Book of Acts in the Setting of Hellenistic History*. Winona Lake, IN: Eisenbrauns, 1990.

Hengel, Martin. *The Pre-Christian Paul*. Philadelphia: Trinity, 1991.

Hengel, Martin, and Christoph Markschies. *The "Hellenization" of Judaea in the First Century after Christ*. Philadelphia: Trinity, 1989.

Hengel, Martin, and Anna Maria Schwemer. *Paul Between Damascus and Antioch: The Unknown Years*. Translated by John Bowden. Louisville: Westminster, 1997.

Hester, James D. "The Rhetorical Structure of Galatians 1:11—2:14." *Journal of Biblical Literature* 103 (1984) 223–33.

Hill, Craig C. *Hellenists and Hebrews: Reappraising Division within the Earliest Church*. Minneapolis: Fortress, 1992.

Hock, Ronald F. *The Social Context of Paul's Ministry: Tentmaking and Apostleship*. Philadelphia: Fortress, 1980.

Holladay, Carl R. "1 Corinthians 13: Paul as Apostolic Paradigm." In *Greeks, Romans, and Christians: Essays in Honor of Abraham J. Malherbe*, edited by David L. Balch, Everett Ferguson, and Wayne Meeks, 80–98. Minneapolis: Fortress, 1990.

——. *A Critical Introduction to the New Testament*. Nashville: Abingdon, 2005.

Jeal, Roy R. *Integrating Theology and Ethics in Ephesians: The Ethos of Communication*. Studies in Bible and Early Christianity 43. New York: Mellen, 2000.

Johnson, Luke Timothy. *The Acts of the Apostles*. Sacra Pagina 5. Collegeville, MN: Liturgical, 1992.

——. *The First and Second Letters to Timothy: A New Translation with Introduction and Commentary*. Anchor Bible 35A. New York: Doubleday, 2001.

——. *Hebrews: A Commentary*. The New Testament Library. Louisville: Westminster John Knox, 2006.

Judge, E. A. *The Social Pattern of Christian Groups in the First Century.* London: Tyndale, 1960.

Karris, Robert. "The Background and Significance of the Polemic of the Pastoral Epistles." *Journal of Biblical Literature* 92 (1973) 549–64.

———. *The Pastoral Epistles.* Wilmington, DE: Glazier, 1979.

Käsemann, Ernst. *Commentary on Romans.* Grand Rapids: Eerdmans, 1980.

Kennedy, George A. "The Genre of Rhetoric." In *Handbook of Classical Rhetoric in the Hellenistic Period 330 B.C.–A.D. 400*, edited by Stanley E. Porter, 43–50. Leiden: Brill, 1997.

———. *New Testament Interpretation through Rhetorical Criticism.* Chapel Hill: University of North Carolina Press, 1984.

Klauck, Hans-Josef. "Zur rhetorischen Analyse der Johannesbriefe." *Zeitschrift für die neutestamentliche Wissenschaft und die Kunde der älteren Kirche* 81 (1990) 205–24.

Koester, Craig R. *Hebrews: A New Translation With Introduction and Commentary.* Anchor Bible 36. New York: Doubleday, 2001.

———. "Hebrews, Rhetoric, and the Future of Humanity." *Catholic Biblical Quarterly* 64 (2002) 103–23.

Kopf, Dietrich-Alex. *Die Schrift als Zeuge des Evangeliums: Untersuchungen zur Verwendung und zum Verständnis der Schrift bei Paulus.* Beiträge zur historischen Theologie 69. Tübingen: Mohr Siebeck, 1986.

Kümmel, Werner G. *Römer 7 und das Bild des Menschen: Zwei Studien.* Theologische Bücherei, Neues Testament 53. Munich: Kaiser, 1974.

Kurz, William S. "Hellenistic Rhetoric in the Christological Proof of Luke-Acts." *Catholic Biblical Quarterly* 42 (1980) 171–95.

Lambrecht, Jan. *The Wretched "I" and its Liberation: Paul in Romans 7 and 8.* Louvain Theological & Pastoral Monographs 14. Louvain: Peeters, 1992.

Lane, William L. *Hebrews 1–8.* Word Biblical Commentary 47A. Dallas: Word, 1991.

Levine, Amy-Jill, and Ben Witherington III. *The Gospel of Luke.* New Cambridge Bible Commentary. Cambridge: Cambridge University Press, 2009.

Lincoln, Andrew T. *Hebrews: A Guide.* London: T. & T. Clark, 2006.

Lindars, Barnabas. "The Rhetorical Structure of Hebrews." New Testament Studies 35 (1989) 382–406.

Litfin, A. Duane. *St. Paul's Theology of Proclamation: 1 Corinthians 1–4 and Greco-Roman Rhetoric.* Society for New Testament Studies Monograph Series 79. Cambridge: Cambridge University Press, 1994.

Long, Thomas G. *Hebrews.* Interpretation. Louisville: Westminster John Knox, 1997.

Longenecker, Bruce W. *Rhetoric at the Boundaries: The Art and Theology of New Testament Chain-Link Transitions.* Waco: Baylor University Press, 2005.

Longenecker, Richard N. *Galatians.* Word Biblical Commentary 41. Waco: Word, 1990.

Lyonnet, Stanislas. "L'histoire du salut selon le chapitre 7 de l'épître aux Romains." *Biblica* 43 (1962) 117–51.

Mack, Burton L. and Vernon K. Robbins. *Patterns of Persuasion in the Gospels.* Sonoma, CA: Polebridge, 1989.

MacMullen, Ramsay. *Roman Social Relations, 50 B.C. to A.D. 284.* New Haven: Yale University Press, 1974.

Malina, Bruce. *The New Testament World: Insights from Cultural Anthropology.* 3rd ed. Louisville: Westminster John Knox, 2001.

Marrou, Henri Irénée. *A History of Education in Antiquity.* New York: Sheed and Ward, 1956.

Martin, Troy W. *Metaphor and Composition in 1 Peter.* SBL Dissertation Series 131. Atlanta: Scholars, 1992.

Mayor, Jospeh B. *The Epistle of St. Jude and the Second Epistle of St. Peter: Greek Text with Introduction Notes and Comments.* 1907. Reprint, Grand Rapids: Baker, 1979.

McCall, Marsh H. *Ancient Rhetorical Theories of Similes and Comparison.* Loeb Classical Monograph. Cambridge: Harvard University Press 1970.

McCullough, J.C. "Some Recent Developments in Research on the Epistle to the Hebrews." *Irish Biblical Studies* 2 (1980) 141–65.

Melanchthon, Philipp. *Commentary on Romans.* Translated by Fred Kramer. St. Louis: Concordia, 1992.

Meyer, Paul W. "The Worm at the Core of the Apple: Exegetical Reflections on Romans 7." In *The Conversation Continues: Studies in Paul and John in Honor of J. Louis Martyn,* edited by Robert T. Fortna and Beverly Roberts Gaventa, 62–84. Nashville: Abingdon, 1990.

Meyers, Ched. *Binding the Strong Man: A Political Reading of Mark's Story of Jesus.* Maryknoll, NY: Orbis, 1988.

Milton, John. "Paradise Regained." In *The Complete Poems of John Milton.* New York: Washington Square, 1964.

Mitchell, Margaret M. *Paul and the Rhetoric of Reconciliation: An Exegetical Investigation of the Language and Composition of 1 Corinthians.* Louisville: Westminster John Knox, 1993.

————. *The Heavenly Trumpet: John Chrysostom and the Art of Pauline Interpretation.* Louisville: Westminister John Knox, 2002.

Moo, Douglas J. *The Epistle to the Romans.* The New International Commentary on the New Testament. Grand Rapids: Eerdmans, 1996.

Morris, Colin. *Epistles to the Apostle: Tarsus, Please Forward.* Nashville; Abingdon, 1974.

Murphy-O'Connor, Jerome. *Paul the Letter-Writer: His World, His Options, His Skills.* Good News Studies 41. Collegeville, MN: Liturgical, 1995.

————. *Paul: A Critical Life.* Oxford: Oxford University Press, 1996.

Murray, Gilbert. *Four Stages of Greek Religion.* Columbia University Lectures. New York: Columbia University Press, 1912.

Neufeld, Dietmar. *Reconceiving Texts as Speech Acts: An Analysis of 1 John.* Leiden: Brill, 1994.

Neusner, Jacob. *Rabbinic Traditions about Pharisees before 70: The Masters.* Vol. 1. 1971. Reprint, Eugene, OR: Wipf & Stock, 2005.

Neyrey, Jerome. "The Forensic Defense Speech and Paul's Trial Speeches in Acts 22–26." In *Luke-Acts: New Perspectives from the SBL Seminar,* edited by Charles H. Talbert, 210–24. New York: Crossroad, 1984.

Nock, A. D. *St. Paul.* New York: Harper, 1938.

North, H. F. "Rhetoric and Historiography." *Quarterly Journal of Speech* 42 (1956) 234–42.

Olbricht, Thomas H. "Hebrews as Amplification." In *Rhetoric and the New Testament: Essays from the 1992 Heidelberg Conference,* edited by Stanley E. Porter and Thomas H. Olbricht, 375–87. Journal for the Study of the New Testament Supplement Series 90. Sheffield: Sheffield Academic, 1993.

Pogoloff, Stephen M. *Logos and Sophia: The Rhetorical Situation of 1 Corinthians.* SBL Dissertation Series 134. Atlanta: Scholars, 1992.

Porter, Stanley E., and Dennis L. Stamps, editors. *Rhetorical Criticism and the Bible.* London: Sheffield Academic, 2002.

Richards, E. Randolph. *Paul and First-Century Letter Writing: Secretaries, Composition, and Collection.* Downers Grove, IL: InterVarsity, 2004.

———. *The Secretary in the Letters of Paul.* Wissenschaftliche Untersuchungen zum Neuen Testament 2/42. Tübingen: Mohr Siebeck, 1991.

Roetzel, Calvin J. *The Letters of Paul: Conversations in Context.* 3rd ed. Louisville: Wesminster John Knox, 1991. 4th ed., 1998.

Rothschild, Clare Komoroske. "Luke-Acts and the Rhetoric of History: An Investigation of Early Christian Historiography." PhD diss., University of Chicago Divinity School, 2003.

Salyer, Gregory. "Rhetoric, Purity and Play: Aspects of Mark 7:1–23." *Semeia* 64 (1993) 117–37, 139–69.

Satterthwaite, P. E. "Acts against the Background of Classical Rhetoric." In *The Book of Acts in Its Ancient Literary Setting,* vol. 1 of *The Book of Acts in its First Century Settings,* edited by Bruce W. Winter and Andrew D. Clarke, 337–80. Grand Rapids: Eerdmans, 1993.

Scharlemann, Martin H. *Stephen: A Singular Saint.* Analecta Biblica 34. Rome: Pontifical Biblical Institute, 1968.

Schnackenburg, Rudolf. *The Johannine Epistles: A Commentary.* New York: Crossroad, 1992.

Seid, Timothy W. "The Rhetorical Form of the Melchizedek/Christ Comparison in Hebrews 7." PhD diss., Brown University, 1996.

Sevenster, J. N. *Do You Know Greek? How Much Greek Could the First Jewish Christians Have Known?* Novum Testamentum Supplements 19. Leiden: Brill, 1968.

Sherk, Robert K., translator and editor. *The Roman Empire: Augustus to Hadrian.* Translated Documents of Greece and Rome 6. Cambridge: Cambridge University Press, 1988.

Siegert, Folker. *Drei hellenistisch-jüdische Predigten: Ps.-Philon, "Über Jona," "Über Simson" und "Über die Gottesbezeichnung 'wohltätig verzehrendes Feuer.'"* 2 vols. Tübingen: Mohr Siebeck, 1980–1992.

Smalley, Stephen S. *1, 2, 3 John.* Word Biblical Commentary 51. Waco: Word, 1984.

Smith, Robert W. *Art of Rhetoric in Alexandria: Its Theory and Practice in the Ancient World.* The Hague: Nijhoff, 1974.

Soards, Marion L. *The Speeches in Acts: Their Content, Context, and Concerns.* Louisville: Westminster John Knox, 1993.

Soden, Hermann von. *Urchristliche Literaturgeschichte: Die Schriften des Neuen Testaments.* Berlin: Duncker, 1905.

Spicq, C. *L'Epitre aux Hebreux.* 2 vols. Etudes bibliques. Paris: Gabalda, 1952.

Stamps, D. L. "The Johannine Writings." In *Handbook of Classical Rhetoric in the Hellenistic Period 330 B.C.–A.D. 400,* edited by Stanley E. Porter, 609–32. Leiden: Brill, 1997.

Stark, Rodney. *The Rise of Christianity: A Sociologist Reconsiders History.* Princeton: Princeton University Press, 1996.

Stegner, William Richard. "The Ancient Jewish Synagogue Homily." In *Greco-Roman Literature and the New Testament: Selected Forms and Genres* 21, edited by David E. Aune, 51–69. Atlanta: Scholars, 1988.

Stendahl, Krister. *Paul among Jews and Gentiles, and Other Essays.* Philadelphia: Fortress, 1976.

Stowers, Stanley K. *Letter Writing in Greco-Roman Antiquity.* Library of Early Christianity 5. Philadelphia: Westminster, 1986.

———. *A Rereading of Romans: Justice, Jews, and Gentiles.* New Haven: Yale University Press, 1997.

Swetnam, James. "On the Literary Genre of the 'Epistle' to the Hebrews." *Novum Testamentum* 11 (1969) 261–69.

Talbert, Charles H. *Romans.* Smith & Helwys Bible Commentary 24. Macon, GA: Smith & Helwys, 2002.

Tannehill, Robert C. *The Narrative Unity of Luke-Acts: A Literary Interpretation.* Vol. 2, *The Acts of the Apostles.* Minneapolis: Fortress, 1990.

Taylor, Robert O. P. *The Groundwork of the Gospels.* Oxford: Blackwell, 1946.

Thatcher, Tom. "The Relational Matrix of the Pastoral Epistles." *Journal of the Evangelical Theological Society* 38 (1995) 41–45.

Theissen, Gerd. *Psychological Aspects of Pauline Theology.* Translated by John Galvin. Philadelphia: Fortress, 1987.

Thiessen, Werner. *Christen in Ephesus: Die historische und theologische Situation in vorpaulinischer und paulinischer Zeit und zur Zeit der Apostelgeschichte und der Pastoralbriefe.* Texte und Arbeiten zum neutestamentlichen Zeitalter 12. Tübingen: Francke, 1995.

Thurén, Lauri. "The General New Testament Writings." In *Handbook of Classical Rhetoric in the Hellenistic Period, 330 B.C–A.D. 400,* edited by Stanley E. Porter, 589–92. Leiden: Brill, 1997.

Thyen, Hartwig. *Der Stil der jüdisch-hellenistischen Homilie.* Forschungen zur Religion und Literatur des Alten und Neuen Testaments 65. Göttingen: Vandenhoeck & Ruprecht, 1955.

Übelacker, Walter G. *Der Hebräerbrief als Appell: Untersuchungen zur Exordium, Narratio, and Postscriptum (Hebr 1–2 und 13,22–25).* Coniectanea Biblica 21. Stockholm: Almquist & Wiksell, 1989.

Vaganay, Léon. "Le plan de l'épître aux Hébreux." In *Mémorial Lagrange,* 269–77. Paris: Gabalda, 1940.

van Unnik, W. C. "Tarsus or Jerusalem?: The City of Paul's Youth." In *Sparsa Collecta: The Collected Essays of W. C. van Unnik Part 1. Evangelia, Paulina, Acta,* 259–320. Supplements to Novum Testamentum 29. Leiden: Brill, 1973.

Vouga, François. *Die Johannesbriefe.* Handbuch zum Neuen Testament 15/3. Tübingen: Mohr Siebeck, 1990.

———. "La réception de la théologie johannique dans le épîtres." In *La communauté johannique et son histoire: La trajectoire de l'évangile de Jean aux deux premiers siècles,* edited by J.-D. Kaestli, J.-M. Poffet, and J. Zumstein, 283–302. Geneva: Labor et Fides, 1990.

Wacholder, Ben Z. *Nicolaus of Damascus.* Berkeley: University California Press, 1962.

Walters, John R. "The Rhetorical Arrangement of Hebrews." *Asbury Theological Journal* 51.2 (1996) 59–70.

Watson, Duane F. "Amplification Techniques in 1 John: The Interaction of Rhetorical Style and Invention." *Journal for the Study of the New Testament* 51 (1993) 99–123.

———. "An Epideictic Strategy for Increasing Adherence to Community Values: 1 John 1:1—2:27." *Proceedings of the Eastern Great Lakes and Midwest Biblical Societies* 11 (1991) 144–52.

———. *Invention, Arrangement, and Style: Rhetorical Criticism of Jude and 2 Peter.* Society of Biblical Literature Dissertation Series 104. Atlanta: Scholars, 1988.

———. "1 John 2:12–14 as *Distributio, Conduplicatio,* and *Expolitio*: A Rhetorical Understanding." *Journal for the Study of the New Testament* 35 (1989) 97–110.

———. *1–3 John.* New Cambridge Bible Commentary. Cambridge: Cambridge University Press, forthcoming.

———. "Paul's Speech to the Ephesian Elders: Acts 20:17–38." In *Persuasive Artistry: Studies in Honor of George A. Kennedy,* edited by D. F. Watson, 184–208. Journal for the Study of the New Testament Supplement Series 50. Sheffield: Sheffield Academic, 1991.

———. "A Rhetorical Analysis of Philippians and its Implications for the Unity Question." *Novum Testamentum* 30 (1988) 57–87.

———. "Rhetorical Criticism of Hebrews and the Catholic Epistles since 1978." *Currents in Research: Biblical Studies* 5 (1997) 175–207.

Winter, Bruce W. *Philo and Paul among the Sophists.* Society for New Testament Studies Monograph Series 96. Cambridge: Cambridge University Press, 1997.

———. "On Introducing Gods to Athens: An Alternative Reading of Acts 17.18–20." *Tyndale Bulletin* 47 (1996) 71–90.

Witherington, Ben III. *The Acts of the Apostles: A Socio-Rhetorical Commentary.* Grand Rapids: Eerdmans, 1998.

———. *Conflict and Community in Corinth: A Socio-Rhetorical Commentary on 1 and 2 Corinthians.* Grand Rapids: Eerdmans, 1995.

———. *Friendship and Finances in Philippi: The Letter of Paul to the Philippians.* The New Testament in Context. Valley Forge, PA: Trinity, 1994.

———. *The Gospel of Mark: A Socio-Rhetorical Commentary.* Grand Rapids: Eerdmans, 2001.

———. *Grace in Galatia: A Commentary on St. Paul's Letter to the Galatians.* Grand Rapids: Eerdmans, 1998.

———. *Letters and Homilies for Hellenized Christians.* Vol. 1, *A Socio-Rhetorical Commentary on Titus, 1–2 Timothy And 1–3 John.* Downers Grove, IL: InterVarsity, 2006.

———. *The Letters to Philemon, the Colossians, and the Ephesians: A Socio-rhetorical Commentary on the Captivity Epistles.* Grand Rapids: Eerdmans, 2007.

———. *The Living Word of God: Rethinking the Theology of the Bible.* Waco: Baylor University Press, 2008.

———. *The Paul Quest: The Renewed Search for the Jew of Tarsus.* Downers Grove, IL: InterVarsity, 1998.

———. *Paul's Narrative Thought World: The Tapestry of Tragedy and Triumph.* Louisville: Westminister John Knox, 1994.

———. *Shifting the Paradigms.* Waco: Baylor University Press, 2009.

———. *Women in the Earliest Churches.* Cambridge: Cambridge University Press, 1988.

———, with Darlene Hyatt. *Paul's Letter to the Romans: A Socio-Rhetorical Commentary.* Grand Rapids: Eerdmans, 2004.

Wright, N. T. "Romans." In *New Interpreter's Bible: Acts–First Corinthians,* vol. 10. Nashville: Abingdon, 2002.

Young, David M. "Whoever Has Ears to Hear: The Discourses of Jesus in Mark as Primary Rhetoric of the Greco-Roman Period." PhD diss., Vanderbilt University, 1994.

Youtie, H. C. "Agrammatos: An Aspect of Greek Society in Egypt." *Harvard Studies in Classical Philology* 75 (1971) 161–76.

———. "Upographeus: The Social Impact of Illiteracy in Graeco-Roman Egypt." *Zeitschrift für Papyrologie and Epigraphik* 17 (1975) 201–21.

Zehnle, Richard F. *Peter's Pentecost Discourse: Tradition and Lukan Reinterpretation in Peter's Speeches of Acts 2 and 3.* Nashville: Abingdon, 1971.

Index of Ancient Documents

Hebrews

Hebrews (*continued*)

☙

RABBINIC LITERATURE

b. Sanhedrin

CPSIA information can be obtained
at www.ICGtesting.com
Printed in the USA
FFHW021249031218
49749638-54197FF